A HERO PERISHED

A Hero Perished

The Diary and Selected Letters of

NILE KINNICK

Edited by Paul Baender

University of Iowa Press Iowa City

University of Iowa Press,

Iowa City 52242

Copyright © 1991 by

the University of Iowa

All rights reserved

Printed in the United States of America

First edition, 1991

Design by Richard Hendel

Printed on acid-free paper

Library of Congress Cataloging-in-Publication Data

Kinnick, Nile C. (Nile Clarke), 1918–1943

 A hero perished: the diary and selected letters of Nile Kinnick/edited by
Paul Baender.—1st ed.

  p. cm.

 Includes bibliographical references (p.).

 ISBN 0-87745-336-5 (alk. paper)

 1. Kinnick, Nile C. (Nile Clarke), 1918–1943—Diaries.

2. Kinnick, Nile C. (Nile Clarke), 1918–1943—Correspondence.

3. Football players—United States—Diaries. 4. Football players—
United States—Correspondence. 5. University of Iowa—Football—
History. I. Baender, Paul. II. Title.

GV939.K44A3 1991

796.332'092—dc20   91-10195

[B]   CIP

Who sees with equal eye, as God of all,

A hero perish, or a sparrow fall,

Atoms or systems into ruin hurl'd,

And now a bubble burst, and now a world.

   — Alexander Pope

CONTENTS

THE DIARY

ACKNOWLEDGMENTS

Many people have contributed information essential to the introduction, headnotes, and annotations to this book, and others have been of important procedural assistance. I am grateful to friends and contemporaries of Kinnick: Ray and Janet Bywater, Celia Peairs Fay, Shirley McKim Gardner, James L. George, James M. Hoak, Robert A. Hobbs, Robert Hogan, Barbara Miller Johann, Thomas A. Louden, Edwin S. McCollister, Edward J. McManus, William L. Meardon, Margaret Kuttler Mills, Elizabeth Charlton Moore, Earle Murphy, Mrs. J. Kenneth Pettit, Erwin Prasse, Dorothy Klein Ray, Ruth Ainsworth Robert, Norman Sage, and William C. Stuart. Two Adel sources, Jim Mitchell and David L. Tetrick, have supplied or led me to information unavailable without their help. In Iowa City graduate student Sarah Coggins has also provided data.

Faculty members at the University of Iowa have provided information or useful contacts with people and resources. They are Professor David G. Rethwisch of the College of Engineering; Dr. Kenneth D. Dolan, Dr. Annette E. Fitz, and Dr. Charles E. Hawtrey of the College of Medicine; Professor Phillip D. Cummins of the Department of Philosophy; and in the Department of English, Professors John C. Gerber, Robert E. Kelley, Carl H. Klaus, and Tom Lutz.

In the University of Iowa Library, I have been guided to reference sources and otherwise assisted by Richard Green, David Hudson, Rebecca Johnson, James Julich, Lucia Marino, Joel Maxey, Keith Rageth, Helen Ryan, John Schacht, and Harlan Sifford.

Other libraries, organizations, and institutions that have provided information and materials are the Adel Public Library, the Alumni Association of the University of Chicago, the Brown University Library, the Center for Research Libraries, the Christian Science Reading Room (Iowa City), the Department of History of Iowa State University, the Library of Congress, the New York Public Library, the Office of the Registrar of the University of Chicago and the University of Iowa, and the State Historical Society of Iowa (Iowa City).

The staff of Special Collections at the University of Iowa Library has my deepest respect and gratitude for their expertise, courtesy, and patience. They tolerated my daily requests for data, access, and advice during the months I worked with the Kinnick Collection. Assistants in the department, all three so kind and helpful, were Susan Hansen, Judith Macy, and Barbara Siebenschuh. The senior staff, Robert A. McCown (Head of Special Collections and Curator of Manuscripts), Earl Rogers (Curator of Archives), and David Schoonover (Curator of Rare Books), saved me from many mistakes and put me on to resources I did not know existed. Genial and professional, they were always concerned that things be done right. These men and women make Special Collections at the University of Iowa an ideal environment for researchers.

Last, and far from least, is Vicky Dingman. Without her this project could not have been completed within a reasonable time. She entered my manuscript into the computer and with never a complaint added my many corrections and revisions in material I should have perfected in the first place. Prompt, effective, and amiable, she is a model collaborator.

INTRODUCTION

This is a book of and about a football player, but it is not a football book. From the accomplishments of a single season, Nile Kinnick became the most famous player in Iowa history, and he is still one of the best-remembered college athletes in the United States. Over the years following his death in 1943, a tradition if not a cult of Kinnick has developed that began in his lifetime. People have written about him as if he was a moral paragon who serenely obeyed all the imperatives and observed all the constraints that give the rest of us so much trouble. This book allows Kinnick to appear as the person he was, so far as the documents permit. The aim is not to discredit him but to make the reputation square with the man, and the man is worth knowing. He is not accountable to anyone's false beliefs.

But like caricatures, the traditional exaggerations about Kinnick have their foundation in fact. In the introduction to follow, I use the phrase "heroic American innocent" in discussing the public estimation of him by the time he died, and in two important ways the phrase was true to the man. First, he tried to live by the codes of his grandfather and the rest of his family's elders. These were codes in which honesty, industry, purpose, dedication, and the greater good of humanity in general were essential aspirations for people of integrity. In late January 1940, just after he returned with his national awards from New York, Philadelphia, and Washington, he wrote his grandmother that "*Nothing* you could say would make me feel happier than your statement that in many ways I remind you of grandpa." Earnest, patriotic, idealistic, hardworking, passionate on behalf of racial and economic equity, Kinnick seemed to friends and to journalists a noble vestige from an earlier America. Second, like such a vestige, Kinnick lived as though he had just awakened to a dazzling new world. He was vivacious and expectant, credulous and trusting, ready for the adventures of college life and the bigger society beyond. Movies, good food, cowboy music, classical concerts, looking at the moon from a Florida beach – he wrote about these and many more incidental delights he savored as he passed in his eagerness to catch up. Mature and boyish, wise and naive, profound and banal, vernacular and stilted, tough and maudlin, Kinnick resembled such American innocents as Henry James's Christopher Newman and F. Scott Fitzgerald's Jay Gatsby.

Let no one invoke the cliché about "simpler and more innocent times." Kinnick lived in a time of terror, desperation, and complexity beyond charting. To maintain one's character in that time was no easy matter. It was easier to be cynical, opportunistic, and urgently indulgent and perhaps healthier to be so. Nor was Kinnick a simple man. He resisted the life of dedication and regretted his inability to be true to it. He knew his own contradictions very well, and with a humorous distance he could laugh at his own floundering. He seemed serene only in the last month of his life, and then not as a paragon of virtue but as a man no longer in a hurry, no longer reaching out to the past or conjuring up postwar futures for himself. In the last letter in this book, possibly the last he wrote, he was writing from a tranquility in which he could recall Iowa City and all it had meant to him and yet let it go with a gentle good-bye.

Kinnick had been born on 9 July 1918 at home, at 219 North Twelfth Street, in the small town of Adel, Iowa, the county seat of Dallas County, about twelve miles northwest of Des Moines.[1] His childhood and adolescence were more or less typical for a boy living in town yet part of rural culture. He had a town education from primary school through high school, and his sports and games involved the groups that develop in town and town school environments. At age nine he had a paper route, as he might have had in Des Moines or Chicago. But because of his father's and relatives' agricultural enterprises he was also put to the chores of a farmboy, and there were the hayrides, camping, and watermelon theft that any such boy would know. For Kinnick these experiences of the immediate and nearby environments were compatible and bountiful together, and given his personality, intelligence, and athletic talent, he might have grown up to be a pillar of his community – high-school football hero, known to all in town and countryside, later an attorney with an office on the town square, a notable whose opinions counted for much in local issues. Figures like that were dignitaries in small towns across the country; he would have been one sort of typical American.

But the two families behind Kinnick shared patterns of motive and accomplishment that both the families and he believed set him on a course of higher and broader development. His father's father, William

Nile Kinnick at age nine. Adel, 25 June 1928. Negative, Kinnick Collection.

Butler Kinnick, had come to Iowa from Indiana with his family at age five in 1854, and while still a young man he became a bank vice-president and an extensive landowner, later a county supervisor. Kinnick's father took a degree in agronomy at Iowa State College in 1916 and was more a farm manager than a laboring farmer. His father's two sisters attended Grinnell, and his mother, Frances Clarke Kinnick, studied at Drake and Northwestern. The figure singled out as the most forceful shaper, again by both the families and Kinnick, was his maternal grandfather, George Washington Clarke. Like W. B. Kinnick an immigrant in childhood from Indiana, Clarke received a bachelor's degree at Oskaloosa College (later Drake University in Des Moines) in 1877 and the next year earned his law degree from the University of Iowa. John Bushrod White and he formed one of the leading law firms in central Iowa, and he rose from justice of the peace to speaker of the state assembly, lieutenant governor, and governor. Sunday evenings in his stately home on North Fifteenth Street became a memorable tradition for Kinnick. Clarkes and Kinnicks assembled for dinner, but Kinnick remembered especially the recitations, games, and conversation. The general talk was never idle, for the occasions were designed to increase knowledge and understanding. Kinnick's parents and their parents could recall their origins farther east, but what they were and might become depended on what they made of their time in their new home.

The Depression forced Kinnick's father to liquidate some of his farm properties, and in 1934 he found salaried employment with the Federal Land Bank of Omaha, appraising farms over a territory covering much of Iowa. The family bought a house in Omaha, and Kinnick transferred to Benson High School there after finishing his junior year in Adel. He had always been an excellent student as well as an athletic leader, and he could have graduated in 1935, but his parents held him back a year to become thoroughly prepared for the university. He considered Minnesota – how seriously is not clear – but he chose the University of Iowa. Perhaps a more compelling motive than his grandfather's law degree there was the stature of Iowa football at the time. Verle Davis, his last football coach at Adel, in the undefeated season of 1933, recalled that "he was determined to go to some school that was 'down.' . . . He didn't want to go to Minnesota because they were on top. . . . He finally went to Iowa as he figured they were at their lowest ebb."[2] The account is persuasive because it was typical of Kinnick. To start from nothing and to test himself against his own weakness as well as outside resistance were challenges Kinnick always pursued if they were available.

There was abundant opportunity to struggle at Iowa. After a promising 1936 season of freshman football (first-year men were not eligible for varsity play), Kinnick entered a program headed by newcomer Irl Tubbs. In 1937 he continued to impress coaches, and he made the United Press All Big Ten Team, but the season record was 1–7. Iowa lacked adequate personnel and, as Kinnick came to see the next year, adequate coaching. The 1938 season was a more severe test, because Kinnick injured an ankle in the opening game. He could not match his previous performance, much less fulfill his promise, and as that dull season wore on, agitation developed in and out of the media for a coaching change. Four days after the season ended, "reliable sources" announced that Dr. Eddie Anderson was the first choice to succeed Tubbs. He quickly accepted Iowa's offer, and on 29 November a large and jubilant crowd welcomed him to Iowa City, for he had the credentials of Iowa birth and upbringing (Oskaloosa and Mason City), Notre Dame training, and six successful years as head coach at Holy Cross, at a time when such a record there brought national recognition.

The 1939 season saw the emergence of the public Nile Kinnick.[3] The situation called for such a figure: an obscure state in the middle of the country that had been a football loser for years suddenly brings in a Notre Dame man from a prestigious eastern program; the team wins its first two games, scoring more points than it had the entire previous year; the one loss, no embarrassment, comes in the third game; after that there are four successive victories, the last two extraordinary upsets of undefeated Notre Dame and Bernie Bierman's strong Minnesota team. Injuries during the streak force Coach Anderson to use several players, including Kinnick, the full sixty minutes in game after game, and in November references to the "Iron Men" begin to circulate in the press. At the focal point of this scene was Kinnick, by that year an improbable hero yet visibly the leader and star performer among other unlikely heroes. Like a character in a play, he was under a cloud from the previous year, but now, in his last season, this man of five feet seven or eight inches and 170 pounds was redeeming his promise and doing more than he ever had – punting, passing, running, tackling, intercepting – and with indifference to the beatings he took from opponents much larger than he. Many things about him had become known: his Christian Science convictions, his small-town origin, his relation to a former governor, his modest poise, his taciturn perseverance, and his academic brilliance (he was nearly assured of a Phi Beta Kappa key as an economics major). Now these conditions and traits became the staples of newspaper profiles, and a fillip of his media arrival was his alliterative nickname. Years earlier, Red Grange had been the "Galloping Ghost," Larry Kelley was dubbed "Laughing Larry" in 1936, Davey O'Brien gained fame as the "Mighty Mite" in 1938, and in November 1939 Kinnick became the "Cornbelt Comet," despite it being common knowledge that he had to make up in shiftiness for what he lacked in speed.[4]

With Kinnick's selection for the Heisman Trophy, and especially after his performance at the ceremony on 6 December, New York and other big-city journalists became the major propagandists of the public Kinnick, an image by then ready-made for general circulation. Writers like Jack Cuddy, Bill Cunningham, George Trevor, and Whitney Martin reiterated his basic qualities of small size, brilliance, devoutness, modesty, and endurance. The qualities were truly his, and to that point the only significant difference between the persona and the man was the selectivity that delimited the public figure. But repetition was not enough for eastern writers with bylines; to the familiar profile they added finer points and moral bearings. Trevor, for instance, noted that the "square cut of Kinnick's jaw, the bulldog set of his mouth, and the look of eagles in his brown eyes, reveal the grim determination and fixity of purpose. . . . Character is stamped in every line of Kinnick's alert, forthright face. Intelligence glows from his luminous eyes."[5] Bill Cunningham proclaimed that "the country is okeh as long as it produces Nile Kinnicks. The football part is incidental."[6]

Kinnick's year seemed so unlikely and the publicity was so insistent that people could become skeptical or irritated. According to Cunningham in the *Boston Post* of 6 December, a rumor was circulating that Kinnick was actually an All-American who had played at Pittsburgh for three years and that Anderson was about to be fired and Iowa's victories canceled because of the imposture. By the twelfth, New York writer Jack Miley could take no more: "The way they have been lugging Kinnick around the country and exhibiting him, practically with a ring in his nose . . . you'd think he was one of those prize shoats who had won all the blue ribbons at the Iowa county fairs. . . . I'm just getting sick and tired of having his square-jawed, dimplechinned kisser staring at me out of the newspapers and having to hear Nile make one of those 34-B speeches of his every time I turn on my radio" (*New York Post*, 12 December).

But the public figure continued to develop, and not just because each subsequent major honor enhanced it – the Maxwell and Camp awards, the Athlete of the Year Award, top votegetter for the College All-Star Game, Phi Beta Kappa, and two scholarships that helped out during his year in law school. Kinnick had become a Hero, and the Hero must have a Lover, even in Iowa, where nine days after the Heisman ceremony the *Sioux City Tribune* printed the false rumor that Barbara Miller of Sioux City, an Iowa student Kinnick dated off and on in 1939 and later, was "engaged to marry her football hero."[7] A photograph taken of them on campus was printed from the *Washington Star* and the *Chicago Tribune* to the *Omaha World-Herald*, with brief stories about her being his "best girl" (see photograph with letter 9). When Kinnick returned to New York in January 1940 for the Captain of the All-Americas Award, he met a young heiress the evening of the ceremony, Virginia Eskridge, who did not take him for a football player. "Oh, you're from the school that has that famous All-American," she was reported to have said. Later that evening Kinnick, Anderson, and she turned up at the Kit Kat Club, a midtown spot in the East Fifties, where a tabloid photographer got him to pose with a glass of milk and thus produce a complication of the persona. There was the "Milk Fed All-America," wearing a tuxedo, amused and at ease, sitting close to a handsome and elegant woman holding a highball. The same day Dorothy Kilgallen reported that "Nile Kinnick . . . and Virginia Eskridge, a Delaware heiress, are yum, yum."[8] Had Kinnick finally yielded to Dan Topping's offer and turned professional with the Brooklyn football Dodgers, the New York press might have pushed the latencies in this picture for all they were worth. The Hero might have become the Sophisticate, at home anywhere, enriched by situations that might compromise lesser folk. This line of publicity was not pursued, but exploitation, fan mail, and lecture appearances showed that the uncomplicated persona was attractive enough on its own, and they showed that the attraction lasted well beyond the usual span of occasional fame.

The exploitation began when Kinnick won the Heisman Trophy. Upon his arrival in New York, the United States Navy took over the outdoor display. He was driven to Floyd Bennett Field, where he boarded a navy transport plane, along with the Naval Academy's football captain, other navy people, and assorted dignitaries. They flew slowly over Brooklyn and Manhattan, accompanied by a dirigible and twenty-five smaller navy planes in formation. During the flight there was to be a national radio broadcast by the Mutual Broadcasting System, and for this the navy had a surprise. Kinnick was given questions to ask as though he was interested in joining up, a routine that he later called "unexpected" and that infuriated his uncle Charles Clarke, listening back in Adel.[9] Afterward a navy source evidently planted the story that Kinnick would soon enlist, for the New York press reported that he would. At that time the item was groundless, but the solicitation may have been the first in a chain of motives that led to Kinnick's enlistment in September 1941.

After he entered the Navy Air Corps in December 1941 the exploitation continued, with navy help or navy instigation. At Kansas City, Kinnick was made available for radio interviews and for photo-story features in the *Kansas City Kansan* and the *Kansas City Star*. At New Orleans, though he was there only two weeks, the *Times-Picayune* enjoyed a photo opportunity: the pairing of Kinnick and Mel Ott. When the commandant at Pensacola learned that Kinnick and Ken Pettit, a fellow player on the 1939 Iowa team, were among his cadets, he invited them to a cocktail party attended otherwise only by officers (see letter 23). Also at Pensacola, Kinnick learned that he could have an easy ride through the war as an instructor if he agreed to play football for the base team but that he could not choose a marine commission on the pretext that he had lost a lottery drawing for the assignment (diary, 11 March and 4 June 1942). And shortly after he transferred to Miami, the *Miami Daily News* did a photo story hailing Kinnick the football star as a "one man gang," to his amusement (Kinnick to the family, 17 July 1942).

Other exploitations were of familiar sorts. In January 1940 the *Allied Youth* used an enlargement of Kinnick excerpted from the Kinnick–Barbara Miller photo of December to preface an article that had him say: "I am a teetotaler . . . and am in no way in sympathy with the use of alcoholic beverages." The quotation may have been spurious, for the journal's masthead announced its dedication to "liberation . . . from the handicaps of beverage alcohol," and at least as early as September 1940 Kinnick took some "anti-freeze" without a qualm and not as if for the first time (see letter 14).[10] In February the Delta Kappa Epsilon chapter at the University of Rochester asked him to serve as judge in a junior-prom beauty contest. Whether he agreed is not known, but he did serve as such a judge for the May Frolic in North English, Iowa. In September Kinnick introduced Wendell Willkie at an Iowa Falls rally, and in November a full-page Elgin watch advertisement showed him in football uniform socializing with two models dressed as "co-eds," with his endorsement in large script: "'I've teamed up with Elgin De Luxe. . . . a real All-American.'"[11] There were at least two failed attempts to use Kinnick. In 1940 a Philadelphia entrepreneur tried to enlist him in his sales force (see letter 12), and in 1941 some "dude in the east" concocted a scheme in which Kinnick would accompany a group of well-known rich boys to Mexico, and the dude would make his money selling or renting newsreel footage of the trip (see letter 15).

In 1940 and 1941 Kinnick received many admiring letters from adults and from boys and girls around the country. There were valentines, requests for autographs, and simple statements of respect. Even an incomplete account of Kinnick's lecture appearances in these years indicates how strong a pull he maintained. He spoke before Rotary Clubs and Lions Clubs, quarterback clubs and YMCA groups, at father-son dinners and high school banquets; and time after time the audiences filled the halls. In the winter and spring of 1939–40 alone he spoke in Evansville, Indiana; Chicago, Monmouth, Princeton, Rock Island, and Sterling, Illinois; Aberdeen and Mitchell, South Dakota; and in Iowa at Charles City, Davenport, Decorah, Des Moines, Dubuque, Mason City (at least twice), Muscatine, Oelwein, Tipton, and Waverly. In late 1940 and in 1941 he appeared at Anamosa, Atlantic, Clinton, Garner, Muscatine, Omaha, Sioux City, Waterloo, and Yarmouth. Kinnick's addresses necessarily became formulaic (see his admission in letter 16). His fame preceding him and his accomplishments a matter of record, he would make wry fun of his shortness and slowness. He would tell how two women in New York failed to recognize him as a football player, how a Des Moines reporter forgot whether he had graduated, and how his College All-Star teammate Bulldog Turner exclaimed: "Holy smoke . . . you're just a little guy."[12] He could argue that only diligence and resolve had allowed him to succeed and that these were qualities the boys hearing him could achieve too. He told them to enjoy their sports and to pursue their studies, to make of their college experience the wonder time it should be. Modest yet articulate, humorous and serious by turns, Kinnick seemed to confirm the persona in the man.

Kinnick took his ensign's commission in the Navy Air Corps in September 1942. On 2 June 1943, near ten in the morning, he died in the Gulf of Paria, between Venezuela and Trinidad. He had become a fighter pilot with the USS *Lexington,* a new carrier on its shakedown cruise preparatory to assignment to the Pacific theater. The day was clear and the waters calm. He had been flying for more than an hour in routine practice when his Grumman Wildcat developed an oil leak so serious that he could neither reach Trinidad nor return to the ship, whose flight deck was in any case crowded with planes about to be catapulted. He made an ordinary wheels-up landing four miles off the starboard bow of the *Lexington* and in full view of the bridge and fellow pilot Bill Reiter (see map with letter 38). The plane sank in a minute, and only paint chips and a gas and oil slick remained when rescue craft arrived. Kinnick either had not gotten out or had been unable to inflate his life jacket. His body was not found.

Most of the press reaction was measured. Writers lamented that the war was killing such fine men, and so young. Editorials were fond retrospectives. There had been many American deaths already, against a background of worse slaughter in Europe, Africa, and Asia. Kinnick was only one among multitudes, yet a few journalists singled him out for a transfiguration. He who had been a relatively secular model was now for Whitney Martin "the typical American boy . . . the kind of young man you would like to have as Sunday school teacher for your boy" (*Des Moines Register*, 7 June 1943). Bob Considine wrote that if Kinnick "had taken a chance and tried to land on deck he might have survived at the cost of other lives and much equipment."[13] Bill Stern reconstituted the events as well as the character: "One summer day in the South Pacific Ensign Nile Kinnick was bringing in his plane for a landing on the deck of an aircraft carrier. He was about to set the plane down when a group of sailors darted directly in front of him. . . . Kinnick chose a hundred-to-one chance of living by crash-landing into a rough sea. Ensign Nile Kinnick lost his life because he thought of his teammates first."[14] In the 1943 or 1944 remarks of a fellow law student, John Evans, Kinnick possibly came as close to ascension and apotheosis as the Hero can in modern times: "Perhaps [God] refuses to allow His special clay to engage in our bloody little game. And you must admit that something would seem out of proportion if Nile Kinnick were to be decorated and famed for killing, burning and maiming. Perhaps he was jerked in the first quarter because war just wasn't his field." [15] Considine and Stern may have been manipulators, and Evans naive, but it was Kinnick who evoked the manipulation and the naiveté. In his case a public figure had evolved that might support any claims, whether false or merely hopeful. A heroic American innocent had run the course from achievement to legend and to myth.

That sort of public figure is superficial. A persona takes form from the qualities attributed to an individual, and an observer respects it without respecting more than its constituent parts. A persona is a set thing, full of itself, and one credulously believes that the living host must also be beyond regret and yearning, his identity complete. But there was a "public" Kinnick more essential than the monumental creature that emerged in his fame. This was the boy and man who assumed the code of his two family backgrounds. A fitting text to introduce him is a passage from a different kind of speech from those he gave on his trips. On 29 May 1940 Kinnick spoke at his Commencement Supper in Iowa City, and near the close of his address he told his fellow seniors that by now "we should have learned that success and happiness and attainment come only periodically not permanently – that they really are only passing moments in our experience. . . . our joy and happiness should lie as much in the struggle to overcome as in the fruition of a later day." [16]

Kinnick was still only twenty-one, yet in these words he sounded older, prematurely wise. He seemed resigned to a life without a hope or desire to say "I have lived to the full – this ecstasy is everything." For him there was no "fruition of a later day" anyhow, because the successful end of one purposive sequence meant the resumption of another that had been in abeyance or the start of something new. When he had his date in New York with Virginia Eskridge, the Delaware heiress, he invited her to come down to Washington and join him at the Camp Award ceremony. On 16 January, the day of the ceremony, she sent a telegram to the Willard saying she could not make it. She told him not to worry about his forthcoming examinations and to enjoy experiences that came once in a lifetime. Conceivably, there in the Kit Kat Club, while singer Velma Middleton was performing, Kinnick had thought out loud to Virginia about what concerned him – not the miracle season that had brought him there, not how good he felt or how good she looked, but the challenges that lay ahead. And when he returned from that second triumphal eastern trip, he began a note to the family (letter 11) by saying that the "final day of reckoning is at hand. . . . whether the Phi Bete Key can be gotten I don't know." He granted that the trip was "quite a bit of fun and the trophies . . . beautiful." "But," he added, thinking beyond the "Phi Bete Key" to still another challenge, "I am . . . pretty sure that Iowa is the place for me to go to law school & probably to live."

No one among the Clarkes and Kinnicks gave him Virginia's advice. By example, precept, and discipline the families taught him early the values of work, organization, and advancement; and from his Christian Science parents – especially his mother, a Christian Science practitioner – he learned also to reject worldly satisfactions as terminal values. And so the goals Kinnick strove for became temptations from the right path once he achieved them. He could not abandon the ethos of concentrated effort, for his religion also endorsed it: man must continually work toward control and transcendence, not through a monkish asceticism but while living in the world. To compete with men in their worldly games, knowing all the time that the true goal lay beyond them, was a reliable way of measuring the genuineness of the inward abnegation, for an air of disdain was not to be trusted in a slacker. People who knew Kinnick remember his modesty and calm when others praised him. Indeed, he was a modest and shy man, but for him the triumphal moments were not quite real, and he did not care enough to be proud.

The influences of the two families worked synergistically in Kinnick. Often he had two or more lines of purposive activity going at the same time – football, baseball, basketball, and academic study in high school; after 1938 (when he quit the Iowa basketball team) football and study, each with dedication, and these while he worked part-time in a bank, a cleaner's, the Iowa fieldhouse, and in 1939 as steward of his fraternity. In spring 1940 there were his lecture trips, for which the travel alone took many hours, and then and earlier there were plays, concerts, and the movies of which he was especially fond. He also took up dancing and became adept in that too. A classmate recalls seeing him with Margaret Kuttler at a formal dance in the spring of 1940. She noticed his moves, the tails of his full-dress suit snapping this way and that. The schedule was never too full for Kinnick to speculate on more lines to follow. In early 1939 he thought he might take a Rhodes Scholarship to make up for the limitations of his economics major, and while abroad he might go over to the Continent and learn German and improve his French (letter 7). While he was in the Navy Air Corps, with departure for battle coming closer, he thought ahead to after the war. He might become a working farmer, yet with an ample library and his own airplane, a Piper Cub or the Beechcraft five-passenger model he admired. Or he might become a flour salesman, with a broad Midwest territory so as to prepare a base of acquaintances and information that might serve him if he entered elective politics.

In the letters to follow, Kinnick often seems indecisive. Should he work in Des Moines or Seattle in the summer of 1939? Should he take the job with the Philadelphia entrepreneur? Should he join a new wheat-milling venture in Georgia? These were some of the issues he mulled over in letters home, hoping for advice. A major reason for his quandaries may have been a reluctance to refuse any line of purposive action not criminal or immoral. He spent more than two months considering even the zany proposal to join the rich boys in Mexico as their celebrity ornament, evidently unaware or not caring how humiliating the scheme was on its face. The need to do, to do more, to do everything available also affected his time away from commitments. Early in 1939 he wrote his family (and as so often, himself) that "too much time is spent getting ready to live and making a living and not enough in living dynamically and enjoyably right now." This could have been Emerson or Thoreau talking, but Kinnick added that "the most important thing . . . is to maintain an active, alert interest in everything going on about you" (letter 8). Accordingly, his idea of "three care-free days" in New York in 1943 was to hear Marian Anderson at the Met; take his brother Ben's fiancée to *Sons o' Fun* at the 46th Street Theater; see two movies, *The Human Comedy* at the Paramount and *Edge of Darkness* at the Strand, together with their accompanying stage shows, featuring Les Brown and Jan Savitt; and go to Sidney Kingsley's play *The Patriots* at the National and the vaudeville-burlesque show *Star and Garter* at the Music Box, topped off with a midnight supper and a performance by Alec Templeton at the Waldorf-Astoria (letter 35). Like the New York weekend, much of Kinnick's free-time reading until he entered the navy was also scattered and once over lightly (see letter 18), often in the *Reader's Digest* and other miscellanies. But far from making him feel broadly knowledgeable, his snippets and glimpses showed him what courses of study he would have to complete when he had the time.

Some of Kinnick's experiences with women were approaches to courtship – like his speculative careers, more form than substance – and here too he welcomed the bounty of opportunities. Shy in general and until he was about twenty especially reticent with girls, he broke out as a frequent dater of many women at Iowa and elsewhere, probably far more than the record indicates. He was immensely charming – witty, intelligent, a very big man on campus, zestful, warm, handsome, unpretentious, a fine dancer in conventional steps, fond of nightclubs[17] and elegant restaurants. Women loved him, and they remained loyal long after his death and during their own happy marriages. But he never let them get too close, and at least once when asked to commit himself, he said nothing.

Some of his comments indicate that he recognized women as another developmental challenge. Early in 1942, for instance, he believed he had reached a "normal" unconcern in telling his parents about his "social activities" (diary, 31 January), evidently recalling a time when he spoke of them with boyish excitement. Two weeks earlier he had written: "I shall not consider my mortal existence complete until I have loved and won a woman who commands my admiration and respect in every way" (diary, 18 January), apparently ruling out Merle McKay, the woman in Kansas City he was seeing then, as well as other women he kept in touch with. In the meantime, enjoying his associations along the way, he was in another kind of training. He put off until later, after the war, when he had sorted out his ambitions and found a career, growing up to the acceptance of someone other than an ideal.

In a life of purpose and dedication, experience became mostly transitional, and the consummations were quickly gone. It was one thing to dismiss successes as "passing moments" or to think little of them as they occurred, but it was another to see them pass beyond recapture and without issue. "Good bye, 1939, there will never be another season like you" – with this Kinnick ended a series of five newspaper articles on the glory year just over.[18] During the very crescendo of adulation, after the Heisman trip and with the January triumphs still ahead, he saw those Saturdays recede when he had joined with circumstances to produce events sufficient unto themselves. Here nostalgia was mitigated only by the knowledge that he had been there. He left so much behind, he knew the sorrow many times over.

Sometimes he tried to escape, through nostalgic tableaux, the onward rush in which nothing seemed stable. On Christmas Day 1942, knowing he would soon be going to sea to whatever that might bring, he recalled a Christmas morning in the 1920s when he was disappointed in a gift, a Luther sled, because he wanted a different make, a Flexible Flyer (letter 30). He was standing on a sofa looking out a window at the sled with his mother on one side and his father on the other. He cried, they cried, and he got his Flexible Flyer. Though trivial, the recollection was formally gratifying because it was of a complete and integral event with all the parties in fixed positions – the boy, the parents, the sofa, the window, and the sled. On another 1942 occasion Kinnick's grandmother, Arletta Clarke, saw in his nostalgia a threat to the family perspective. He had written her of "how you used to fix all of us brown sugar and toast when we were small children. . . . And the first time I ever mowed your lawn, I'll never forget that. It seemed an interminable job then, and I never could have lasted had you not called me in for ice cream and cookies every now and then." Kinnick told his parents that she replied with advice "not to look backwards very much, that forward was the watchword"[19] – this from a woman in her eighties to a young man of twenty-four.

The watchword was in no serious danger from Kinnick's nostalgic moods, frequent though they were, for at most they gave him occasional redress. But as early as 1938, among a gathering of random reflections, there was a potentially subversive one in which he associated quiescence and contemplation:

Why the constant hurry and intensity of present day life? I suppose it is a result of . . . the general philosophy of "do" and then "do" some more, to accomplish, then start something else. The general idea seems to be that he who accomplishes the most, visibly and materially, is the closest to being the ideal man. Personally, I discount this viewpoint and fail to see the desirability or worth of . . . being on the "go" all the time. Why not "take it easy" and attempt to "be" for awhile? . . . enough time MUST be set aside, it seems to me, for a little contemplative thought and speculation, a little thoughtful inquiry as to whither art we bound and are we on the right track. How are we to develop a sense of appreciation, of human understanding, of rationality, of true, harmonious living if we don't slow up and philosophize now and then. – June 1, 1938[20]

At that time the doctrine of "being" rather than "doing" was the means; the end was "contemplative thought and speculation," through which Kinnick might determine the things needful to all people. He was close to naming a way not to discard the ethos of "doing" but to avoid its oppressiveness and its selfish tendency. The way was a political career, which he elsewhere explicitly considered before he became famous (for instance, in a letter to the family dated 22 March 1939). In this alternative line, his success and his transcendence would start with his articulation of the needful things. He might for a time have to have a career in private life, but it would lead to his becoming a spokesman like his greatest hero of the war, Winston Churchill. And he might both speak and help get done what he spoke of if he became a public official, able to affect the "doing" of his state and his country.

Speaking – whether through writing or oratory – was essential to Kinnick for more than this pragmatic reason. His family and religious codes set much store by normative words. The words *principle* and *mind* might not have had exact referents, but when Kinnick used them he endorsed his grandparents and his parents and also put himself under the obligation of practicing what he preached. And when he wrote to his brother George, eight years younger, and advised him with undeniable stuffiness to shape up, the very stuffiness made his own challenge the more demanding. As a young man himself, and a fallible one, he had not yet established a public character to his own satisfaction. At that time in his life, his highest accomplishment could only be to state his principles and state them again; each statement was a pledge to be made good.

After Kinnick entered the Navy Air Corps pilot training program, the range of his purposive activities of course became restricted. There were ground school, aerial lessons, watches, cleanup, and other navy obligations, and he had to exercise his push to excel mostly on these duties. He had hours to himself, and he was able to catch up on such big fictions as Santayana's *The Last Puritan* and Tolstoy's *War and Peace*. But after his transfer to Miami for the final phase of his training, the tedium became overpowering. In August 1942 his diary entries marked the time, and some days he could not muster enough interest to write anything. The strongest feelings he registered were disgust and impatience: "uninteresting, dull, senseless ground school – ugh!" (16 August) and "The days creep by – will we never finish?" (24 August). When the course ended on 1 September, he also ended his diary. It had become part of the creeping, and he considered himself well shut of it.

But eight months later, less than a week before the *Lexington* sailed on 11 May 1943, he resumed his diary. Why he did so is not altogether clear. Some of the material was characteristic "thought and speculation," and there was even a final recitation from the family code in "A man must *never* cease growing, developing, looking ahead" (6 May). Some of the entries were wholly given over to reading notes and reflections during his engrossment in *War and Peace*, Willkie's *One World*, and Thurman Arnold's *The Folklore of Capitalism*. In these respects the May diary was like the previous portion and like much of his correspondence. But now Kinnick also recorded trivial sense impressions, navy slang, song titles, an Errol Flynn joke, and vagrant phrases he may have heard or invented, such as "restless as the sea" and "pay with the ring of my money for the smell of your roasting goose." In these materials the May diary was not a communication to his parents [21] or an organization of experience, hardly a conversation with himself. He saw and heard things, he had things pop into his mind, and so he put them down, without connectives or other signs of structuring. He had become relaxed, his schedule out of his hands, and now "being" rather than "doing" was both means and realization. In slowing up, he opened to whatever entered his field, and anything was worthy of notation.

Kinnick also opened to himself. At the end of the remarkable entry for 9 May he recorded images from "Wild dreams," one of them a dream of forced landings, in possibly the only account of his dreaming he ever wrote. A few lines earlier he wrote of flying high and alone among cumulus clouds, and what welled up during the flight was a self-assessment that crossed a span of seven years. He formed an obvious association of the clouds with snowy mountains, and if a visual association had been dominant, he might have been reminded of Long's Peak in Colorado, snow-covered when he ascended it in 1935, and with which he had associated Alec Templeton's "Trout Streams" the month before (letter 35). Instead, naming a range he had never seen, he wrote that he felt "like an Alpine adventurer." He was and had always been like the solitary traveler in Longfellow's "Excelsior," a poem his grandfather transcribed for him in a letter of 1936 (see preface and letter 17). But this condensation in a reverberant phrase did not trigger an elaboration on the duty to climb or a reminiscence of his grandfather, much less a recollection that the solitary traveler reached his triumph only through dying. Here and in the dream account, Kinnick seemed no more or less involved in what he was writing than he did in the accompanying list of song titles and the women and places he associated with most of them. The title "Chattanooga Choo-choo," all by itself between the accounts of his flight and his dreams, had as much right to be included as they did. Each item received brief mention and gave way.

In the entry for the day after his flight, Kinnick wrote that "the happy, peaceful, kindly mind is the one which loses all sense of self and takes no thought of the physical body." Many passages in the May diary imply, if not a loss of self, a slackening of consciousness, a loss of inhibition, and an indifference to judgment. Through evacuation came an indiscriminate acceptance, a "kindliness" toward things, and though his advocacy of losing the sense of self may suggest a Christian Science influence, Kinnick represented the desirable condition not as transcendence but as vacancy. These signs of a possible disorientation in the May diary could have been incidental. In that month Kinnick entered an unprecedented situation, for all his months of training, and some shakeup in his canons of relevance and importance is hardly surprising. But it can also be that the May diary, written for his eyes only, disclosed a change that had started some time before and that would have ended with his becoming a more urbane and less driven man. In any case, where he was heading remained to be seen. If he had fought and survived through August 1945, he might have taken up where he had left off, and with a reaffirmation of the family ethos; or he might have found restoring his cultural ties difficult and problematic, like many a veteran of that war. His death was a sad and ridiculous accident, one that left him unfinished and so beyond our full grasp. But better that than at twenty-four to have died completed, with nothing more to become.

Even so, Kinnick lived long enough to be a familiar American man of a type manifested in every generation and in every region: the man of talent who is told to rise, who wants to rise, who refashions himself in order to do so, and who, the higher he climbs, becomes unsure of what he wants and of what true rising is. He enters a psychic limbo, yearning for some still more subtle glamor just beyond and looking back to what he wishes he had never left. He may resort to activity for the sake of activity, and sooner or later he may make a virtue of quiescence. Dead a month before his twenty-fifth birthday, Kinnick precociously matched this profile item for item, and readers of a certain age who recognize themselves in it will agree that it was not designed to match him. It is up to them, nevertheless, to keep their vivacity, their humor, and their convictions of what is best for society in their time, as Kinnick did in his.

The Nile Kinnick Papers Collection

The Kinnick Collection at the University of Iowa is the only large holding of Kinnick manuscripts and memorabilia.[22] The first acquisition came in January 1959 and resulted from a solicitation of Kinnick's parents by George M. Sheets, Collector of Iowa Historical Documents at the University of Iowa Library. On 4 November 1958 Frances Kinnick wrote Sheets that she felt "very humble and grateful that you wish to establish such a file." She and Nile Kinnick, Sr., looked through their son's papers for an appropriate selection, and on 30 December she sent off the first installment of their donation. But she told Sheets that there was an omission within the chronological period of the shipment: "The active correspondence between Nile and me I chose to destroy not long after he was lost. I have always flinched from biographies which lay bare the innermost feelings of people after they are gone" (covering letter of 30 December 1958). Her statement may mean that she destroyed only her letters to him, for none survives in the collection, whereas several letters from him to her are there besides the four in the present selection. She may have destroyed some of his letters that she thought too intimate for the public to see.

That first consignment consisted of thirty letters dating from 1922 to 1940, twelve speeches, several news releases and clippings, and eight miscellaneous papers (George M. Sheets memo to Leslie W. Dunlap, Dir. of the Univ. of Iowa Library, 21 January 1959). Sheets did not prepare an inventory, but he indicated that the following were in the lot: Kinnick's 1935 essay on his trip west with his brother Ben titled "A Motor Trip thru the West"; the Commencement Supper address; a letter from Erwin J. Gottsch to Kinnick, 18 September 1940 (see letter 13); a letter from Alice Dagwell to Kinnick, 28 September 1940 (see letter 14); and "some thoughts on philosophy, in diary form" (probably the gathering of random reflections cited above, in which each reflection is dated). The earliest Kinnick letter in the collection is from 1935; those of earlier dates have only family association value.

After Sheets's retirement in 1959 and Frances Kinnick's death in 1966, correspondence regarding further donations passed between Kinnick's father and Robert A. McCown, Manuscripts Librarian. Between 1975 and 1977 Mr. Kinnick gave the library most of the remainder of the collection. This included an unspecified number of letters dated before September 1942 and, for the first time, correspondence from September 1942 through May 1943; carbon copies of letters from Mr. Kinnick to Nile and Ben Kinnick; photographs, evidently including two albums of the Kinnick boys' baby and boyhood pictures, together with newspaper clippings about Nile's and Ben's athletic activities from 1931 to 1935; Kinnick's navy diary; additional loose newspaper clippings; tape recordings made from Mr. Kinnick's records of the Heisman Award address and of Kinnick's interviews with Merle Miller and Arch Ward; and three scrapbooks. Mr. Kinnick signed the Consignment of Papers form on 12 August 1977. In 1983 he made a final donation of seven Kinnick photographs, including four of the 1939 Iowa–Notre Dame game. More recently there have been donations to the collection by Celia Peairs Fay, Robert A. Hobbs, Earle Murphy, and William C. Stuart. These include a Kinnick telegram to Celia Peairs dated 21 February 1941 (photocopy); a letter and a postcard (Hobbs); a twelve-minute sound film of game action, a campus rally of 1939, and the Heisman Award address (Murphy); and letters, student legal briefs, and other memorabilia (Stuart).

The bulk of the collection consists of the correspondence, the diary, and the three scrapbooks. There are more than two hundred letters and postcards from Kinnick alone, most of them to his immediate family, and nearly as many of Mr. Kinnick's carbons, which frequently contribute information necessary for a full understanding of Kinnick's letters. The letters and carbons, together with the diary (in three notebooks), occupy the first of four file boxes. The other boxes contain the speeches and miscellaneous manuscripts, loose clippings and association items, photographs (including the two albums), and the audiotapes. The three scrapbooks are very large ledgers, with pages measuring 14 × 15¾ inches of usable space and with so many pages that the first two scrapbooks are 3 inches and 2⅛ inches thick, not counting their board covers. A label on the front cover of the first scrapbook gives the inclusive dates of its items, September 1936 to 26 November 1939. The second covered 27 November 1939 to 31 December 1942, and the third, 5 June 1943 to 1975.

The scrapbooks contain indispensable information as to Kinnick's three varsity football seasons, the 1939–1941 awards and lectures, his fame among journalists and the public, and his Navy Air Corps career. The notion of starting the scrapbooks evidently began with both Kinnick and his father, and both contributed material to them. The elder Kinnick regularly cut items from the *Omaha World-Herald*, the *Des Moines Register*, the *Des Moines Tribune*, and any other paper or magazine to which he had access. Kinnick apparently took items from the *Daily Iowan*, the *Iowa City Press-Citizen*, and newspapers he saw on his trips and then sent them on to his father in Omaha, where the scrapbooks remained. It was probably Kinnick, for instance, who sent the clippings (see illustrations with Heisman address) and telegram relating to Virginia Eskridge, as well as a flyer from the Kit Kat Club advertising singer Velma Middleton (all in scrapbook 2). Early in the project, Kinnick told his parents that the scrapbooks should not be restricted to favorable publicity: "I rather hope that you have saved the unfavorable newspaper comment along with the rest. If the scrapbook is to give a true picture the bottom as well as the top should be shown" (letter of 1 October 1938, after Kinnick's inadequate performance in the Iowa-UCLA game on 23 September). Thus the Jack Miley diatribe cited above was included, along with a postcard to Kinnick of 20 January 1940 from an anonymous "Football Fan and World War [I] Veteran" in Fort Dodge who objected to the pacifist slant of his Heisman and Camp speeches: "I have up to now thought quite a bit of you and your achievements, . . . but when you keep saying something about football medals and grenades and fighting for your country etc., I want to state here that I prefer my honorable discharge to any trophies" (scrapbook 2).

The collection lacks some significant documents. Frances Kinnick's destruction of her letters leaves her a shadowy figure whose personality and place in the family structure must be inferred from what Kinnick and others said about her. The collection also lacks the Navy Department telegram to Kinnick's parents announcing his death. Apparently

Kinnick's father quoted it in a letter to Ben of 3 June 1943, but that letter is not now available, and the one transcript that has been printed therefore cannot be verified.[23] But a letter from Kinnick's squadron commander on the accident is in the collection and is evidently more descriptive than the telegram. Its information agrees with the log of the *Lexington* for 2 June 1943, so it has been introduced as letter 38 in the present selection.

There are deficiencies in the collection more serious than these. Aside from the Virginia Eskridge telegram, there are no communications from any of the unrelated women he knew, and very few from anyone he knew well. There are no letters from his brothers, Ben and George, and if his father had not made carbons there would be none from him either. Kinnick's policy evidently was to discard his mail after he read it, except for his mother's letters, apparently. Occasionally he forwarded letters home, including one that "attests to my charm" he sent with a letter to his parents in March 1941, possibly on 4 March. He told them to "Keep it!!!" and beneath this request his father wrote "(see personal letter file)." The "personal letter file" is not in the collection and may no longer exist. Further, aside from photocopies of a telegram and a letter to Celia Peairs, there are no Kinnick letters to the women he dated and few to anyone outside the family. Thus some of the earlier statements about his relations with women are inferential or depend on correspondence and interviews that developed during this project.

Despite its deficiencies, the collection permits a selection representative of Kinnick's primary dispositions. A reliable sense of him emerges during the seven years covered in the thirty-eight Kinnick letters of the present volume. Those omitted merely confirm the impression.

Editorial Policy

The foregoing introduction is only selectively biographical and explores no events in close detail. Such exploration is reserved for the headnotes to the letters, which in their sum serve as a consecutive, though still quite limited, biographical account. In several letters Kinnick alluded to minor matters that would be obscure without explanation. In cases in which the explanations would unduly clutter the headnotes, they have been placed after the letters in the relevant order.

Such annotation can become obtrusive if it explains what every reader knows or can easily learn, and thus many historical events, people, movie titles, book titles, and the like have been left without comment.

The letters and the diary are printed without abridgment. Missing words are enclosed in square brackets, and where conjectural they are followed by a question mark. Kinnick's simplified spelling is kept (*nite* for *night* and *thru* for *through*, for example), as are his technically incorrect plurals (*philosophys* for *philosophies*), on the assumption that they were part of his simplification system. Another unusual styling remains: the feminine plural *alumnae* for the usual masculine plural *alumni*. Kinnick had two semesters of high school Latin (with grades of A), enough to know that the Latin *-ae* sounds the same as American English (but not Latin) *-i* in that word. He may therefore have chosen *alumnae* in the belief that *alumni* was unlearned or inconsistent. Some punctuation normally regarded as incorrect is also kept, such as possessives and contractions without apostrophes, again assuming that they were simplifications. Another eccentric styling not emended is the occasional terminal question mark where a period is customary (see, for instance, letter 1). In all such cases there is contextual reason to believe that the question mark signaled a wry intonation or pointed to an irony or joke in the preceding sentence. And Kinnick's contractions (*pchse* for *purchase*, for example) are not spelled out.

Dates within square brackets and included without comment are those inscribed during the organization of the Kinnick Collection on letters he failed to date. Other dates within square brackets are, as indicated, his father's or are the editor's inferences, and a date especially uncertain is followed by a question mark. All dates without brackets are Kinnick's.

Many misspellings have been corrected. Kinnick had occasional difficulty with surnames and more difficulty with place names, such as Duchess, Macqueripe, and Venzuela for Dutchess (the New York county; see letter 34), Maqueripe, and Venezuela. These and several other misspellings do not appear to have the warrant of his schematic simplification. But when he wrote "(sp)" after a misspelling (after Deehl in letter 6, for example), the incorrect form is kept and the correction, if needed, is supplied in an annotation. In the text, all corrections of misspellings and of Kinnick's other slips are silent. An apparatus listing these changes – what textual critics call changes of "accidentals" – is not necessary or appropriate for this edition.

Notes

1. Kinnick's father's name was Nile Clark Kinnick, the "Clark" deriving from his paternal grandmother's maiden name. Nile Clarke Kinnick (the Clarke coming from his mother's family) was technically not a "junior," but everybody considered him one, and in Adel his boyhood nicknames were "Jun" and "June." For details of family history I have used *Adel Quasquicentennial, 1847-1972* (Adel, n.d.); G. W. Clarke's obituary in the *Des Moines Register*, 29 November 1936; the *National Cyclopaedia of Biography*; D. W. Stump, *Kinnick: The Man and the Legend* (Iowa City, 1975); data supplied by David L. Tetrick, an Iowa honors student from Adel; and correspondence and other documents in the Kinnick Collection at the University of Iowa.

2. *Council Bluffs Nonpareil*, 20 December 1939; clipping in scrapbook 2. Here and hereafter citations to the scrapbooks are to ledgers in the collection, discussed later in the introduction.

3. For details of the season, see Stump, *Kinnick*, and Scott M. Fisher, *The Ironmen* (Lincoln, 1989). Fisher provides game-by-game statistics and gives the best overall account of the 1939 season.

4. For example, in the *Daily Iowan*, 11 November 1939; clipping in scrapbook 2.

5. *New York Sun*, 9 December 1939; clipping in scrapbook 2.

6. *Boston Post*, 8 December 1939; clipping in scrapbook 2.

7. Clipping in scrapbook 2. Evidently the rumor began with a release by the National Editorial Association, cited as the source in the *Tribune* article.

8. See figs. 8 and 9. The statement by Virginia Eskridge was in the *Evansville Courier*, 20 February 1940; clipping in scrapbook 2. The *Courier* synopsized Kinnick's speech in Evansville at a YMCA banquet in the First Presbyterian Church. Kinnick added a note to a 1941 speech he wrote for delivery in Sioux City: "Another instance – girl in New York after the Iowa alumnae banquet" (typescript in box 2, Kinnick Collection). He was discussing the brevity of his fame, and there as elsewhere he exaggerated the brevity in his ingratiating rhetoric of self-deprecation.

9. Kinnick to his parents, 13 January 1943; carbon of Kinnick, Sr., to Kinnick, 14 December 1939.

10. Clipping in scrapbook 2. Readers will notice later convivial occasions described in the letters and diary in which there is no reason to believe Kinnick did not take part.

11. *Saturday Evening Post*, 16 November 1940, p. 89; clipping in scrapbook 2. Kinnick stands between the girls, facing slightly to his left; the girls, both blond, are turned toward him; they are all laughing. The girl on the viewer's left wears a white blouse with open collar, cardigan sweater, knee-length plaid skirt, bobby sox, and saddle shoes. The other girl wears a white blouse with open collar, tartan blazer, knee-length skirt, bobby sox, and saddle shoes.

12. From the typescript cited above in note 8.

13. INS dateline 11 June 1943; undated clipping from an unidentified newspaper, scrapbook 3.

14. *New Argosy*, May 1945; clipping in scrapbook 3.

15. Statement by John Evans, killed on Saipan in 1944, in Stump, *Kinnick*, p. 118. Another fantasy about Kinnick's death was enclosed in a letter from Illinois Superior Court Judge Michael L. McKinley to Max Hawkins, 26 October 1948 (box 2). Frank Balazs, a former Iowa football player, brought an ex-sailor on the *Lexington* to Judge McKinley's court, where the sailor deposed that he saw Kinnick crash about 100 yards from the ship just after takeoff and that he saw him jump from the wing of his plane in his Mae West (i.e., life jacket) to avoid being drowned when the plane sank. While Kinnick was floating he suddenly raised his arms and disappeared, evidently dragged down by a shark. For Balazs and McKinley, see letters 19 and 28.

16. For the complete speech, see "The Commencement Supper Address," following letter 12.

17. Compare Kinnick's disclaimer in his diary for 29 January 1942: "Must say I'm not much of a nightclubber." He may have meant that sometimes he did not feel at ease, for he often went to nightclubs in Chicago and other cities.

18. *Des Moines Register*, 19 December 1939; clipping in scrapbook 2. The other installments appeared in the *Register* on 14, 15, 16, and 18 December.

19. Kinnick to Arletta G. Clarke, 25 July 1942; Kinnick to his parents, 8 August 1942.

20. In box 2.

21. Kinnick began the diary portion for 4 December 1941 to 1 September 1942 almost as a serial letter to his parents, whom he allowed to read it during his leave before he transferred to New Orleans.

22. The history of the collection is based on correspondence and other documents in file MsC 112, Special Collections, University of Iowa Library.

23. Stump, *Kinnick*, p. 115.

PREFACE

In 1936 G. W. Clarke and his son Charles F. Clarke sent Nile Kinnick high school graduation presents, which he acknowledged in separate letters. Only his letter to his Uncle Charles survives (letter 1). The grandfather probably wrote the following response to Kinnick's letter in July, when the day and date coincided that year. The tenor of the response suggests that he also had in mind Kinnick's eighteenth birthday, forthcoming on 9 July.

Born in 1852 and a farmer and attorney by profession, G. W. Clarke had been governor of Iowa for two two-year terms, from 1913 to 1917. The main issue in his first campaign was his support for expansion of the capitol grounds in Des Moines, and a measure to that end succeeded in the state legislature. A progressive Republican, he supported workers' compensation, rural school improvement, and state highway development. After his governorship he served briefly as dean of the law school at Drake University in Des Moines. By 1936 he was passing his time largely in the vast personal library of his Adel home, where he may have copied out the Longfellow passages. What may seem the fifth and sixth lines of the poem were Clarke's comments, and there are other interpolations and minor errors in the transcription. Governor Clarke was in failing health, but he wrote his letter in a large and firm nineteenth-century hand. He died on 28 November 1936.

By July 1936 Kinnick had moved from Omaha to Iowa City, where he worked as a dishwasher and ditchdigger before his freshman enrollment at Iowa that fall. He kept relatively few letters from any correspondent, but the survival of this letter was no accident. It was probably kept safe in Omaha, and what it meant to him is indicated in letter 17. For quotations from Governor Clarke's first inaugural address, see letter 25.

Thursday 2nd 1936

My dear Nile:

I fully appreciate your being recognized and labeled as "Junior," that is, possessing and exemplifying all the fine qualities and ambitions of your most estimable father, yet I still think that at this time in your life when you are just beginning to take a real, deep, thoughtful look at the

*George W. Clarke in 1931. Negative, State Historical Society of Iowa,
Iowa City.*

Arletta G. Clarke in 1915. Negative, Kinnick Collection.

world and the years of your life just beginning to unfold – at such time I just think you are entitled to a name wholly in your own individual right, and I, therefore, address you as my dear Nile, at the same time begging to assure you that the qualifying word is used in all its fullest and deepest meaning by us – grand-pa and grandma – for you are, indeed, very dear to us. We most confidently look forward to a finely developed and outstanding manhood in you as the years go by. We are so much encouraged in this by the fact that such clearly seems, even now, to be your own inspiring ambition. You put behind you, dismiss, all and definitely, that would entangle you, harass you, prevent you.

Are you familiar with Longfellow's poem "Excelsior"? It is inspirational. Read it again some day.

"The shades of night were falling fast
As through an Alpine village passed
A youth, who bore, mid snow and ice
A banner with strange device," – "*Excelsior*"!
   (means higher, ever upward) I interpret slightly
He went on up the Alpine mountain; was that life?
   In happy homes he saw the light
Of household fires gleam warm and bright,
Above the spectral glacier shone,
And from his lips escaped a groan – "*Excelsior*"!
   (Stop not for the bright, happy homes)
"Try not the Pass! The old man said;
Dark lowers the tempest overhead,
The roaring torrent is deep and wide"
And loud that clarion voice replied – "*Excelsior*"!
   Stop not for the tempest and roaring torrents of life
"O stay," the maiden said, "and rest
Thy weary head upon this breast"!
A tear stood in his bright blue eye,
But still he answered, with a sigh – "*Excelsior*"!
   I must to the peak, I must gain the peak
Beware the pine-tree's withered branch
Beware the awful avalanche"!
This was the peasants' last good-night;
A voice replied, far up the height, "*Excelsior*"!

A traveler, by the faithful hound,
Half buried in the snow was found,
Still grasping in his hand of ice
That banner with the strange device, – "*Excelsior*"!

There in the twilight cold and gray,
Lifeless, but beautiful, he lay
And from the sky, serene and far,
A voice fell, like a falling star, – "*Excelsior*"!

I have not quoted all the poem – only parts of it. "Excelsior"! The "youth" was bound to reach the top. Nothing stopped him, nothing could. Nothing did, for

There in the twilight cold and gray,
Lifeless, but beautiful, he lay,
And from the sky, serene and far,
A voice fell *like a falling star – Excelsior*!

For all such ambitions, all such resolves, all such persistent efforts even against stubbornest difficulties-hardships the whole world shouts praise – *Excelsior*! – So may it be to you. But we would like to witness the *Triumph as it will come to you.*

We appreciate very much your sincere "thank you" for our little gift.

With all good wishes we are

Grand-pa and Grandma

The Letters

1 ✳ To Charles F. Clarke, 26 May 1936

The occasion was the Senior Banquet of Benson High School in Omaha in May 1936. The letter perhaps indicates Kinnick's early attraction to the law, but it may simply show a diffuse ambition here attaching itself to a family tradition. Charles F. Clarke, son of G. W. and Arletta G. Clarke, had practiced law in Adel for many years and was a noted outdoorsman who supported conservation causes. Auntie Kate was Kate Macomber Clarke. The "scintillating General Counsel for Peanut Amalgamated" was Kinnick's father, who was with the Federal Land Bank of Omaha. *The Cockle Bur* was and still is a monthly brochure sent to friends and customers by the Cockle Printing & Typesetting Company of Omaha. It contains jokes, songs, and miscellaneous items. See *The Best of the Cockle Bur*, ed. Harry B. Otis (Omaha, 1987), [p. iii].

May 26, 1936

Dear Uncle Chas:

Thank you for the necktie you and Auntie Kate sent me. I can always use a cravat.

Our banquet was held last nite and it was a huge success. Counting the faculty there were 201 in attendance. Each member of the class had to "kick in" $1.75 but I guess it was worth it. The girls were all in formals but the boys paraded in just their regular suits.

When they asked me to be toastmaster they said I would be competent because I had some subtle humor. I was afraid it might be *too* well hidden but everything went off nicely. In fact, with all due modesty, I had them under the tables half the time. I got off to a good start and things "broke" just right so as to make my cracks effective. I started off by saying that even after this bounteous banquet, with our esteemed class president on my left, I can still honestly say I have eaten *next* to nothing.

I wish very much that you might have been present. You would be surprised at the talent in this school. All the after dinner speeches were very clever. Nothing lagged at any time. I appreciate your response to my letter of a week or so ago. Father got a few back numbers of the Cocklebur and I was able to find a few appropriate jokes.

Here is a crack that went over pretty good and that you will appreciate. (From the standpt of the reference to the New Deal).

Nile Clark, Nile Clarke, and Frances Kinnick in Omaha in June 1936. Print, Kinnick Collection.

In referring to a boy who is known for his drinking I stated that he was now a reformed man. And that this all came about thru attendance in Chemistry class. The teacher said alcohol was $C_2 H_5 OH$ and the boy being a radical anti–New Deal refuses to have anything to do with any more *alphabetical regimentation.*

Another: Voltaire, that great French philosopher, says that whiskers are like ideas – women don't have them.

Again: A minister & a banker were having a hotly contested round of golf. The minister had the hard luck to lose by one stroke on the eighteenth hole. He didn't take his defeat very graciously and bemoaned his luck lustily. The banker, of course being in the best spirits, tried to console him. Saying, don't take it so hard old boy, we can't always win. Why, he said, John you'll probably live to bury me. Yes, sadly replied the minister but it would still be your *hole*.

May 26, 1936

U. Chas: –

One of the speakers retaliated with the remark, that she still thought the best toastmasters could be bought at the electric shop?

The Benson male quartette sang their cannibal song – *men u et*.

We all liked your picture very much. It is very good. I hope that the brilliant son of this scintillating General Counsel for Peanut Amalgamated will be of invaluable service should he decide to practice with you. At any rate he should dispel any vestige of the senile atmosphere that might have pervaded your law suite heretofore.

Be sure and thank Auntie Kate for me. Her selection, or yours, was excellent.

Yours,

Nile Jr

2 ✳ To George Kinnick, 18 July 1938

During the summer of 1938 Kinnick worked as a counselor at Camp Highlands, a boys' camp on Plum Lake in far north central Wisconsin, whose letterhead stationery he used for this letter. He had had a similar job in Minnesota the previous summer at a camp run by Ossie Solem, a former head football coach at Iowa. Also in the Camp Highlands area was Red Arrow, a camp run by Rollie Williams, the Iowa head basketball coach, where Kinnick's group stayed a night during the canoe trip described here. Camp Highlands was operated by W. J. Monilaw, M.D., of Chicago (familiarly "Doc," as in this letter), a college friend of Kinnick's uncle Fred Clarke. George William Kinnick (1926–1987), going on twelve that summer and visiting first with his grandmother in Adel, was to receive cautionary asides and letters wholly given over to advice on his studies, prose style, and general conduct for the rest of Nile's life (see letter 37 for the final example). The Bices, with whom Kinnick urged George to behave in a manner befitting lofty and unfamiliar hosts, were Uncle Don and Aunt Ruth (Kinnick) Bice of Atlantic, southwest of Adel. Kinnick's poor singing voice, treated here with a self-ridicule that might please George, was a lack he always regretted. The day before his death he would write, "How I wish that I could sing and play the piano!" (diary, 1 June 1943). Ben was Benjamin Greene Kinnick (1919–1944), Kinnick's other brother. Bob in the postscript was Bob Hobbs of Omaha, already Kinnick's close friend.

July 18, 1938

Dear George: –

I am so glad to hear that you are having so much fun. There is no place like a small town for a boy to have a fine time during the summer time. I hope you are working on your swimming, diving, tennis, and occasionally some golf. You will want to be proficient at them some day and it doesn't come without a good deal of practice. Are you helping Grandma a little each day? Consideration and helpfulness are great virtues and well worth cultivating. When you go with the Bices – if you have not already gone; I have forgotten; remember that you are their guest. Be obedient, quiet, and helpful. Nothing stands out so much in a small boy as being quiet, reserved, instantly obedient and cheerfully helpful. I only have one in my cabin and to him I have naturally become quite attached. To be a tough, rugged boy is every lad's ambition. But to be a gentleman, to be kindly, charitable, thoughtful as well as tough and rugged is much more to be desired. And he who can be both is much the better man and usually much tougher in the long run. He is admired and respected by all but those who are too "small" to acclaim fine characteristics. I have been so pleased to find you improving in many ways each time I come home. Keep it up; never cease to strive for the best. You – as well as Ben and I – have a wonderful heritage from parents, grandparents, relation, associations and religion. Make the most of all them. You have much to live up to. I expect much of you in the years to come and I am sure you will not fail. When I was your age I could not meet and introduce people as well as you. Nor be at ease and converse with the girls as I am sure you can. Nor could I play tennis or swim as well. Develop in all these channels – this seems to be your forte. Be at ease, joyful, and composed in all your activities and associations. Do not quibble and quarrel over trivialities but stand firm as the rock of Gibraltar on matters of principle. That is, do not argue vociferously over a referee's decision or a difference in

From left: Frances, Nile, George, and Ben Kinnick in Omaha in 1936. Print, Kinnick Collection.

size of dessert but stand solid and unflinching when it is a question of absolute honesty, truthfulness, kindliness, compassion, thoughtfulness, etc. It is time you are thinking along these lines, and I am sure you are.

Tonite you should have been here for supper. You would have rolled in the aisle. It is customary for those late to meals to sing a little song. I vowed at the first of camp I would never, never be late, but lo and behold who should be late tonite but yours truly. Fortunately, Don Warfield a pretty competent vocalist was late also which saved my skin. We went to town on the Iowa Corn Song which luckily I knew in a sort of haphazard manner. I was quite careful not to sing too loud so that they would only hear Don.

Friday morning I returned from a five day canoe trip the route of which I shall outline on a map and inclose if I remember it. I suspect I passed thru a little bit of Uncle Charlie's heaven. We made 4 or 5 portages ranging from just a "pull-over" (a bridge or road) up to a mile and a half which is pretty tough going. The canoes weigh about 90 lbs & the packs which we usually had to go back and get if the portage was very long weighed about 80 lbs. As I watched these city boys struggle

& stagger I wondered how well you would have done. Have you learned to compete? To work hard & keep going even when it isn't easy? I hope so. We paddled thru many lakes which were connected by rivers or gradually tapering from one to the other. We paddled on lakes that were calm and smooth as glass and then again directly into white caps which would have overturned us had we not kept our bow headed right into them. Again when the boy in the bow slacked in his paddling I wondered how you would have done. Would you have quit as soon as you were just a little tired? We slid thru lakes thick with wild rice. So thick in fact it was about like paddling across a football field in a heavy dew. Now we rush down a fast stream dodging rocks (most of the time), sticking on sand bars, getting out wading along and then in again. About 5 or 6 oclock we land & pitch camp, cook & wash dishes & then to bed. There is not much spare time but it is pretty much fun. Many times I wished the whole family were along – especially father. I know he would have enjoyed it *so* much. The last day out we paddled up Trout River. It was raining & pretty cold. I just had on a quarter sleeve & no raincoat but it was fun & very refreshing to stick out my chin & pull ahead. Now & then a duck would get up out of the wild rice along the banks; and every so often a large blue heron would lazily & ponderously flap along ahead of us. As we proceeded up stream the river ran faster & faster. Finally we had to get out & pull our canoe against the shallow rushing water for a mile where it opened into Trout Lake. Many times as I was wading up this swift stream pulling my canoe behind me I thought of the pioneers of this country – Geo. Rogers Clark, Lewis & Clark, etc. and the Indians. It was great fun. I wish you could have been along. As we came into Trout Lake we turned left 100 yds or so & there was Red Arrow – Rollie Williams' camp. We camped there that nite – played bridge with Rollie that evening – paddled across the lake the next morning where a camp truck picked us up. A fine trip & lots of fun. A trip including just grown fellows or say, you Ben and father would be ideal. Perhaps sometime we can do it. Tomorrow I go out on a *camping* trip with a bunch of little snipes which I don't relish very much. But perhaps it will be more fun than I think.

My sweatshirt arrived as did also my toothbrush, etc. Thanks very much.

I planned to write just as soon as I got back from the trip. I was full of a lot of good things to write then, but since my return I have been busy writing letters to parents at Docs request which has taken up most of my time. Hence, I haven't said as much about the trip as I had planned.

Here is a puzzle for you.

New Door

Make one word out of these two. I'll send the answer on request.

Well take it easy, sonny boy.

Yours,

Nile.

P.S. Bob has written me twice – both fine letters. Tell him I'll write him as soon as I can – and that my golf game is still punk.

See map: –

Started at noon. We paddled across Plum Lake; portaged to Star; paddled across Star L. into Mud L.; portaged from Mud to Ballard; stayed all night on far side of Ballard; portaged next morning over to Partridge; paddled across Partridge & portaged a mile $\frac{1}{2}$ along Nixon Creek until it was deep enough to put in; thence down Nixon Creek into Nixon Lake, on into Manitowish R & into Boulder Lake where we stayed all night, (about 20 miles in all – 60 miles, covered in entire trip) Thru Boulder L. into Manitowish R. again; all night; then thru Alder L., Big-Rice & up Trout R. to Trout Lake (all night at Red Arrow) Across T. Lake & picked up.

3 ✻ To Frances Kinnick, 23 October 1938

During the 1938 and 1939 football seasons Kinnick usually wrote his mother or both parents after Iowa games she or they had not attended. The day before this letter was written, Iowa lost at home to Colgate, 14–0. Kinnick had seriously bruised an ankle in the first game of 1938, a road loss to UCLA, 27–3, and though he played throughout the season, that and later ankle injuries affected his performance. The phrases "good work" and "Fine work" evidently refer to his own therapeutic religious exercises and to his mother's "absent treatment" of his injury in her role as a Christian Science practitioner. His request that she stand by him and his suggestion that they work jointly to produce a "fine demonstration" also refer to Christian

Science observances, and these expressions often recur in his correspondence. The term "demonstration" here means a display of the power of transcendent Mind or Truth over "error" or a "claim" of pain and injury issuing from what Christian Scientists call "mortal mind."

Kinnick and Bob Hobbs had pledged Phi Kappa Psi in the spring of 1938 and would be initiated on 30 October. The "hard times party" was an annual Phi Psi event, for which Kinnick's date that year was Era Haupert of Marshalltown (see letter 9), who had been selected for a full-page photograph in the "Beauties" section of the 1939 *Hawkeye* yearbook (published in the spring of 1938; during this period the date on the university yearbook was the graduation year of the junior class, because the editor and staff were chosen only from that class).

The last paragraph of this letter introduces a sensitive matter in letters 4 through 6, the adjustment of Kinnick and his parents to the removal of Irl Tubbs as head football coach and his replacement by a Roman Catholic, Dr. Eddie Anderson. Tubbs's first season, 1937, was unsuccessful, and by the fourth game of 1938, the Colgate game, his position had become tenuous. In the remaining half of the season, Iowa scored only three points, lost three games, tied one (0–0 with Purdue), and Tubbs was out. Kinnick's references to "micks" and "some Notre Dame man" suggest an anti-Catholicism easy to see but difficult to assign to this or that family member, and Anderson's faith becomes an explicit consideration in letters 4 through 6. Was it a prejudice Kinnick held at first, and was it something he sensed in one or both of his parents? The record does not permit a sure answer, but letter 6 indicates that Kinnick was quick to drop this religious issue. It never returns in his extant writings, and he and Anderson became good friends.

[23 October 1938]   Sunday

Dear Mother:

I felt just about really ready to go yesterday, but by golly I got cracked right off the bat and again later in the game. However, there was good work done previous to the game and my ankle feels as well today as it did last Sunday, I believe. This morning I had breakfast with friend Tubbs at his invitation. During our conversation he asked me if I was a Christian Scientist. He was just verifying what he already knew, I suppose. After a little discussion about this and that he asked if my laying off until I felt perfectly ready to go would more harmoniously fit my plans. I said yes, definitely, but said I couldn't so very well ask that. He said why not! Of course you can; your situation & outlook is considerably different from the other boys. He suggested that I not come out this week until I felt perfectly ready to go, and that if I didn't feel like playing Sat. to let him know and it would be "ok." – Fine work *has* been done, hasn't there? – He lamented that my ankle injury had occurred; that I seemed set for such a fine season – so much faster the 1st ten days than last year; that people were beginning to wonder what had happened bet. last year & this. Well as far as I am concerned neither Iowa nor Nile Kinnick has been whipped by error yet – nor will they be. I am grateful that there has been little publicity of my injury – that my mind has not been able to hang any excuses on me for a poor showing. Help me to handle the belief that the Iowa team play & spirit is dependent on my being able to go at top speed. I wish so fervently that we could get going for the coaches sake – they are as fine a bunch as ever lived. The papers and wolves are after them hot and heavy – the rats. Oh well, enough of this. Stand by me in culminating a fine demonstration. I should come out a bigger, better man in every respect – including football.

Last nite the Phi Psis had their hard times party and little Nileo was in there "swinging it." We started off with a hayride and danced afterwards. All a lot of fun. I had a date with a pretty darn nice girl – a Hawkeye beauty queen last year, to be exact. She invited me to the Delta Gamma party next Sat. nite – so I guess my social debut is inaugurated with a bang. Rah, rah, for the college boys.

I am in need of my jacket and will soon need my overcoat, maybe. Better send them down one of these days.

Received your two bucks and thank you. Could use more sox any day – (Size 11-½). Yes, I pchsed a sweater before going to Calif. I finally got a slip on – but like it very much. Am getting along quite well – studies are lining up a little better as are things in general, despite the football situation. Gee how I want to get in there and really go.

The "micks" all over the state are of course all set to run in some Notre Dame man. Perhaps we can beat them to the punch by winning two or three upset games. We should battle with a joyous feeling of confidence and absolute lack of apprehension – shouldn't we.

Yours,

Nile

4 ✹ To the Family, 14 November 1938

Iowa nearly defeated Indiana on a hot afternoon in Bloomington, 12 November 1938, but Indiana scored on a sixteen-yard pass with two minutes left in the game and won, 7–3. Ernie Nevers and Pat Boland were backfield coach and line coach respectively under Irl Tubbs. There is no evidence that either man was considered to succeed him. In a 16 November reply to this letter, Kinnick's father stated that both parents wanted him to accept the 1939 captaincy if it were offered. There is no indication in November of a parental concern that a Notre Dame man might replace Tubbs. (In December Erwin Prasse was elected captain.) Kinnick's "trying mental problems" again had to do with his lingering ankle injury, and he may have been thinking in part of his inability to confine his self-treatment to Christian Science methods. Ray Bywater (Iowa '33), a Phi Psi who then lived at 715 North Linn Street, recalls visiting Kinnick more than once that fall at the Phi Psi annex four doors away and finding him wrapping his leg in hot compresses (interview, 22 March 1990). His father's carbons before and after this letter do not identify whatever he was supposed to acknowledge, and as noted in the introduction, no Frances Kinnick letters survive in the collection.

[14 November 1938]   Mon. – 5:30 P:M:

Dear Family:

The game at Indiana was a heartbreaker. The boys fought harder than I have ever seen them. It was hot and it seemed as if they were on our goal line all afternoon. But we dug in and held them time after time. We hung on even tho we were all so tired we could hardly move. After getting that field goal we thought surely we had them beaten – and then by golly they scored on one of their many passes.

I played the only *real* game I have played all year – blocked and tackled with a reckless abandon and ran spontaneously and unhampered whenever necessary. How good it felt. This week I should be ready to make up in some measure for the poor game I played against Nebr. last year.

There is little doubt in my mind that the reign of Ira Irl is at an end. Personally, I believe it is best for him and all concerned. He is fighting a losing battle – he just *isn't* the man for this job contrary to what I thought at first. I would like very much to see Ernie or Pat take over –

they both understand the situation down here now and both are good coaches and would use a single-wing back – however, it is difficult to see how such a setup could come about.

There is, without a doubt, a strong movement to get a Notre Dame man in here – Buck Shaw for instance. What the actual outcome will be is pretty much beyond prediction. The alumnae will begin to roar as soon as the final game is over, regardless. They will "gun" for a big name coach undoubtedly. Happily, I feel that I am *established* now in the way that I should be. Consequently, I am not apprehensive about the choice at all. Whether you would want me to play under a N.D. man I do not know. And, another thing, do you think I should avoid the captaincy of next years team if possible? – relative to the statement above and probable necessity of spring practice if elected. On the face of it, it seems a dubious privilege anyhow; but I don't believe I would consider it as such. I want so much to help lift Iowa out of this situation.

Despite a poor season and trying mental problems I have had a pretty good time. Everything seems to be clearing up quite a bit and I am looking forward to many happy times after football – experiences, normal experiences, that I haven't enjoyed for several years. This year will see a much more equitable & normal division of time between my rightful college activities.

Monday 10:30 P.M.

A radio broadcast just stated that the *new* Iowa football coach would be announced right after the Iowa-Nebr. game. The consensus of opinion seems to point to Buck Shaw of Santa Clara – a former Stuart boy & player at Notre Dame.

I trust that I shall hear from you soon as to whether you are coming down for the Nebr. game. As for Thanksgiving – if you find it at all convenient I should like to meet you all in Adel. There are several things I should like to talk to you about.

In your last letter you mentioned something that I should acknowledge. I don't remember what it was but do recollect that I mentally noted at the time that I had received it – whatever it was.

Iowa State must have a fine team – power to them. I wish that I could revel in the fun & success of a good team. In four years of high school & two years of college football I have played on only one GOOD team – my jr. year in high school.

Best of everything to everyone.

Love

Nile

5 ✳ To the Family, 30 November 1938

Iowa ended its 1938 season with a record of 1–6–1, losing to Nebraska, 14–0, on 19 November. The only victory was over the University of Chicago, which would shortly drop intercollegiate football. On 23 November the *Des Moines Register* announced the selection of Eddie Anderson as head coach. Raised in Mason City, Anderson had played under Rockne at Notre Dame and had been a successful head coach at Holy Cross. He arrived in Iowa City on 29 November to a tumultuous reception, bringing with him his backfield coach, Joe Sheeketski, and his line coach, Jim Harris. (In December Sheeketski would accept an offer to succeed Anderson at Holy Cross, and Frank Carideo would replace him at Iowa in February 1939.) Among Anderson's remarks quoted in the *Register* on 30 November were these that Kinnick must have liked: "It's a clean start. Past performances don't mean a thing. We want hard runners. And speed. . . . You've got to have your offense ready when the season starts. I want the players to enjoy the game on Saturdays. They ought to get a kick out of confusing, outhitting and outrunning the other team." At that time Kinnick's father was also pleased with the selection, writing on 2 December: "It would appear that a smart choice has been made, as I don't know where it can be faulted, from the general point of view." Of course, the limiting "general point of view" may imply another, less satisfied point of view.

A "board job" was an employment privilege to help cover a student athlete's costs. Kinnick's job consisted of janitorial work in the Iowa fieldhouse. His C grades in two semesters of intermediate accounting (fall 1938 and spring 1939) were his lowest in his four years at Iowa.

[30 November 1938] Wednesday 5:30 P:M:

Dear Family:

I have time to dash off a few lines before I go to my beloved board job. Its been quite awhile since I have written but there has been little of interest to impart.

Yesterday afternoon the new coaches arrived amid much fanfare & enthusiasm. Before a large and spirited student gathering they were presented from the steps of old capitol. I met and talked with them only briefly. Head coach Anderson impressed me very favorably. Both he and I took an immediate liking & respect for each other I am quite confident. His assistants are quite inferior to him in polish and appearance, however, they seemed alright and probably know their football. The backfield coach seemed like a pretty good gent. The assistants are below the quality of Nevers & Boland I am afraid but I believe Anderson will have more on the ball than any of them. I liked very much what he said in his speech yesterday and his quotations in the paper this morning. He talks as if he appreciates the athlete's viewpoint. I hope this proves true. He has a lot of fire & enthusiasm & looks to be a very determined man – in actuality he isn't as tough looking as the newspaper photographs would indicate. Aside from the R.C. angle the situation seems to look pretty good. I am quite certain the experiences of the past few years have established me firmly on what I know to be right & true. There is no reason why everything shouldn't work out quite harmoniously.

I have been busier in the past week and half than during football season – if that is possible. However, I am having a better time than last year. Once or twice a week I rush over & play a little handball which keeps me toned up in pretty good style. I took 3 tests this week and did pretty well in all but the intermediate accounting exam. That stuff is really tough & for the first time in my scholastic career I am struggling to keep my head above water. All fine experience – just as the football season was – don't you think?

Thanks very kindly for the shirts, underwear & socks. All are appreciated very much.

Yours,

Nile

Send me some envelopes in the next laundry, please.

6 ✳ To the Family, 7–8 January 1939

The letters that roused Kinnick to the irritation and extended argument of this reply are missing. The absence of his mother's letter is not noteworthy, for again none of her letters survives in the collection, but the absence of the elder Kinnick's carbon is striking and may indicate a suppression. Also, no known quotation of Eddie Anderson in the *Daily Iowan* (the university newspaper), the *Iowa City Press-Citizen*, or the *Des Moines Register* from 23 November 1938 through 8 January 1939 remotely suggests Kinnick's comment in the second paragraph or his father's concession in his reply to this letter that Anderson's statement was an "involuntary one, made without knowledge of the person he referred to" (carbon of 15 January). Unless a relevant Anderson quotation turns up in print, the incriminating remark, whatever it was, must be taken as hearsay.

Yet a rough history can be drawn. On 5 October 1938, after Kinnick sent his parents the news of his bank job, his father wrote that "Mother's eyes were shining when I came home this aft and when I had read your letter we both rejoiced." So Kinnick was right to notice a switch in his mother's attitude from fall to winter and right to speak as though the issue was not the job as such but the job as a factor in a new environment of constraint. Anderson's remark may have seemed prejudiced against a Protestant, so now that a Catholic had indeed succeeded Tubbs and now that he had been heard from in an ominous way, both parents came to see Kinnick's position as difficult, and they evidently suggested that he quit both the bank and board jobs to keep his independence should there be any religious or cultural pressure. This reconstruction fits Kinnick's letter and his father's reply of 15 January, in which he surrenders to Kinnick's argument but tries to explain why Frances and he wrote as they did earlier. One may suspect that a prejudice in the parents led them to jump to conclusions about prejudice in their son's coach, but there seems to have been a good end to their action. They brought matters into the open that Kinnick exorcised, and the amicable relation that developed between Anderson and the Kinnick family may have owed much to the resulting clean start.

Persons mentioned by name are Otto Vogel, the head baseball coach; Frank Williams, a Phi Psi and president of the First Capitol National Bank (now the First National Bank); Chester A. Phillips, dean of the College of Commerce and a member of the Board in Control of Athletics; and Jim Diehl (not Deehl), a real-estate salesman and former Minnesota football player (Kinnick, Sr., carbon of 15 January). Ben Kinnick was at that time a student at Iowa State College; the absence of the elder Kinnick's carbon leaves unclear the allusion to a Webster scholarship.

The first quotation in the second paragraph is from Matthew 7:20. The other is not biblical and cannot be traced from concordances to

Mary Baker Eddy's works. It may have come from a serial like the *Christian Science Sentinel*, which Kinnick frequently read.

The catalog date is 8 January, but Kinnick began the letter at 11:30 P.M. on Saturday, 7 January 1939. This may be the only occasion when he timed both the start and the end of a letter, here to imply the deliberation he put into his argument.

[7–8 January 1939]   Saturday 11:30 P:M:

Dear Family:

I have your two letters, received today, in hand. I have read and re-read them both carefully. That their contents, correlative and supplementary in nature and import, were written after due delay and consideration and animated by fervent desire for my own best interests and welfare, there can be no doubt. The suggestions therein proposed are sound; however, that the steps outlined are correct and the best – of that I am a little dubious. Inasmuch as you did say in your letter, father, that the aforementioned suggestions were being presented for my consideration, and inasmuch as I have been intimately connected with the general situation here for three years, permit me to add my comment and arguments.

First of all may I say that if Coach Tubbs had been the participant in the conversation attributed to Anderson and his "buddies" in Chicago – when *he* was on his way to Iowa three years ago he very likely would have commented in a similar vein. There are few coaches who wouldn't probably. (That Anderson is a R.C. very likely added vehemence to his remarks – that may be assumed I suppose) However, I feel quite strongly that he (Anderson) and I will get along very well. That we can forestall any clash of opinions I am quite confident. When I met him several weeks ago and spoke enthusiastically in his behalf I am sure that he was well impressed with me – as I was with him. He and I will of course differ in opinions, beliefs and convictions. However, that we must clash personally can be metaphysically obviated. He and I both have good reputations; the development of which each of us attributes to diametrically opposite causes and convictions. Nevertheless, we both will be aware that our continued success may lie in cooperation and mutual effort. The belief that such harmony and unity of effort is impossible should not be accepted. Religions, convictions, philosophys may differ – widely and bitterly; but never, in my belief, should such differences be allowed to assume the personal aspect. Disassociation from people for such reasons is inexcusable; it is representative of bigotry and intolerance. They need not become your intimate friends, but neither should they immediately be added to your list of "untouchables." For three years, nay for fifteen years, I have been preparing for this last year of football. The season just past has removed much of the tension that might have attended this last effort. I feel confident and free from the pressure of "absolutely necessary success" and falsely accepted responsibility. I anticipate becoming the roughest, toughest, all-around back yet to hit this conference. That is a little strong, of course, but nevertheless I am not planning to be robbed of my consummation. That "ye shall know them by their fruits" is not an empty and obsolete phrase. It is only just and right that right thinking shall be provocative of just rewards. Truth and Love ARE efficacious; reliance thereon *is* PRACTICAL. The law of "Divine Principle is as powerful in the material world as in the spiritual." Victory shall undeniably be ours.

Now as to the sources of my income allow me to say a few words. It will be best, I think, at the very outset to inform you that I am working daily at the bank for at least one hour. I have been typing and serving as a messenger boy each day. First let us look at your contention that my athletic job and bank job constitute for the opposition – the new regime, as it were – a "hold" upon me. It is my firm belief that neither constitutes any such "hold" over me. I am not in the final analysis dependent thereon for my continued schooling as you very patently disclose in your letters. Speaking bluntly they are paying me to play football; I am not playing football for my means of sustenance. They are very definitely seeking good football players; I am no more interested in them than any other instructor. I have demonstrably proved that I am down here for the primary purpose of getting educated. Loss of my athletic jobs (I am considering for the present that the bank job is also an athletic job. However, I have more to say on this later) would hardly break my stride in my educational pursuit. They know this and will say nothing relative thereto. Otto Vogel once told me that Iowa was proud that her jobs were granted in the interest of the college's student and not for the exclusively athletically minded chap; that a boy receiving a job in the fall could hold that job the remainder of the year regardless of what happened – whether he finished the year in active competition or not. And his statement is borne out by actual cases – with which I am quite familiar. Incidentally, Vogel is in charge of the athletic jobs at present. In actuality they have no hold on me except a possible personal fear of unfavorable publicity and resentment among the players and my associates. This particular situation has been well met and handled in the season just past. The likelihood of having to cope therewith next fall is remote – based on spiritual understanding and not the law of averages, of course. Assuming both of the jobs mentioned above to be athletic jobs – for that is the light in which you consider them is it not – I don't believe you can say that I am overpaid, that I receive more than is merited by the effort expended. Anyone familiar with the arduous hours of college football practice could hardly conscientiously so aver. Now let us deal with the crux of my financial status; that matter which so perturbs my mother – my beloved bank job; that which seemed so fine and good early in the fall. Has it suddenly been revealed as debasing my character and a shame to my pride and integrity. I dare say not; and will endeavour to so prove.

Mr. Williams personally called me up and asked me to drop in and see him. I did not solicit the job or ask anyone to so do. At the time I was not in dire need for funds or a job; I had both – and both were satisfactory. Therefore he could not have been actuated by any moral obligation felt by ardent alumnae in the interest of the needy athlete. In the past three or four years he has had no athlete in his employ – therefore it has not been his custom to give just any athlete a free ride every year. He was under no compulsion to employ an athlete because all the other business men were making a concerted effort to so do – for no such activity was in evidence, nor is it now. He is getting a return for his money in some form or he wouldn't have hired me. Certainly he has no axe to grind. That I can be of any measureable benefit to his bank or to him personally thru reputation or otherwise in the near future is a rather silly contention. Hence, how could I entertain any obligation in that respect. Dean Phillips told me he considered it an honor to have me connected with the bank. In what way I couldn't say, but if he thinks so I feel highly flattered. I shall continue to stand on those principles from which I believe the external characteristics have sprung that resulted in my being selected for the job rather than some other athlete or some other student. Any time that they or any other employer of mine or my associates disapprove or become intolerant of the principles which give birth and foster those characteristics which they originally professed to so admire – they making no correlation, or appreciation of the cause and effect between principle and external characteristic – we then have met the parting of the ways. However, to explain all this at the time of employment is not feasible for that would be akin to apologizing for your very being. (This is somewhat of a digression but nevertheless a worthy observation, don't you think?) Now back to the Williams subject. I firmly believe that thru suggestion from someone else or active interest he became familiar with my reputation and character in athletics and in scholastics. (I have it on good authority that he made inquiry as to how I was getting along financially last year BEFORE Nevers of the athletic dep't spoke to him – as you know he (Nevers) did from my conversation with you) He appreciated my aims, ambitions, and accomplishments and resolved to find out if he could help me along in any way – this is my reasoning, of course. If you were reading the biography of some great man and read that at the age of twenty while he was in college one of the professors or prominent business men became interested in him through what?, why his accomplishments, his fine character, high ideals, etc – and took him into his house and boarded and lodged him (and bought him a new suit of clothes) for the remainder of his college career, you would strongly exclaim that thru adherence to the "best" this man had progressed in the world; that most of a certainty it was just and fine that he should have been helped along – even tho he only fired the furnace as a tangible means of return for the beneficence extended. Suppose Ben had rec'd that $500 scholarship given by John P. Webster. You would have said isn't that fine of that man that he should want to help deserving boys along. Would you have questioned whether Ben was entitled to it? Of course not? What would he give in return? Certainly not work or anything materially tangible? And yet Ben's high ideals, good character, would be known and an inspiration to oh so many fewer people than a good athlete. Good character and fine ideals are much more common in the fraternity and classrooms than among athletes. It is much more difficult to cling to your convictions when surrounded by the defaming circumstances, mental influences and general atmosphere and publicity of the athletic setup. Inasmuch as manifestation of such characteristics is the only return a man animated by the desire to help worthy students & prospective good citizens along can gain from his beneficence who should be worthier of more. Please overlook the very evident vanity attending these statements and try to accept my inference as valid argument that I should keep my job at the bank. Personally, I can see no other reason for my being extended that job. If expressing good character, ideals, good scholarship, plus an ability on the athletic field is Williams', Phillips', the bank as an institution's (or whoever is responsible for my present employment) return for the money expended, I would say that I put in all of 16 hrs a day fulfilling the contract, but it is of course *easy* for me to do so – that I will grant.

Well I have spoken; I have presented my side of the case. However, if you still believe your course of action the better I'll follow it. Nevertheless, at the present time I feel strongly for the arguments I have just set forth. These jobs – all of them – represent to me manifestation of right thinking about supply. They are the culmination of three years consecration, effort and prayer. I am grateful for them. Thru them I am able to join a fraternity, pay all my living expenses and have enough left after to go out socially, to buy myself the best suit I have ever had. Let me again repeat if you feel you are absolutely right we'll toss them overboard nonetheless. Personally, it seems wise to me to hang on to them, rejoicing all the while, and pray for guidance and protection until such time it shall be definitely revealed as to our proper course of action.

Isn't it nice that Ben stepped into a board job on his return? Power to him!!!

Father, you did not enclose the name of the personnel mgr of Sears. Will you try to do it next time you write?

Incidentally I saw Jim Deehl (sp) at church in Des Moines last Sunday.

Best wishes and love to you all.

Yours,

Nile

2:30 P:M: – Sunday

7 ✳ To the Family, 13 January 1939

This letter introduces Kinnick's uncertainty in 1939–40 as to his postgraduate future. Among options he seriously considered were law, sales, and professional football. He proposed a choice of law schools, should he choose law, that he would later withdraw. Before his ultimate decision to study law at Iowa rather than Washington, he also thought of Harvard (letter 10). Perhaps Kinnick would have pursued a Rhodes Scholarship had World War II not started for another year or two, but the Rhodes Scholar elections were virtually suspended shortly after the war began. At this time Kinnick was also undecided about a summer job for 1939. He considered working again as a camp counselor and working at whatever suitable job might turn up in two equally attractive places, Des Moines and Seattle. He finally took a job with the Omaha Grain Exchange, sampling wheat in boxcars.

Kinnick was made steward of his Phi Kappa Psi chapter, as he seems to have expected. The "house" he regretted that he would need to move into was the Phi Psi house proper, a crowded facility at 830 North Dubuque Street, whereas in the nearby annex at 228½ Brown Street he was enjoying a room to himself.

The catalog date is 20 January 1939, but that is impossible, for Kinnick's father's letter of 16 January quoted from the last paragraph of this one. An earlier Friday than the thirteenth is unlikely because a three-day interval between posting and delivery was normal in 1939. Kinnick's father wrote "(Jan-1939)" beneath Kinnick's partial dating.

[13 January 1939]   Friday 10:20 P. M.

Dear Family:

You are the recipient of correspondence from a lad whose mind is very much in flux. Constantly, I am inquiring, wondering, speculating, philosophizing about what my future education, if any, should be; toward what I should really point as an occupation; for what line of endeavour am I best equipped, apart from my formal education; is a happy, normal, honest upright life of the average man a sufficient goal toward which to strive, or is man duty bound if he is capable to try to serve his fellowman by serving his government and his country. Out of such musing and meditation I believe I have reached this definite conclusion. Man should be motivated in searching for employment and finding his place in society by the desire to benefit his fellowman and society, to leave his community and country a better place in which to live insofar as his effort, humble as it may be, will help produce that result. This service to society and country can be exercised in private business as well as in government affairs. Certainly, a business man should strive for honesty in his advertising and to market a worthwhile product as economically as reasonably possible. This idea of working just to make money or setting up in business just as a means to a livelihood is all wrong. There is no doubt that a majority of our corporations and business establishments have been fostered on such a premise. However, that such a thought animated their endeavours is one of the main causes for our distressing predicament today. It seems to me absolutely necessary, and in reality a joy, that a young man starting out in the world should be imbued with a desire to benefit mankind and society by his work and service – whether that be in the field of business, law or something else.

Yesterday I thought I would take some graduate work here at the University; study history, literature and perhaps get a Phd in economics. The day before I thought I would like to get my B.A. and go into law school the following year. The week previous I had decided to finish up in another year and immediately go into business, preferably, I thought some large merchandising concern. Today, I am all enthused about the Rhodes Scholarship again. My grades are in a rather dubious shape much to my chagrin – now – but I have decided to really "bear down" for final "exams" and see what I can salvage. My plan, now, is to finish all my commerce courses this year, take a good deal of history and literature next year and then sail for "merrie" England for two or three years of enjoyable but conscientious study of economics, history and literature. In the summer I will study in France and Germany and learn the language. I will then return to the U.S. with a wealth of experience and cultural education to my credit. Soon I shall next take myself to the U. of Washington in Seattle and there study law. At the age of twenty-seven or eight I shall then be ready to venture forth and put my experience and study to practice. Just what form my endeavours shall then take my mirror of the future here becomes nebulous. A noble thought, don't you think? And who knows it might come to pass. In some way my athletic knowledge and coaching ability shall pay for my education in this country – I think.

There is a very excellent possibility that I shall become the steward of this fraternity next Monday evening. Such a job would yield $25 per month. It would give me excellent experience and a worthy responsibility. It would entail quite a good deal of work, but would enable me to drop my board job and cleaners job. I would undoubtedly have to move into the house and probably room with someone else. This is to me a rather unsavory factor, but I believe I am ready & prepared for such a move. I am quite anxious to get the experience but more especially to serve this fraternity. It direly needs leadership and I am becoming well enough established to gently move forward.

Just what I shall do this summer I do not yet know. For some reason I favor some kind of business job in Des Moines. I wouldn't make as much money nor enjoy it as much as if I were to work in Omaha. However, I think D. Moines is where I should be making my contacts and associations rather than Omaha. I think I have much more of a heritage and opportunity there – if it should develop I should want to go into business.

I think I feel better physically and mentally than at any other time since I came away to college. I am enjoying my rather minor bank work each day and also my board job. Once more I am getting *something out* of ALL my studies. The world is alive, alert and dynamic. So must we be. It is an opportunity, not a problem.

Yours,
Nile

8 ❋ To the Family, 16 January 1939

Here in January 1939 Kinnick shows his customary link between a pragmatic orientation in scholarship and a desire to affect the world of affairs. Though as a Christian Scientist he grants that "right thinking" alone could improve the lot of mankind, he insists that present conditions be studied from "an economical, sociological and historical point of view" (compare the diary entry on Christian Science and "Yankee pragmatism" of 24 May 1943). The article he quotes is "Young Man in a Hurry Backwards" in the *Reader's Digest* for December 1938. H. L. Mencken gives a variant of Kinnick's adage about experts: an expert is "an ordinary man, away from home, giving advice" (*A New Dictionary of Quotations* [New York, 1942], p. 372; author unknown). Ted is his cousin Fred Clarke, Jr., in Seattle. Kinnick's father dated the letter.

Monday 4:15 P:M: [Jan. 16th 1939]

Dear Family: –

Last night I did something that I have never done before, something I have often sworn I would never do. However, necessity and other circumstances often alter convictions. I stayed up and studied Intermediate Acct'g until 2 A:M: Even then when I retired I was far from confident. Happily the test wasn't as difficult as it might have been, and I believe I got along quite well.

On Thursday or Friday of this week I shall register for the second semester. I think I have enough money to get by alright. If I run short toward the end of the month I'll let you know. During the month of February my income should be right around $80. Not a bad little sum in any league.

I have spent a great deal of time during the past month wondering just what I have been getting of value from college; just how a man should study, etc. Certainly it is practically impossible to answer dogmatically. However, I think I have some good ideas on the subject – realizing, of course, that the answers to such questions would have to differ from individual to individual – and am hoping you will tolerate good-humoredly my observations on the problem. My letters home are about the only opportunity I have for written expression of my sentiments on such matters. Again I woo your tolerance and urge expression of your own feelings on the subject if you so desire.

It is my belief that the essential thing to be gained from a college education is to learn to think, to think for yourself; to develop an active, alert, inquiring mind. In an article about Robert Hutchins by J. P. McEvoy in the Readers Digest, Hutchins is quoted as saying: "You come to college to learn to think – think straight if possible, think always for yourselves – to learn to read, discuss and understand – and to do this the old disciplines are needed – Grammar, Rhetoric, Logic and Mathematics – but don't let that scare you – for these are only the arts of Reading, Writing and Reckoning." I think he is pretty close to correct. It would seem quite natural that we should turn to the writings of the great minds of the centuries gone by to discipline and guide our own mode of thinking. However, the little experience I have had with Plato, Socrates, etc. leads me to believe that the subject matter about which they argue and upon which they exert their mental effort is of little consequence and interest. Hence, study thereof is imbibing of the art of skilled sophistry and results ultimately in nothing but issues for further argument. I should think a mild study of such writings would serve to order and discipline your thinking somewhat but certainly not prove the universal catalyst for the turbid waters of logic and reason. Mathematics also provides a fertile field for mental gymnastics and development of logic. But that there is a close correlation between intensive study of calculus and clear and concise reasoning on practical problems in later life, I seriously doubt. The important thing, it seems to me, is to study both of these fields enough to start you on the right track – the processes of scientific logic, etc., and then eagerly to turn to the current problems facing your locality, your state, nation and world today. Develop an active, dynamic interest. Read, discuss and understand; think for yourself and gradually form your opinions and convictions about them. Study history and economics in order that you may see the possible why and wherefore of the current events of the day. Study literature in order that you may improve your mode of expression; in order that you may more clearly and conclusively express your ideas and convictions on the problem of the day. The economists and sociologists weakly admit that our entire problem is lack of a "good neighbor" policy, a "love your neighbor as yourself" philosophy, then proceed energetically to label everything as a social and economic problem and attempt just as energetically to solve it on that basis. The great men in literature and philosophy claim our problems to be entirely philosophic and religious, and proceed to analyze everything on a philosophic basis but can't offer a thing on the practical, positive side. The ministers of today maintain that religion is the universal solvent of our problems and then proceed to preach a marvelous sermon on economics and deliver an excellent homily on philosophy utterly devoid of practical value and inspiration. Inasmuch as we know the whole thing is a philosophic and religious problem and how to dynamically and effectively improve conditions little by little by right thinking should not our educational energies be directed toward a better understanding of this science? Well, there is little doubt about that. However, there is still the practical necessity of understanding and studying present conditions from an economical, sociological and historical point of view. An adequate knowledge and application of these studies is desirable, certainly. However, the memorization of all minute detail connected therewith is for the scholar, the future instructor and technician, but it [is] not for me. I am very much in favor [of] studying history and economics in the light of present day conditions, in comparing and evaluating a similar period of the past with the future, in absorbing the fundamental principles of economics and analyzing the present economic problems in that light. A careful and constant reading of the newspaper and current periodicals is most desirable. It is evidence of an active mind. Decide what should be gotten from each course, ie what you desire to get, and study it with that goal in mind and not the ultimate grade. In reality you have to educate yourself. College only presents the opportunity. Only you, yourself, know the best way for you to get what you want and to what degree you are getting it. Business and commerce courses, unless you are planning to teach or be an accountant, should be studied for the underlying principles in order that you can pick them up readily when next you encounter them in the business world. I am firmly convinced that I have not kept myself well enough informed on current happenings. In the future I shall do my best to read as often as possible the daily newspaper – which is an excellent textbook in itself – the Fortune, Time & Readers Digest magazines – and use my classes and instructors as a means of clarifying and explaining what is mentioned in the current publications. More time should be spent trying to understand the problems of universal import – economical, physical, social, etc – in order that we may live better and more fully and interestingly; in order that we may be better prepared to aid humanity and the world; and perhaps less time on the subjects which are supposed to prepare you to make a living. I do not mean neglect them, but rather spend just enough time thereon to gain the underlying principles & essence of the course. Too much time is spent getting ready to live and making a living and not enough in living dynamically and enjoyably right now. The most important thing – and I am sure I am right – is to maintain an active, alert interest in everything going on about you. Analyze and think for yourself. Read and listen only insofar as it stimulates and aids your own thinking. Don't read and parrot back in the language of another; don't think and explain thru the already formed concepts of someone else all the time. Don't be afraid to grasp, develop and expound your own ideas. "An expert is often just a glib fellow away from home." Be alert, inquire, question, read, discuss, understand.

There you have rather roughly and incoherently expressed some of the thoughts that have come to me in the last month or so. As you can see I am more and more becoming set against obscuring initiative, imagination and ideas by too much detail, mediocre conservatism and directed study. All this is not a camouflage for laziness or an apology for possible low grades in the future. It is at present my firm conviction. I trust [I] have the courage to practice it.

Some time in the future I should like with your approval to write my feelings on what I have gotten from athletics, what good is a knowledge of the classics, art, and music.

More and more every day I feel that I would like to take law at U of Washington in Seattle. Would you object to my writing Ted concerning possible employment this summer? It would lay the foundation for future employment and association if I decided to take law out there. Either D.M. or Seattle would be *the* place, this summer it seems to me.

Thank you for your kind, inspiring letters, and love to all.

Yours,

Nile

9 ✳ To Frances Kinnick, 8 October 1939

On another hot afternoon, 7 October 1939, this time in Iowa City, Iowa defeated Indiana, 32–29. With four minutes to play, trailing 29–26, Kinnick passed to Erwin Prasse for the winning touchdown. He also passed for two others, ran for one, and dropkicked two extra points. Iowa was undefeated after two games, having beaten South Dakota, 41–0, on 30 September. The only loss of the season would come on 14 October to Michigan at Ann Arbor, 27–7.

"Gus" was Kinnick's longstanding nickname for his father. The elder Kinnick told D. W. Stump that it derived from an occasion when he was inspecting a farm under foreclosure for the Federal Land Bank. The tenant farmer asked him for shingles to repair a roof, but Kinnick refused because the bank did not own the land. Nile was there and asked why his father could not help the man, who had been helpful during the inspection. He began calling his father Gus, the tenant's name, at first to remind him of the man and his need (Stump, *Kinnick*, pp. 25–26).

The first quotation in the second paragraph is not biblical and cannot be traced from the Eddy concordances; the second slightly varies from Isaiah 40:31. Jim George was Kinnick's fraternity brother, fellow athlete (co-captain of the 1939 baseball team), and friend beyond college years. This occasion may have been Kinnick's first date with Barbara Miller of Sioux City (see the introduction), but later he sometimes writes about her to his parents as though he has never mentioned her before. Kinnick's father dated the letter.

Dear Mother:

I am terribly ashamed that I haven't written you a personal note long before now. I hope that father has spoken of the love I send to you each trip he makes. I wish that I might be living at home so that you all might experience first hand the joys that I have had this fall. It seems so good to see Ben and father, and father and George and Bob the week before. If I did not know of the fine and loving duty you perform each

Nile Kinnick and Barbara Miller at the south entrance to Schaeffer Hall on the University of Iowa campus, probably on 12 December 1939. Proof print, Kinnick Collection.

Sunday I should feel piqued at your absence on these trips. The radio no doubt gives you almost as much pleasure as seeing the game yourself – for that I am glad.

Things are going along very well thus far and I have no fear for the future. We won a glorious game yesterday as Gus will relate. This week will be even tougher but we may sneak by; if we do we will be a very tough team the rest of the year. I came out of this game unscathed and ankle untouched. Thank you for the good work you are doing. Today I feel pretty good but tired and with a claim of a cold. Please help me to know that I "rest in right activity" and may "run and not be tired." It looks as if I will be in there pitching the whole route most of the time. I am thankful for the blessings that are mine – I have more stamina and feel better physically than I have for 4 or 5 years.

We had a nice weekend or rather a nice Saturday. We all went to the Dad's day banquet and all had a reasonably good time I'm sure. Jim George & I had dates after the banquet and it is remarkable what a refreshing tonic a pretty girl can be. I escorted Barbara Miller of Soo City whose picture I think I have pointed out in the yearbook. She is a very charming and likeable gal. Also I introduced father to Era Haupert – now Mrs. Henry Wolfe – with whom I had several dates last year. I think father will agree my taste is good even though she married someone else.

I enjoy the sentinels very much – try to send one in each laundry will you please.

Much love,

Nile

10 ✳ To Frances Kinnick, 4 December 1939

On 28 November 1939 Kinnick learned that he had won the Heisman Award. He was in Adel that week for the family Thanksgiving dinner to be held at grandmother Arletta Clarke's house. Now back in Iowa City, he still had limited upper-body movement because of a shoulder separation in the last game of the season, a 7–7 tie with Northwestern on 25 November at Evanston – the only game his mother attended that year. The game was anticlimactic, following two weekends of the most boisterous reveling in Iowa City football history.

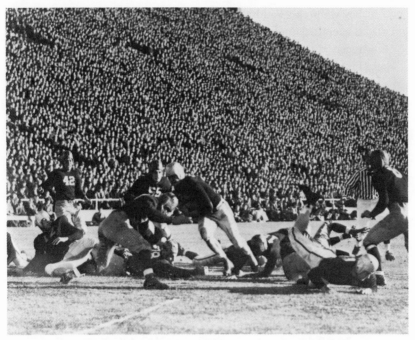

Nile Kinnick scores the winning touchdown against Notre Dame in Iowa City on 11 November 1939. Print, Kinnick Collection; Des Moines Register *photograph by John Robinson.*

First there had been the national shock of the 7–6 victory over Notre Dame in Iowa City on 11 November (the score flashed on the Times Building in New York well into the night; see letter 31), and then came what Kinnick called the "sweetest" win of the year, the 13–9 upset of Minnesota in Iowa City on the eighteenth, with Kinnick's famous touchdown pass to Bill Green in the closing minutes. The 1939 season settled a score with 1938: from 1–6–1 to 6–1–1.

Eddie Anderson was to be named Coach of the Year, so he was more than Kinnick's ex officio attendant at the Heisman ceremony and other occasions in the East. A calendar for December and January shows how full a time it would be: departure from Iowa City on 5 December; arrival in New York, the air procession over Manhattan, the Heisman evening, and then out on the town – all on the sixth; to Washington on the seventh for a tour of the Anacostia Naval Air Station and the Naval Academy at Annapolis; on the ninth to a Newark hospital, where Kinnick gave his All-America sweater to a high school boy whose leg had been amputated because of a football injury; on the tenth, dinner at Ruppert's Brewery in New York, where Anderson received the *New York World-Telegram* Coach of the Year award; a flight back to Iowa City on the eleventh; departure for Philadelphia on 7 January; the Maxwell Trophy ceremony at the Warwick on the ninth; on the tenth to New York, where Kinnick and Anderson watched Iowan Lee Savold knock out Big Jim Robinson in Madison Square Garden; Kinnick and Sec Taylor of the *Des Moines Register* saw the movie *Raffles* at the Roxy on the twelfth (letter 31); on the thirteenth the Iowa alumni dinner at the Western University Club, where Kinnick received the Captain of the All-Americas award, followed by the date with Virginia Eskridge (see the introduction) that took Anderson and him to the Kit Kat Club; to Washington on the fourteenth; the Camp Trophy dinner and presentation at the Willard on the sixteenth; finally, back to Iowa City late on 17 January. At some point in the first trip he saw the Rodgers and Hart musical *Too Many Girls* at the Imperial, and sometime during the second he went to Billy Rose's Diamond Horseshoe at the Paramount Hotel in New York (letter 35).

The Bulova watches were illustrated in *Life*, 4 December 1939, pp. 54–55. The list price of Anderson's watch was nearly that of the four-door Buick sedan given him by Davenport fans the evening before the Minnesota game. (Frank Carideo and Jim Harris also received new cars in late November at a presentation in Des Moines.) The list price of Kinnick's watch ($49.50) was ten dollars more than a Philco console radio.

Monday   Dec 4th '39

Dear Mother:

Coach and I leave for New York tomorrow morning at 9 oclock. We will take the Rocket into Chicago; the Twentieth Century out of Chicago at 5 oclock and get into New York City 9 AM Wednesday. I am going to try to stay till Sunday or Monday & then fly back.

I have pretty well snapped out of the daze that beset me for several days after learning of the award; have caught up on my mail; made arrangements concerning my studies, and in general feel all set for the trip.

Today at a small informal lunch the Bulova watch company presented Prasse & me with fine wrist watches. If you will look in the current issue of Life magazine you will see them in a fine advertisement.

Mine is the Am. eagle model & Prasse's the Ambassador. On the left hand page is a $1000 watch – pure platinum studded with diamonds. They gave that one to *coach*. This coaching racket is truly lucrative.

My shoulder is coming along excellently. Each day sees fine improvement as far as I can tell with it taped the way it is. The bump hasn't gone down much but I can tie my tie and move it with considerable freedom nonetheless.

I wish you would help me in the line of proper guidance as to the future. From this experience I feel that pro ball is not the right direction and yet I don't want to pass it by if it seems to be the ultimate consummation of my endeavours in this field. I hardly think it is however. I have no desire to play nor hesitancy about passing up the money though I suppose it will look awfully big in a few years. I shall continue saying I have no intention of playing, regardless, as long as this seems to be the RIGHT thing.

Possibly opportunities will present themselves in the East which would make it possible to go to Harvard. We shall have to wait & see, I guess.

Banzai to you,

Yours

Nile

The Heisman Award Address, 6 December 1939

The text transcribes an audiotape (box 4) of Kinnick's address before the Downtown Athletic Club in New York on 6 December 1939. The audiotape derives from an electrical transcription made at station KSO in Des Moines of the WOR radio broadcast in New York for the Mutual Broadcasting System. The audiotape directly copied 78-rpm records, which the station manager at the Register and Tribune Building made from the transcription (Kinnick, Sr., carbon of 14 December). Kinnick's father loaned the records to Robert A. McCown, Manuscripts Librarian at the University of Iowa Library, who had the tape made at the university audiovisual center (Robert A. McCown to Kinnick, Sr., 22 September 1976).

Kinnick spoke without a prepared text or notes (Bill Cunningham in the *Boston Post*, 8 December 1939; clipping in scrapbook 2). Most printed texts of the complete speech have copied a written transcript taken at the ceremony, and the rest have some of its inaccurate readings. The writer was probably a journalist who did not know shorthand and who may not have been in a position to hear well, for several words and phrases were omitted or misconstrued. That version began to circulate on 7 December, and part of it – "I thank God that I was born to the gridirons of the middle west and not to the battlefields of Europe" – was excerpted for release by the Associated Press and the United Press. The printed text closest to what Kinnick said, in Fisher's *The Ironmen*, pp. 116–17, has the mixed reading "born on," and though some reporters relying on their own notes quoted the passage correctly, in its erroneous form the passage has become the expression most often associated with Kinnick. What he actually said was an equally surprising entry into a peroration that the audience received with a protracted roar. He would use a similar construction in his address before the Touchdown Club of Washington, D.C., on 16 January 1940, when he accepted the Walter Camp Memorial Trophy as the Outstanding All-American Football Player for 1939: "Young men would rather fight and bleed for a trophy of this kind than for all the war medals in the world. . . . I thank God that this past year I have been dodging tacklers and not bullets, throwing passes and not hand grenades" (*Dallas County News*, 17 January 1939; scrapbook 2). The Camp address survives only in this and a few other newspaper quotations. "Mr. Holcombe" and "Mr. Prince" in the Heisman address were Walter P. Holcombe and Willard B. Prince, the president of the club and the chairman of the award committee.

Thank you very, very kindly, Mr. Holcombe. It seems to me that everyone is letting their superlatives run away with them this evening, but nonetheless I want you to know that I am mighty, mighty happy to accept this trophy this evening.

Every football player in these United States dreams about winning that trophy and of this fine trip to New York. Every player considers that trophy the acme in recognition of this kind, and the fact that I am actually receiving this trophy tonight almost overwhelms me, and I know that all those boys who have gone before me must have felt somewhat the same way.

From my own personal viewpoint, I consider my winning this award as indirectly a great tribute to the new coaching staff at the University

*Eddie Anderson, Nile Kinnick, and Virginia Eskridge at the Kit Kat Club
in New York on 13 January 1940.* New York Daily News, *15 January 1940,
microfilm, Library of Congress.*

of Iowa headed by Dr. Eddie Anderson, and to my teammates sitting
back in Iowa City. A finer man and a better coach never hit these
United States, and a finer bunch of boys, and a more courageous
bunch of boys, never graced the gridirons of the midwest than that
Iowa team of 1939. I wish that they might all be with me tonight to
receive this trophy. They certainly deserve it.

I want to take this grand opportunity to thank collectively all the
sportswriters and all the sportscasters and all those who have seen fit,
have seen their way clear, to cast a ballot in my favor for this trophy.
And I also want to take this opportunity to thank Mr. Prince and his
committee, the Heisman Award Committee, and all those connected
with the Downtown Athletic Club for this trophy and for the fine time
that they're showing me, and not only for that, but for making this fine
and worthy trophy available to football players of this country.

Finally, if you'll permit me, I'd like to make a comment which in my
mind is indicative perhaps of the greater significance of football and

The Voice of
Broadway
By Dorothy Kilgallen

Broadway Bulletin Board

David Niven's British intimates are bulletining his betrothal to Ursula Slaney, an English society girl now working as a volunteer war nurse . . . Betty Allen, the "DuBarry" beauty, has shelved Mack "Killer" Gray, George Raft's bodyguard, in favor of Hank Greenberg, the dream prince of the Detroit Tigers. Meanwhile she and her estranged groom, Gus Bivonne of the Teddy Powell crew, are flipping coins over who'll start annulment proceedings.

Norma Shearer underwent a minor operation of her photogenic jaw yesterday. She's at Hampshire House . . . Artie Shaw, the errant swing bandleader, will return to his jiving public in February, via a Chicago engagement.

Nile Kinnick, the U. of Iowa All-American, and Virginia Eskridge, a Delaware heiress, are yum, yum . . . Geraldine Spreckles, of the sugar fortune, left Midtown Hospital last week, suffered a relapse, and is back again. Palmer Dixon is the lad who's doing all the worrying.

GERALDINE SPRECKELS
Relapse forces her return to bed in hospital

Eddy Duchin's deal to buy the Detroit Lions, pro football team, probably will be clinched within a fortnight. The maestro is putting up $100,000, which is a lot of piano solos.

Dorothy Kilgallen's column in the New York Journal-American *of 15 January 1940. Microfilm, Center for Research Libraries.*

sports emphasis in general in this country, and that is, I thank God I was warring on the gridirons of the midwest and not on the battlefields of Europe. I can speak confidently and positively that the players of this country would much more, much rather, struggle and fight to win the Heisman Award than the Croix de Guerre. Thank you.

11 ✳ To the Family, 19 January 1940

The "unfamiliar notes" Kinnick mentions in this letter may have been his own notes he had been unable to review, and he may also have enlisted classmates to take notes during his eastern trips as part of the "arrangements concerning my studies" he mentions in letter 10. On 3 May 1940 H. J. Thornton would notify him of his election to Phi Beta Kappa (scrapbook 2). Ahead were further university honors: on 29 May he was to speak at the Commencement Supper; on 30 May university president E. A. Gilmore would write that he qualified for a degree with distinction (scrapbook 2); and on commencement day, 3 June, the Associated Press announced his selection for a John P. Laffey law scholarship (several clippings in scrapbook 2). As letter 12 shows, Kinnick already knew about this award, but a personal notification cannot be traced in the collection. Later he would receive an additional law scholarship endowed by Iowa alumni (*Christian Science Monitor*, 23 August 1940; clipping in scrapbook 2).

The Aberdeen, South Dakota, engagement mentioned here was on 5 February 1940. Kinnick spoke at a dinner of the local Quarterback Club (*Aberdeen Morning American*, 6 February 1940; clipping in scrapbook 2). He was planning to see Bob Hobbs over Saturday and Sunday, 3–4 February.

Friday 1/19/40

Dear Family:

Well the trips are all over and [the] final day of reckoning is at hand. I will get along ok but whether the Phi Bete Key can be gotten I don't know. It is pretty tough to make up half a semester in two or three days – especially by using unfamiliar notes.

The eastern trip was quite a bit of fun and the trophies are beautiful but I am happy to be back and pretty sure that Iowa is the place for me to go to law school & probably to live. I will go into that in more detail when I come thru Omaha on my way to Aberdeen – about the 3rd probably. If you have time phone Bob that I am so pressed for time I haven't as yet been able to answer his letter but am looking forward to seeing him on the 3rd & 4th.

Love to all

Nile

12 ❋ To Frances Kinnick, 26 May 1940

With this letter Kinnick ended a tortuous job consideration that began at least as early as March 1940. Possibly struck by his performance at the Maxwell ceremony in Philadelphia, a man named
R. Baum contacted him about employment with his company after
graduation. How soon Baum made his first solicitation is unknown,
but a letter to Kinnick from his father of 24 March indicates that the
subject was already familiar. The father-son exchanges from March
through May reveal that Baum's company marketed folding ma-
chines by agreement with another firm and that he wanted Kinnick
to join his national sales team. From March through May, Kinnick
went back and forth between enthusiasm and doubt, depending upon
the tenor of Baum's letters and according to his own metronomic tendencies. In May, Baum apparently showed signs of backing off, following Kinnick's acceptance of an offer in principle. Kinnick's father
suspected that the German western offensive, begun on 10 May, led
Baum to think Kinnick might soon be subject to military service and
hence too great a risk. In any event, on 26 May Kinnick finally decided against the offer.

The "Weaver deal," another possibility, would have taken Kinnick
to Decatur, Georgia, in a wheat mill venture contemplated by Joe
Weaver of the Omaha Grain Exchange (Kinnick, Sr., carbon, 29 April
1940; see also headnote to letter 7). But this letter shows him moving
closer to the law option he would choose in the fall. The "'separation'
business" refers to his shoulder separation in the Northwestern game
the previous fall, which he seems to blame for seducing him into a
reluctance to play professionally so as to support his proper choice of
the law. Yet he would accept the Laffey scholarship and a post as assistant coach under Eddie Anderson, and by these and other means
later available he was able to avoid professional football. The College
All-Star game of August 1940 would be his last as a player.

The present letter actually is two letters in that there were two
mailings, but the second mailing obviously contains second thoughts
and belongs in an immediate conjunction with the first. In the postscript Kinnick suggested an itinerary relating to the graduation ceremony on 3 June, to be held as usual in the basketball and armory
areas of the Iowa fieldhouse. "C.R." in the itinerary is Cedar Rapids,
twenty miles north of Iowa City.

Dear Mother:

I am an awful trial to you I'm afraid – I almost hesitate to write. But here is another enclosure from Baum. I could still make a deal probably but I wonder if it hasn't been proven not the place – I kind of feel that way. I don't know what is left – if it weren't for the All-Star & pro football – which I don't want to play in – I suppose I would go into law. I'll be daggoned if I can figure out what to do. If I were sure that law is my direction economic logic would say play a year of pro ball. I don't want to & I don't know how the shoulder would hold up – it doesn't bother me in movement but I don't know about contact – the physical manifestation seems to be just the same. I'll have to – or rather should – let the coaches down here know what I want [to] do about the coaching job before coming home – also there is a $90 scholarship to law school that I should accept or reject one of these days. If I should go to law school how can I get out of this football tieup – All-Star, etc? Possibly by starting to school this summer would be an alternative? Wouldn't be much fun, however? Possibly I should look into this Weaver deal further. The only thing that bothers me about going into business is could I do people more good somewhere else – I think that is the main pt naive as it may seem. Incidentally, I am beginning to believe anything mechanical might not be down my alley – probably wouldn't like that aspect even if I could understand it.

Last time I wrote I acted like I was going to make my own decisions & now I am back to you again. I guess I am just a little boy still. Sometimes I wonder if I am not just one of these nice guys whom the parents like & wish their children would emulate but doesn't seem to have much idea how to make a living. The main pt or question is that idea of service, mother? What do you think – otherwise that Weaver deal might look good.

Yours,

Nile

What is a man's obligation to society – I know your answer but does it run farther than that practically.

Sunday 11 PM

Dear Mother:

The thought came to me rather forcibly tonight that possibly we are on the wrong track. My feelings when strongest on what I want to do are always toward the law – and those feelings are usually much more than just an interest or enthusiasm – usually much stronger than that and looking farther ahead. Do you think all this "separation" business might be from another angle – keeping me from the path along this line? Now if that means hooking on here as an assistant coach, playing in the All-Star game, etc – I *can* do it – and enjoy it. I would much prefer – and think it would be best – if I go through without any outside work whatsoever. If that path demands a year of pro ball I *can* do that too – and *enjoy* it. I know that with a few weeks rest I can whip myself up for another season of football ok. The money that I could make that way would take me through in style – married if I wanted to be – and leave me some over. It sounds like logic alright. The problem there is what to do about my shoulder – and you know what I mean – I believe I can take either path with courage. What do you think? In any event with the am't of money I have I think I probably should forget the coaching job. If the pros don't offer me what I want I can still get by ok. It may be that *matter* is trying to put the "*squeeze*" on me – make me run away or depend on it to establish the structure. Or it may be that this physical demonstration is a little beyond us – which I hate to admit.

This is a new outlook I know – but think it over. This letter will arrive after the other one I suppose but answer both as quickly as you can, please.

You know in reality our problems are rather small in comparison with the people across.

I am afraid I definitely can't see the Baum deal anymore.

Yours,

Nile

P:S: I think you had better plan to go directly to C.R. & down to Iowa City Mon-morning. Inasmuch as we have to assemble early you had better go directly to the fieldhouse and I'll see you right after the exercises at the North door on the east side of the fieldhouse.

———

Just another thought – if I wanted to avoid all this football – I probably could enter law school this summer. I wouldn't mind *too* much.

The Commencement Supper Address, 29 May 1940

As president of his senior class, Kinnick was one of five speakers at the Commencement Supper in the Iowa Memorial Union on 29 May 1940. His name appears third in the program, under the heading "For the Men Students" (scrapbook 2). He typed the first paragraph on his own elite machine; the remainder is a typescript (box 2) done on a pica machine borrowed possibly to allow easier reading at a podium. Another preparation for delivery was his underscoring to signal oral stress, here rendered in italic type. He may have added the first paragraph within a day of the supper, for the German campaign in the Low Countries and France was by then clearly succeeding. Holland capitulated less than a week after the German invasion; on 28 May the *Des Moines Register* announced the unconditional surrender of Belgium; and the British army was conducting its evacuation at Dunkirk. The remainder of the address dates from before or shortly after 10 May. "Ding Darling's cartoons" refers to the work of Jay N. "Ding" Darling, the editorial cartoonist for the Des Moines Register and Tribune Company who was nationally syndicated by the *New York Herald-Tribune*. Kinnick may have had in mind Darling's use of a common image for a "Brain Truster" in the Roosevelt era: a small, slight male youth wearing a mortar board and with protruding eyes, exposed teeth, and a maniacal expression. An example of that figure can be found in the *Des Moines Register* for 13 May 1940.

The remarks I have to make tonite are very brief, but, nonetheless, with your permission I am going to read them rather than attempt to render them without the benefit of a text. I prepared this short talk several weeks ago but since then so many events of terrible and ominous significance have taken place in the world that I almost revised it. The bloody holocaust raging in Europe with its possible repercussions in this country tends to exert depressive influence on all of us – and as a result many of you will scoff at many of my remarks as foolish hopes and mere fictions. However, whether we know it or not, or like it or not, we in this country live by idealistic hopes and by fictions. And it may be that in the last analysis these seeming fictions and idealisms will prove to be the only realities. With this thought in mind I shall read this speech with absolutely no apologies for the hopes and aspirations expressed.

Tonight we seniors are gathered here as college graduates. Four short but dynamic years have gone fleeing by – it seems only yesterday that we entered this University as the *very greenest* of freshmen. Each one of us has treated and experienced these four years in different ways. To some it has been one grand holiday at father's expense marred only by the necessity of a certain amount of study and classroom attendance; to others it has been a grand opportunity to fulfill the hopes and aspirations of posterity-minded parents, and to still others it has been a stern and intense experience – an opportunity, yes – but realized on only by treading the rough and rocky road of unmitigated hard work. I speak of you courageous boys and girls unfavored by financial assistance from home who have earned your way by outside work on this campus; who have struggled desperately to meet your physical needs and at the same time maintain a decent classroom average – no social activities or frivolous pleasures have been yours – but you have asked for no quarter nor given any. You have been willing to pay the price for that which so many of us take as a matter of course; you hold your heads high tonite – and rightly so – for you have fought and won.

But regardless of what this college experience has meant to different students, this evening we stand as one body; and in a few days we shall stand together once more to receive that which is emblematic of four years of academic study well done – *our diploma*. Some of us will *treasure* this scrap of paper, some will be indifferent, and some will be cynical and unappreciative. But to all of us it will serve as a sort of "union card"; hence forward, we are members of that great group who have "*been to college*." Unfortunately, it can't honestly be said that we are now educated – but certainly, at least, this diploma indicates that we have been satisfactorily *exposed* to the process.

And what now – where do we go from here? Certainly, it isn't a very pretty picture – unemployment and uncertainty here at home and international anarchy abroad. What part are we to play in this dynamic everchanging world? We are told on the one hand by the pedagogues of this University that the salvation of this nation is on our shoulders, and on the other hand depicted in the honorable Ding Darling's cartoons as naive, intellectually doped youngsters without any ideas of practicality. But be that as it may I know that we are full of ambition, courage, and a desire to do well for ourselves and for the society of which we are a part. We shall struggle to be sufficient unto the need – if it means better government we shall be active there, if it means a more enlightened business leadership we shall strive for that; and if it means a broader, more responsible international outlook, count on us to be alert and ready.

Are we capable of successfully meeting the problems that face us? Have we been adequately equipped to fulfill our manifest duties and obligations? Only time can honestly answer. But we may be sure that if this great University is succeeding in her aims then we shall be successful in ours. Fundamentally, all true education is composed of (1) mental discipline and (2) inspiration – and one is of no avail without the other. All successful teaching must hinge on these two necessary fundamentals. Nobly have our professors endeavored to embody these principles in their lectures and personal associations with us. Hopefully, now they will watch our progress to see if we make use of the tools with which they have tried to provide us.

However, the successful use of what we have learned here will be contingent entirely upon the addition of another element which we alone can provide. For whether we realize it or not we have lived a rather sheltered life here at the University; here our ideals are lauded, appreciated and *protected* – the development and expression of a *social consciousness* has been easy. But *you know* and *I know* that this period of *easy* idealism is now at an end. And it is here that this other *element* of which I speak and which can be provided by the individual and the individual alone enters into the picture.

I refer, fellow graduates, to a *real, positive, mental courage.* We all seem to have the courage to face the physical forces of life – sickness, poverty, unemployment – even war itself – but how about courage of conviction, of morality, of idealism, courage of faith in a principle tangible proof of which is slow in appearing. Herein lies that phase of these problems which we must meet by ourselves, unaided by any university-given tools. Here is that angle of the greater difficulty which most often has proven the weak point in graduates of the past. True, we must learn to face adversity with equanimity, and even philosophically, but at the same time never for a moment losing sight of the ultimate goal, never failing in our ambition, or our ideals. By now we should have learned that success and happiness and attainment come only periodically not permanently – that they really are only passing moments in our experience – and that therein lies the explanation of the law of progress, and human dynamics. By now we should realize that the "battle is life itself" and that our joy and happiness should lie as much in the struggle to overcome as in the fruition of a later day. So let us confidently take courage in what we deem to be *right* and no matter what our line of endeavour may be cling to its concomitants of persistence, desire, imagination, hope and faith. Our competitive urge must not only be objective but subjective, not only physical but spiritual. Injustice, oppression and war will ultimately bring on their own destruction – suffering and misery eventually awaken the human race. But that is the long, sad, unenlightened road we have taken in the centuries past. *Now* is the time for these problems to be solved by enlightened thought and understanding. We can accomplish much if we implement mental discipline and inspiration with *real mental courage.* The task is not easy – wishful thinking will not do the job – we shall have to battle until we seemingly have reached the end of the line, then "tie a knot" and "hang-on." (This is not just a figure of speech but an imperative necessity.)

13 ❊ To Erwin J. Gottsch, 22 September 1940

After letter 12 there is no Kinnick letter in the collection until late August 1940, when he was in Evanston preparing for the College All-Star Game. Earlier that summer he attended the Phi Kappa Psi national convention in New Jersey, then went to New York to visit the World's Fair (letter 31). The Green Bay Packers defeated the All-Stars, 45–28, on 29 August, and though Kinnick played well, he made his final decision at that time to forego professional football (several clippings in scrapbook 2). In July or August he made a brief trip to Colorado, and by 17 September he had taken his room in the Iowa Law Commons (see his guest column for Ted Ashby's "Getting Around," *Des Moines Register*, 4 August, clippings in scrapbooks 1 and 2; and Kinnick to his father, 17 September).

On 18 September a stranger in Shenandoah, Erwin J. Gottsch, M.D., advised Kinnick against involvement in politics. He had read in the *Des Moines Register* that morning that Kinnick was to appear with Wendell Willkie, the Republican presidential candidate, at an Iowa Falls rally on 27 September. Dr. Gottsch warned that neither Willkie nor Roosevelt could help him, whereas he stood to lose half his national popularity by endorsing either candidate. Kinnick's reply survives in a handwritten copy he sent to his father, who admired it and urged him to type all his letters, with carbons, to help assure their preservation (Kinnick, Sr., carbon, 25 September). He often typed his correspondence thereafter but apparently without making carbon copies. Dr. Gottsch also admired the reply: on 23 September he wrote that if Kinnick held the same principles ten years later, he would vote for him in any election. Kinnick's father dated the letter.

Sunday   [9-22-'40]

Dear Mr. Gottsch:

I am answering your letter not because I feel the need of justifying my decision to you but because I feel that you were more than sincere in your advice. It is good advice and presents reasoning that has been in my mind since I was approached by the Young Republicans. On the other hand I am not introducing Mr. Willkie because I expect him to do me any good but because I am a Young Republican and expect him to do this country some good. I am addressing the Young Republican state convention not because I think that so doing will boost my prestige but because I am interested in government and have some ambition in that direction. Politics are not very clean but they should be; politics need integrity and idealism; politics more often than not disillusion those who enter with those ideas. Of that I am fully aware. But that does not alter the situation – if my path seems to lie in that direction I shall proceed as best I can – and whether I lose 50% popular favor shall not deter me. My grandfather was a Republican governor of this state – he was honest, fearless and competent. He lost many friends but regained most of them and in the end won the respect of all. I have benefited many times since from the heritage he left all his grandchildren here in Iowa. It is my hope, if politics proves my lot, that I can advance always on the same principles that he did. The feeling that politics and government is not the place for gentlemen has too long been accepted.

Anything I might enter at present – business, coaching, politics, selling, etc – would expose me to criticism because of the publicity I have received. That is unfortunate – but if I have any ability apart from the field of athletics I should be able to overcome this handicap.

Perhaps I have made a mistake. If so it will not [be] the first and I shall recoup. However, I am doing what I think is the thing to do.

Yours,
Nile Kinnick

14 ❋ To the Family, 4 October 1940

This is the first typewritten letter in the present selection. Kinnick typed it on his elite machine, single-spaced, evidently at great speed, perhaps in one sitting, and he covered three 8½ × 11 sheets of Iowa athletic department letterhead paper from top to bottom. He even typed over the letterhead on the second sheet. The letter contains numerous errors, more than any of his typescripts hereafter – misstrikes, strikeovers, omitted characters, wrong characters, and elided words. According to the policy stated in the introduction, missing words are supplied within square brackets, other errors are silently corrected, and word particles regarded as Kinnick's abbreviations are kept. Kinnick's father dated the letter.

Scrapbook 2 contains abundant news clippings relating to the Iowa Falls rally, together with many photographs of Kinnick, Wendell Willkie, and Republican governor George A. Wilson. Kinnick's speech before the Young Republicans is also there. The Iowa Falls occasion was Kinnick's only prominent involvement in a political campaign, and the scrapbooks otherwise rarely cover domestic politics.

Because of the number of names and other particulars needing explanation, annotations follow the letter in order of relevance to the text. People sufficiently identified in the text or regarded as commonly known, such as George Van Nostrand, Wendell Willkie, and George Wilson, are not identified further.

Friday 10:30 PM [10-4-40]

Dear Family:

At long last I have been able to find a little time in which to let you know what I have been doing since I left you early in Sept. and how things have been going with me. Billy Stuart, my roommate from Chariton – an excellent boy, and I have just returned from a cinema downtown. From the way things look this will constitute my only recreation throughout the year. We saw Brigham Young which is an excellent show to my way of thinking. I suggest that you all see it if you have the opportunity. There is very little up town tonite to suggest that there is going to be a football game tomorrow. But next week the night before the game with Wisconsin – Dads Day – will be much different. A spirit of fun and enthusiasm will be in the atmosphere; a huge pep meeting will be held and all will look forward with interest and expectation to find out how Iowa will stack up this year against good competition. Everybody will be wondering who will be the new stars, how

Green, Couppee, and Enich will look, etc. – and yours truly will feel now and then the desire to be back in the harness – but immediately a feeling of peace and contentment and satisfaction of a job well done and many fruits enjoyed will displace it and I shall be glad that things are as they are. Tomorrow just before the game starts, at the half, and for about two or three minutes after the game is over I am going to be on the Iowa Broadcasting hookup giving my comments on the game and the team. The broadcast is sponsored by the Dairy Producers of Iowa and I am to get $25 per game which is not so bad but nonetheless I feel a wee bit chagrined that they got me so cheaply. I am sure that if I had played it halfway smart I could have done much better – but so much for that, it will be good experience.

Starting Thurs at four oclock last week I began an intensive, interesting and thoroughly enjoyable weekend. I got Tom Louden of Fairfield, a friend of mine and a law student to drive me up to Adel immediately after the last law class. I gave him ten bucks for that – feeling that he was being most kind in agreeing to drive me up – especially after I had failed to get any of the beloved fraternity bros. to do that little trick. On arriving in Adel I caught a quick bite at Macks, ran up to see Grandma and Uncle Charlie for a few minutes, grabbed the coupe which Mitch had tuned up for me and took out for Iowa Falls. I managed to get up there about 10:30 and looked up Geo. Van Nostrand, Chairman of the Young Republicans for Iowa. He introduced me around to the local politicos with whom we went out to the Boat Club on the edge of town near the Iowa River where everybody had a little anti-freeze and gabbed for two or three hours. And whom do you think I ran into for the first time in at least ten years – Cliff Powers – remember him. He is just as big as ever and is running a funeral parlor in Iowa Falls. I finally got back to the hotel about 12:30 then found that I was rooming with a couple of young Repubs from Cedar Rapids and with whom I had to gab until about 1:30 and so finally to sleep. Up at 7 for breakfast and then to car to drive to Webster City to catch the train bearing Willkie into Ia. F. While he was making a rather brief appearance from the back platform for the benefit of a nice crowd I along with many others climbed aboard. Whereupon I ran onto several people I knew from around the state including Harrison Spangler and Mike Cowles. I had a nice visit with the latter and reaffirmed my first impression that he is very much alright. The Cowles family is quite a family from many standpoints. Finally, I went back – once the train had started – with several others to meet the "Big Bear" himself. I was well impressed though I didn't get much of [a] chance to say anything more than hello and some general comment on this [and] that. He is a very gracious sort of fellow and meets all with the same genuineness and sincerity. Under a terrific strain I should say he is doing a marvelous job. He is a huge fellow but just a small boy in stature compared to his brother Ed who is 6′5″ and weighs 256. He seems to be a sort of gen-bodyguard and handy man. All of [a] sudden we found ourselves coming to a stop in Iowa Falls where we tumbled out onto the rear platform and thence to the tracks and into an open car. The meeting was to be up in the park hence the crowd was divided which I think was too bad for he otherwise would have gotten a much more spontaneous and stimulating welcome. Well, we proceeded slowly up the street with Willkie and his wife and Governor Geo. Wilson's wife in the back seat and with me and the Gov in the front seat. As we rode along everybody was yelling hi Wendell, etc. but not with as much enthusiasm as I had anticipated. Arriving at the park we climbed up on the platform and before I could get my breath some dude was saying "and this is Nile Kinnick" and somebody shoves me in front of the mike whereupon I presented "your friend and my friend and the present and future governor of this state the Hon. Geo. A. Wilson"; I turned around and stepped down expecting his Honor to blat off a little but he just smiled and waved and sat down and somebody shoved me up there again. Whereupon I once more delivered myself of an introduction which went in substance as follows: "This state of Iowa is a great state and her people are a great people and they demand a great leadership. The Republican party offers that kind of leadership to you this year. We have as our presidential candidate a man who is a friend of labor, a friend of business and a friend of the farmer; and he will translate that friendship into positive action when elected this fall. He has gained everything in the Am. way and epitomizes our ideal of Americanism. It gives me great pleasure to introduce to you the next president of the U.S., Wendell Willkie." I liked what he said up there and have liked generally speaking those speeches that I have read throughout the campaign. As an old time stump speaker, a personal debate campaigner, as it were, he would be unbeatable. However, as I have said before I am afraid that there are too many who just come and admire and respect but aren't enthusiastically convinced enough to vote the right way. The cause of course isn't lost at present but it doesn't look too good. If there should be a lot of enthusiasm whipped up in the next few weeks it may be closer than most people think. Following Willkie's departure I fought off the autographers for about three quarters of an hour then went back to the hotel to get something to eat. There I ran into Bob Hogan who had come up with Clint Knee head of the Ia. highway patrol. Bob is doing some publicity work for them. We had dinner together and I convinced him that it would be a good idea for him to go on up to Soo City with me and I would take him back thru D. Moines on Sun. as I headed for Ia. City. He agreed much to my enjoyment. After dinner I gave a short address at a small gathering of Young Repubs – it was supposed [to be] a state convention but kind of weak in that respect – a copy of which I am enclosing as printed in an Ottumwa paper. Not good but not bad. Immediately after that we started for Soo City. We got in about seven oclock, took up our reservation at the hotel, I made a phone call to the Miller residence and we both had dates – Bob with Barbara's sister – she has two of them and both are as pretty as she is. The next morning I had breakfast with the coach and [the] President of Morningside and made some plans for the game that night. At noon Bob and I and Barbs took out for Vermillion where for 15 minutes before the game started I was busy signing autographs. At the half I was interviewed over the radio but in spite of all this I managed to do a fairly decent job scouting. We had to drive like mad back to Soo City where I was to be on a broadcast at 5:30; we made it with a minute or two to spare. Following the first broadcast I was rushed to another station for the same thing. Finally I got to the hotel and was given 5 minutes in which to clean up before the banquet at which I was to get to eat and wouldn't have to talk. As I got off the elevator on the mezzanine lo and behold here was another radio interviewer. Finally into the banquet we went and after the meal they changed their mind and decided they would like to hear a little about the All-Star game – I obliged them having figured on it all along. I met Barbs father following the talk whereupon without more ado he asked Bob and me out to breakfast on Sun. morning before we left. Feeling the need of some substantial nourishment before starting such a long trip we accepted. A rush upstairs to change into my refereeing outfit and a dash out to the stockyds for the game I was going to headline between Morningside and Midland which the former won quite handily. I called an offside and in general got along quite alright. At the half I kicked punts, dropkicks and did a little passing with either hand. The punting was the best I have done at any time anywhere – just happened to be hitting them just right. I worked clear back to the opposite thirty and could still put them in the corners. After the game a wade thru autographers to Bob and the girls, a rush to the hotel to change clothes and thence out to a dance. After dance out to Miller's house for bacon and tomato sandwiches and ice cream – to bed in the early morning. Out to breakfast at nine and there met Mrs. Millers brother and his two boys – as fine a looking lads as you ever saw and on their way to Sunday School. Her brother went to school with you, his name is McCorkingdale. Finally, we got started for Ia. City. We alternated driving and getting a little shuteye until we got to D. Moines where I left Bob and went on alone getting into Ia City about 6 oclock. The car used only a quart of oil all the way up and back and I came from Soo City clear to Brooklyn on the same tank of gas. I rolled in here in time to do some studying and so to bed about 11:30 and up at 6:30 and I felt fine and not tired. Some weekend, eh what. I netted a little over 2 Cs I should say. I got expenses from three sources plus my exhibition and officiating fee of $150.

And how is the law school going – pretty good I should say. I am enjoying it as well as I could anything that involves a lot of close, tedious work. It is doing me a lot of good apart from the subjects themselves. It is forcing me to read more closely and is once again getting my thinking organized and logical which I must admit in the past two years has been somewhat scattered. I am enjoying my coaching also. As outlines and freshmen arguments come on in the law school I am going to find myself terrifically busy once again but I guess I shall always find myself in that predicament. Out of this tedious work – briefing, analyzing, etc. – is coming the general principles and philosophy which I want. The practice should be much more interesting than going to law school. There is no doubt that it is pretty tough and it will tax my capabilities to do as well as I have done in the other schools – but I'll be in there pitching.

I had a letter from Ben the other day which I should answer but won't have time to do so at any length so why don't you forward this when you have all seen it.

You must have [had] a wonderful trip, mother. I am so glad for you. It certainly was your turn for something of that kind.

I have bought a new study lamp with a goose neck arm which can be extended if wished. It really is a dandy and should be of use for many years to come.

I am planning to register for the draft down here and have registered here to vote. I think it best to affiliate as an Iowan in every respect with the possible future there might be for me in this state. Just an idea – can't see that it will make much difference one way or the other.

Each year brings new blessings upon our family. The success of one is the success of all and the problem of one is shared by each of us. How happy we have been. Through thick and thin we have come and so it shall be. But let us not forget the struggle that is going on in the world today. Portentous times are these and we are sluggards in the race if we do not [do] our part mentally to the best of our ability. Two civilizations are at stake – Truth and error are at bay – and Truth will come thru triumphant only thru us daily affirming for ourselves and all the absolute supremacy of Truth, Life and Love – the utter inability of any anti-Christ, materialism, or mesmerism to shackle man or to do battle against God.

I today received a letter from the little apron peddler I told you about. It seems the publicity I unwittingly gave her in Ashby's column has helped her business considerably. What she says and the way she says it brings a lump to the throat. It is the best thing of this kind I have yet received. Ted Ashby is coming down tomorrow and he will want to see it but after I show it to him I shall forward it. If I am slow in getting this mailed I shall enclose it tomorrow nite.

This is just about as lengthy and newsy a letter as I have ever written. Make the most of it for I don't see how I am going to have the time to write another like it this year.

Love,

Nile

Billy Stuart: William C. Stuart (Iowa '41), a Phi Psi, now a senior federal judge in Des Moines, has donated letters and memorabilia to the collection.

There is very little up town tonite: On 5 October Iowa would again open a season with South Dakota, winning 46–0. About 20,000 attended, according to the 1942 *Hawkeye*, an unusually large first-game crowd. The following week Iowa would defeat Wisconsin, 30–12.

Green, Couppee, and Enich: Bill Green, Al Couppee, and Mike Enich, also players on the 1939 team. Enich was team captain in 1940.

Macks: Mack's was a restaurant near the center of town in Adel, a few blocks from Arletta Clarke's and Charles Clarke's homes.

Mitch: Golden Mitchell, owner of Mitchell Motor Company, the Ford agency on the town square in Adel. The coupe was the elder Kinnick's Ford V-8.

Harrison Spangler and Mike Cowles: Two important figures in the Willkie campaign. Spangler was a Cedar Rapids attorney and a member of the Republican National Committee. Cowles was Gardner Cowles, Jr., in 1940 the publisher of the *Des Moines Tribune* and one of Willkie's early supporters and organizers in the national campaign.

Bob Hogan: In 1937–38 sports editor of the *Iowa City Press-Citizen*; by 1940 a reporter for the *Cedar Rapids Gazette.* He appears several times in the letters and diary.

Clint Knee: An Adel resident and former sheriff of Dallas County, in 1940 he was chief of the Iowa Highway Patrol. During his time as sheriff he headed the posse that captured Buck and Blanche Barrow of the Bonnie and Clyde gang. See *Adel Quasquicentennial, 1847–1972* (Adel, n.d.), [p. 95].

we both had dates: News of Kinnick's doings traveled fast and far: on 29 September the *Daily Iowan* reported that "Nifty Nile is being seen this weekend in old Sioux City. . . . 'tis said that he's stepping out with his All-America girl memory. . . . Barbara Miller, D.G. [Delta Gamma]" (misdated clipping in scrapbook 2).

Vermillion: Kinnick was assigned to scout South Dakota in Vermillion in preparation for the 5 October game.

You must have [had] a wonderful trip: The word *had* is supplied because Frances Kinnick was supposed to return on or about 4 October from a tour of the East Coast with friends. She left on 17 September, as Kinnick knew; before she left he sent her a fifty-dollar check to help with costs (Kinnick to his mother, 9 September).

success of one is the success of all . . . sluggards in the race: Phrases from Mary Baker Eddy, *Science and Health.*

mesmerism: Another Christian Science term, deriving historically from a nineteenth-century suspicion of mesmerism, or hypnotism, as an invasive and possibly evil practice. Mesmerism in a Christian Science context means a metaphoric sleep, the reverse of Mind, a lack of spiritual awareness.

the little apron peddler: In his guest essay for Ted Ashby's "Getting Around" column (see headnote to letter 13), Kinnick spoke of a hitchhiker, Alice Dagwell, he picked up north of Ames the previous spring. She made aprons and peddled them around the state, relying on free rides. On 28 September she wrote Kinnick to thank him because his article helped her sales and because he was "big enough to stop by the way-side and befriend a Lady." She wished him "a long life time ahead."

15 ✳ To the Family, 14 February 1941

Kinnick met Celia Peairs early in 1940 through his cousin Kingsley Clarke (often called King), a son of Charles F. Clarke. While studying law at Drake, Kingsley lived across the street from the Peairs family in Des Moines and made their acquaintance. The earliest mention of Celia in the collection is in a letter of 29 March 1940, in which Kinnick writes his parents that a date with her went well. They had many

Celia Peairs in about 1942. Negative courtesy of Celia Peairs Fay.

more dates from that time until shortly before Kinnick entered the Navy Air Corps in December 1941, and they continued to correspond until a few days before his death. Celia graduated from Vassar in 1937 and in 1940 enrolled in the School of Social Service Administration at the University of Chicago, where she took a master's degree in 1942. She shared her sister's apartment in Hyde Park, near the university. She was three years older than Kinnick, but despite the "disparity in our ages" he cites in this letter, he visited her over many weekends in 1940 and 1941. He drove there, and a statement to his father in a letter of 19 September 1940 – "It develops that I probably should have a car down here for reasons that I shan't elaborate. They are personal reasons." – may have had to do with the Chicago trips, for when he visited her he would stay with his aunt Mary (Kinnick) Lindsay on the far North Side, many miles from Hyde Park. His father in effect gave him the Ford V-8 coupe he picked up in Adel on his way to the Iowa Falls rally (see letter 14) and used on his speaking engagements thereafter. The trip Kinnick mentions here occurred on 1 and 2 February, and on the twenty-eighth he would go to Chicago again (Kinnick telegram to Celia Peairs, 21 February).

Kinnick did well academically that semester. His percentile rank was 83.07, which he estimated put him third in his class (letter to his parents, 27 May). Stuart and he were "Attorneys for the Appellant" against Hilton Moeller and Millard Hills, the "couple of dudes who are fairly sharp," in a case before the "District Court of the State University of Iowa" (student brief donated to the Kinnick Collection by William C. Stuart).

The "dude in the East" is unidentified, and all that can be learned of his scheme is in this letter and in another of 20 April 1941, in which Kinnick tells his parents that he had finally decided against the offer because the man "plans to get quite a bit of publicity including newsreels and I can't see myself being held up to the public as taking it easy with a bunch of rich boys when I possibly should be in the Army."

Kinnick occasionally signed letters home "SB" or "S. B." The initials stood for Sonny Boy of the famous Al Jolson song, the nickname his father gave him. In letters Kinnick occasionally addressed him by that name. Kinnick's father misdated the letter 15 February, a Saturday in 1941.

Friday nite 9:30   [2-14-'41]

Dear Family:

Thank you so very, very much for the Valentine box, mother. It was so very thoughtful of you! And full of the best things I can think of. It makes me very ashamed that I haven't written for such a long time. My excuse as per usual is lack of time. I spent all last weekend getting our appellant brief ready for our freshman argument starting a week from Tuesday. I am arguing with my roommate against a couple of dudes who are fairly sharp I think. So if I don't get another letter off right away you can charge it up to the impending argument. Also spring football is going to start next Tues. so that will add to my obligations.

Well, since I wrote last many things have happened – not much of consequence but the days have been full. The tests are all out of the way and as yet the grades haven't come out yet. I don't feel that I did extraordinarily well – as a matter of fact the grades may be quite average but nonetheless I felt that I knew the material very well and that is the imp. thing. I also have made a couple of speeches – one in Muscatine on last Monday night at a father and son banquet and the one at Waterloo at the Millers convention which I may have already mentioned. I also took a little trip to Chicago which I MAY have omitted to mention in my last letter. Tests ended on Sat. noon so I took off for Chi to see Aunt Mary, of course, and didn't get back until Monday night. I left Chi. on Monday morning and drove to Waterloo in time for the afternoon speech I mentioned above. Miss Peairs is quite a remarkable girl and were there not such a disparity in our ages she might have something on her hands. Haven't any other definite dates for speeches lined up – tho there is a very good possibility that I shall go over to Freeport, Ill. for a talk on March 3rd. Spring vacation starts April 9th I think, but am not sure – will in all probability come home tho it is a very short respite – and then again something might come up. Did I write you that I had another letter from that dude in the East who wants me to be companion to the Fords, Rockefellers, etc. – I'd refuse if it would turn out to be just a Du Pont and an Astor. He said that he hadn't expected me to make up my mind right away but that he wanted me to go and for me to brush up on my Spanish for we would spend a couple of weeks in Mexico. Said he would be out in the spring to see me – I think I'll try to do a little checking on him too. Just returned from the Ia.-Minn. track meet – don't enjoy them much – nor basketball either anymore. Have played a little squash now and then – a lot of fun – will take it up a little more seriously sometime, maybe. Looks like Hitler is going to try to put on the big push soon now – its going to be tough going this spring and summer – good old England – boy how they can hang on. Churchill is marvelous – heard him talk last Sun. – he is wonderful. When he lowers his voice for emphasis it makes my back tingle. Am proud of Willkie and disgusted with the majority of the Republican party – they better snap out of it or they won't be anymore. Some sort of parliamentary system will eventually show up out of this – no longer can this country afford to have two parties whose avowed principle is always to stand for the exact opposite of the other regardless of what the stand is. Speaking of England did I tell you about my Eng. bull dog. – I bought him about a month ago. He is cast in bronze and about 4 or 5 inches high. He is noble, defiant, strong, persevering in every line – makes a nice piece for my desk. About time for bed so will sign off – thanks always for the clippings, goodies, etc. that you send every now and then – love to all – it also gives my back a tingle now and then to realize what a fine family I have been blessed with – would like to see all of you. Bear down George – and get hot if they ever let you in a game again.

SB

Enclosing some letters & clippings – keep or throw away doesn't matter.

SB.

16 ✳ To the Family, 25 April 1941

Kinnick was still more than four months away from joining the Navy Air Corps, but this letter shows his attitudes and motivations becoming established toward that end. The collection does not disclose what training program his parents mentioned, but there is no evidence that he considered the army. A radio address the previous evening by Secretary of the Navy Frank Knox moved him to the declarations of this letter. Kinnick may have been reminded of Jeremiah 6:14 – "Peace, peace; when there is no peace" – from browsing in Bartlett's *Familiar Quotations* (11th ed., 1938, p. 1112), evidently a 1940 Christmas present from his parents, to whom he mentioned his new "quotation book" with fondness in letters in January 1941. Bartlett would remain one of his resources.

Bob Hobbs left Iowa after his third year to enter the University of Nebraska Medical School. In 1940 he moved to Seattle, where he worked in the building materials industry until late 1941, when he returned to the Midwest to join the Navy Air Corps. The picture he sent of Ted Clarke, a clipping from a Seattle newspaper, is in scrapbook 2, but the reference to a medal is unclear.

Kinnick thought better of going to Des Moines to watch the Drake Relays, an annual spring event. The Friday trip to Yarmouth would leave little or no time for study that evening because Yarmouth is fifty miles southeast of Iowa City. His companion on that junket was Billy Stuart, who knew he was hearing time after time the same mix of reminiscence, advice, and encouragement but who liked going along anyway. Kinnick's father dated the letter.

Friday [4-25-41]

Dear Family:

It is noon and I have just finished my lunch. Inside the Commons everyone is lolling around taking it easy before getting back on the books. Some are playing cards, some are reading the paper, and some are just sitting. Outside the sun is bright and warm. It is a glorious spring day. Some of the boys are knocking out flies and some are just basking in the sun. It makes one want to breathe deeply and be happy that he is alive.

I just received a long letter from Bob Hobbs. In fact it was quite long written in response to a quite lengthy epistle I sent him a couple of weeks ago. His ideas are just as sound and healthy as they ever were I believe altho he is fed up on the administration and consequently distrusts Roosevelt on his foreign policy. I might add that he not only writes interestingly but his style is good also. He still misspells quite a few words but he certainly is realizing on his desire to improve his mode of written expression. When I wrote him I mentioned the bare possibility that I might come out this summer and asked if he thought he could get me a temporary job of some kind. He now replies that he is sure he could – so that is a possibility if I so desire.

There is no football practice this weekend and I would enjoy going up to the Relays but better judgment bids me stick around and get in a little studying. Tonight I go down to Yarmouth to give a talk. Bill is going down with me. He seems to enjoy going along altho I would think he would get awfully tired hearing just about the same thing each time. In any event it should be a most pleasant trip. This is the last speech I have scheduled and it is probably best that way. It will give me more time for undivided attention to my subjects.

I am not familiar with the officers training plan you mention – altho I believe I heard a fellow talking about something this morning which must have pertained to it. I shall plan to look into it. I talked to a fellow the other day who had just been called in by the draft board and from the way things are going I should judge that normally I would be called in Sept. As for volunteering – it is at present just an embryo idea. I realize that it might involve the longer period – even if I went into the air corps or the marines it probably would be for the duration of the emergency. It looks like we'll be in for that long anyhow. I suppose you realize that when I say that I might volunteer it is for the officers training corps in that particular division. Each branch of the service is periodically sending out men to the different Universities to get fellows to go into the training period and get their commissions. Did you hear Knox last night? He speaks with courage and forthrightness. I agree with him even tho I realize what it involves. We either must jump in this mess strongly regardless of the risk or refuse to take our rightful place in the world. More than at any time since the Napoleonic period Western Civilization and Christianity are at stake. That puts it strongly but is no exaggeration just the same. Lincoln was a moral and upright man. He was a pacifist at heart. But when there was no other alternative he did not equivocate nor cravenly talk of peace when there was no peace. He grabbed the bull by the horns; realizing that the nation could not endure half slave and half free, he threw down the gauntlet and eradicated the evil. We are faced with the same thing and the longer we wait the worse it becomes. We are not people apart; there is no reason in the world why we shouldn't fight for the preservation of a chance to live freely; no reason why we shouldn't suffer to uphold that which we want to endure than it is anyone else. And it is a matter of self-preservation right this very minute. Those are my sentiments – and they are RIGHT. May God give me courage to do my duty and not falter. This isn't a dramatic speech – it is honestly the way I feel.

I took a few swings with the golf club last night and once again think I have it all figured out. I sure would like to get out and play a few holes but probably won't make it until after exams.

I bought Churchills new book – or rather a collection of his speeches yesterday. I refer to the book Blood, Sweat, and Tears. Some of the passages in those speeches are just beyond any description that can be given. They are marvelous. It makes my spine tingle just to read those lines over to myself. I'd rather write a speech like any one of those than do anything I can think of.

Enclosed is a picture of Ted that Bob sent me some time ago and also the medal I spoke of while I was home.

Yours, Nile

17 ✳ To Arletta G. Clarke, 29 April 1941?

Kinnick typed the body of this letter, dating it "Tuesday" and adding the postscript by hand. His grandmother wrote "April 1941" after "Tuesday," but there is no catalog date or date by Kinnick's father. The most likely Tuesday would be 29 April, inasmuch as Kinnick did not mention Arletta's letter to his parents before then but did in a letter of 8 May. Kinnick's article in the *Davenport Daily Times* (10 March 1941, clipping in scrapbook 2) was a guest column he supplied for Bill Rivkin's regular feature, "Red and Blue Among the Gold," wherein he describes the transition from fame as a football player to obscurity as a law student. The "fade" was gradual, he says, and such events as the College All-Star Game (August 1940) and public speeches in the winter of 1940–41 provided him "a parachute on the way down." Elizabeth was Kinnick's cousin Elizabeth Van Meter, daughter of Portia Clarke Van Meter.

[29 April 1941?]   Tuesday

Dear Grandma:

I enjoyed so very much your letter telling of your trip to Omaha. Driving through the cloudburst which you described must have been quite an experience. I am glad to hear that you got through without mishap. Mother has written what a fine time she had visiting with you and Elizabeth.

You made me very happy by telling me of your reaction to sleeping in my room amongst the trophies and by saying that you thought my article in the Davenport Times was of merit. I have spoken before of the wonderful heritage which you and grandpa have given all the grandchildren. It is All-American in every way – morally, physically, and mentally. I know that each of us realizes that whatever his achievement may be that it in a large measure stems from this background. Anything which I have done which bids you write in the tenor you did makes me very proud. It was especially good to hear that you liked my article in the Davenport paper. I expect I would rather be able to write well and speak well than anything I can think of. A well written and well delivered speech on something of import gives me a bigger thrill than just about anything. When I listen to Churchill give his incomparable speeches I can hardly remain seated in a chair. What frankness, what defiance, and yet withal what inspiration is in each utterance. May we all prove worthy of the cause he is espousing in the trying times ahead. It is very sobering to realize just what the future holds for a boy of my age. On the other hand it is a practical challenge to a man's courage and personal integrity. A man who talks but is afraid to act, who sacrifices principle to expediency whenever real danger threatens is not worthy to keep and enjoy what he has. He is not worthy of his background and heritage who kowtows to tyranny in order to cling to his temporary safety and comfort. This is no expression of oratory or emotionalism but cold, hard truth. I trust I will have the courage to act as I speak come what may. It will not be easy – but *should*, therefore, can be done.

Your mention of Sunday supper at your house brought back memories of the years gone by. What wonderful times we used to have. Do you remember when each member of the clan had to get up in front and recite some piece of poetry? That was a grand idea, and lots of fun. And do you remember the time I gave my high-school commencement address on the Constitution of the U.S. and grandpa with tears in his eyes said it was very good. I certainly do! And that brings to mind the time he wrote me an inspiring letter the theme of which was epitomized in a quotation from Excelsior by Longfellow. I remember the time Uncle Chas. wrote me after our game with Nebraska at Lincoln when I was a sophomore. I had had a fine year but in this final game we were licked soundly on a cold, snowy day and I had looked very poor. He said it reminded him of Napoleon's failure at Moscow after a series of victories. The comparison was, of course, humorous and intended so. But he also told me to keep my chin out and that there would come another day. Kingsley has written me several times with ideas and suggestions that have proven of value. And of course my mother and father have counseled and comforted to say nothing of inspiration through all these years. Yes, my friends, family, and relatives have been most kind and thoughtful in their criticism, praise and consolation. Life has been good to me – full, enjoyable, happy. Your letters of sincerity and tender love always bring this fact home to me.

Much love,

Nile

P.S. I took the liberty to type this letter because I am pressed for time. Please forgive. Incidentally, I live at the Law Commons this year & not at the Phi Psi house.

18 ❧ To Ben Kinnick, 13 June 1941

With the academic year 1940–41 the Phi Psis took up residence at their current more spacious location, 363 North Riverside Drive, on a hill overlooking the west bank of the Iowa River. In a letter to his brother George of 22 June, Kinnick writes that at the end of the month he is returning to Omaha, where in late July he is said to be "visiting his parents, playing golf and talking occasionally about football" (*Omaha World-Herald*, 20 July 1941; clipping in scrapbook 2). In August he would attend the College All-Star Game in Chicago with Celia Peairs. The 22 June letter indicates that George responded favorably to Kinnick's writing proposal expressed in the following letter, but Ben evidently did not, and nothing came of it or of a similar proposal Kinnick would make on 21 March 1942.

The Smitty mentioned here was Roland Smith, in later years a well-known realtor. Clare Marshall was the manager of the *Cedar Rapids Gazette*. The pairings in the foursome balanced ages: the older Smith with the younger Kinnick and the older Marshall with the younger Hogan (see annotation to letter 14). Charles Brady (Iowa '39), a Phi Psi, had been a reserve on the football team. The route to Iowa City from Independence took Kinnick through Cedar Rapids, where he visited his cousin Clarke Van Meter, a son of Portia Clarke Van Meter.

The row of periods in the next to last paragraph does not represent an abridgment. This styling is Kinnick's here and elsewhere, but its significant difference from a dash is unclear. Kinnick's father dated the letter.

Friday   [6-13-'41]

Dear Ben:

A letter from mother tells me that you are home for the summer once again and that you have already gone to work for the Nebraska Power and Light Co. It sounds to me like your job for this summer is going to [be] more enjoyable than any you have had for quite some time. You have been so extremely busy both during the summer and winter for the past two or three years that I hesitate to tell you how leisurely I am taking it at the present time. I am staying on the third floor of the Phi Psi house and have the whole fraternity to myself except for two families living on the lower floors. They are young couples living here during the summer while the men get their Master's. I am completely free from responsibility and obligation. I go to bed when I please and I get up when I want to. I go to a show, play golf, or read just as I choose without any other duty pressing me for time or effort. It is absolutely heavenly. However, I do not feel that I am completely wasting my time. I am doing a little extra reading that I have been wanting to do for some time, and I, also, am trying to learn shorthand. I have just started so as yet I haven't made much progress, but if I lend effort to my resolve I should soon move along quite rapidly. And I might add that I am improving my golf game which may or may not be of any importance. Wednesday Smitty, who runs Smith's cafe, and I went up to Cedar Rapids and played Bob Hogan and Clare Marshall out at the Country Club. I had the best score I have ever had over a tough course. But it certainly was a strange round I must say. Listen to this. I had a 76 on a par 70 course. My score at the end of the first nine holes was 33 which is one under par. On the second nine it follows that I had a 43. But here is the peculiar story of the round. I had 13 one putt greens out of 18; I had a ball in the creek which I could not find on number 11; I had three balls in the river on number 15, and I took four putts on number 17. Number 15 was a long par 5 running parallel with the Cedar River. My woods which had had a slight "tail" all afternoon suddenly began to slice abruptly, hence, a catastrophic 8 followed. Yesterday I drove up to Independence for Charlie Brady's wedding. On the way back I stopped to see Clarke at his office and learned that next week Mary is going to be in Clear Lake with her folks so I think that I will plan to stay a few days with Clarke beginning next Tuesday. Now that I have given you a bit of the news I shall come to the main purpose of this letter.

For some time now I have been distressed with my ability to read and write. It is not because that I am poor at either that I feel this way but rather because I am at best only mediocre. I am disappointed in my reading thus far because I don't seem to read to remember; I don't read closely enough, nor with a keen and alert perception. This faculty I can only develop by myself. However, when it comes to writing a man must have some opportunity to practice in order to improve. None of my courses seem to provide a satisfactory outlet for the practice I need. I want to learn to set down my ideas clearly and plainly and withal develop some beauty and power of expression. Thus far the best that I do is to record what disorderly [idea?] comes to my mind. Now I have intimated that I believe reading and writing and speaking to be the very essence of an education. (Figuring or computation should be included also.) I believe this because an effort to excel in each of these develops a disciplined mind and demands orderly thought and expression. Now it has occurred to me that through writing periodically to George and you I can get the practice in setting down my ideas that I desire. I have already written to George a quite lengthy letter containing counsel and advice that I thought might be of interest and value to him. I am hoping that the idea will appeal enough to you, and George, so that you will want to reciprocate with letters of your own containing your ideas on different subjects. If we all three entered wholeheartedly into the idea we would benefit much, I am sure. Not only would the exchange of ideas be beneficial but the practice in written expression would be most desirable. The theme of the letters could be anything that we wished individually to write on. It could be advice and suggestion based on past experience, or your views on politics, government, war, literature, love, women, athletics, religion, philosophy, mathematics, or even a description of the view from your window or a trip that you may have taken. In other words any subject that would be of interest or instruction and which would provide a stimulant for power and beauty of expression would be alright. However, they must be something more than just ordinary letters both in content and construction if they are to be of real worth. Just news and expressions of felicitations should be separate from the main body of the kind of letters I am suggesting. The scope of such an undertaking would be rather large. It would take time and thought. Twenty or thirty minutes for a letter would not near be sufficient. It may be that the idea would peter out but I think it would be worth a try. What do you think? I, of course, haven't written you a letter of the type I mean as yet so it may be that you don't quite understand what I am driving at. You might ask to see the letter I wrote George and thus get some idea of what I mean. I should add that the tone of the letter I wrote George is too fatherly to interest you much, or even him, for that matter. But on the other hand it will indicate that we should pass on to each other the profit of our individual experiences. We could add to, criticize, and take issue with what the other writes. I think it is a grand idea but realize at the same time that I am more interested in this sort of thing than you and George. If neither of you feel that it is worth the effort don't hesitate to say so, but I hope, nonetheless, that you won't mind if I write to you in this vein now and again. Everything said would of course be considered strictly personal although I think most of the letters could be shown to the folks if we wished. It seems to me it would be a good idea to file them away for future reference, also. One more thing. . . . they wouldn't necessarily have to be long. Just some effort to set down clearly, powerfully, and with some beauty of expression an idea or thought that would be of interest and value.

I am afraid that this [is] a rather labored effort [to] get across my plan. There is little power and no beauty in the way that I have said it. However, I submit it to you for what it may be worth and hope that you view it favorably. May I hear from you soon.

Yours,
Nile

19 ✳ To the Family, 9 November 1941

The Iowa-Illinois game in 1941, a 21–0 Iowa victory, was played in Champaign. Rail transportation took the team through Chicago, where Kinnick usually made the most of his layovers. The girl he met at the station on Friday and took out that evening was Elizabeth Charlton of Manchester, the "Bibba" of Kinnick's later references. His date the next night may have been Celia Peairs. Bill Stauss was an Iowa halfback. Other players mentioned were Bill Parker (an end who caught two touchdown passes) and halfbacks Bill Green and

Bus Mertes. The "flaxen haired little lass" and "Uncle Will" are un-identified, and the telegram is not in the collection.

Kinnick was assistant backfield coach in the 1941 season, and scouting the opposition was among his responsibilities. He was not enrolled in law school, for in early September he had enlisted in the Navy Air Corps and was waiting to be called up. He roomed in the Law Commons during the interim.

Sunday afternoon, Nov. 9, 1941

Dear Folks:

It was quite a relief to me to watch Iowa defeat Illinois so handily. I find that taking full responsibility for a scout report stimulates my interest in the outcome of the game a good deal. Until Parker scored that first touchdown I was a bit apprehensive that Zup would come up with something that I hadn't forewarned the coaches about. After it was all over I was quite pleased with the completeness of my report. With a little more experience I think that I could soon feel confident of always doing a good job.

The team, for the most part, looked quite good. The backs were running hard and the line was doing a pretty fair job blocking. Illinois doesn't really have much of a ball club, and I would have been quite disappointed if Iowa hadn't scored at least three touchdowns. The field was a bit slippery which slowed up Green and Mertes no little. Had it been a dry field, I think one of them would have gotten loose for a long run. It certainly is nice to win. Everyone's disposition is so much better, and the whole trip seems much pleasanter. Nonetheless, as we were rejoicing in our dressing room after the game, I couldn't help thinking, and sympathizing, with the Illinois boys and old Zup. What a dismal and unhappy trail their's has been this fall. The prospect for the rest of the season must bulk over them like a huge storm cloud. . . . . they finish up against Northwestern and Ohio. Poor Zuppke is undoubtedly one of the finest coaches in the business, but even he can't make a go of it with the material he gets. It is a lamentable situation. We will be intensely busy this week trying to get ready for Minnesota. It is not beyond the realm of possibility that we could beat them, but they will probably bounce back with a vengeance after their poor showing against Nebraska. Whether I shall be here or in Lincoln scouting this weekend I do not yet know. Will inform you as soon as I can.

Friday afternoon in Chicago I spent visiting with Dick Evans and Frank Balazs, two former Iowa players whom you will undoubtedly remember. It was very enjoyable sitting high over the city in the Morrison Hotel exchanging views and recollections while the rain and snow fell without. Dick and Frank are both playing pro ball with the Chicago Cardinals. E. Charlton got into the La Salle St. station on the student special about 5 oclock, where I met her. We went out to dinner at the Blackhawk and then to see Louisiana Pchse at the Erlinger. It was an highly enjoyable production. Very humourous and replete with good music and dancing. Zorina the famed modern and toe dancer had one of the leads. She is the acme of grace and rhythmic movement. The squad got back into Chicago about 8:45 Sat. night, and since the train didn't leave until 1 AM Bill Stauss [and I] went out for awhile. We both had dates and planned to go to a show or something quiet and inexpensive. However, every decent show had a long waiting line so we headed over to the Blackhawk again. In case you don't know the Blackhawk is a restaurant and cabaret. Les Brown and his band were playing there. I gathered from the enthusiasm of the females that he is supposed to be plenty good. The upshot of it was that we sat around listening to him for about three hours, dancing now and then, and I caught a check which looked like a government budget. The dance floor was about the size of our living room. I never took such a beating in my life, nor have I ever felt more strongly that the art of dancing is for others and not me. The more I see of that kind of entertainment the more I am glad that I was an athlete. You most certainly would have to be tight to think it was enjoyable. (I must be a little owly this afternoon. It must be more fun than that. I'll try again sometime.)

I have a date tonight with some Delta Gamma. I guess I can be a little more specific than that. She is the same flaxen haired little lass that I had out last Sunday night. I wish that I didn't have the date now. In fact the way I feel today I would just as soon not have any more dates ever. I seem to be pretty moody about going out with girls. I suppose that is due to the fact that I never find anyone with whom I really want to run around. Oh well, so it goes, now up and now down. Bob Hogan is coming down tonight from Cedar Rapids, and we plan to go out to the Amanas for supper. Will be glad when 10:30 rolls around, and I can fall into bed for some protracted sleep.

Ben and I weren't able to get together in Chicago. He left me a note at the Morrison saying that he had to pull out on Friday. I shall be interested to hear if he had a good time while he was in there.

Enclosed is a telegram which was mistakenly sent to Iowa State College. Uncle Will, or whoever he is, evidently thought I was coaching at Ia. State rather than at the U. of I.

Appreciate your long letter very much, Gus, will reply when I have a little more time. Won't be long until I see all of you again.

Love,
Nile

20 ✳ To the Family, 26 December 1941

Kinnick entered the Navy Air Corps at Fairfax Airport in northeast Kansas City, Kansas, on 4 December 1941. He and his group were given leaves from 24 December until 10 P.M. Christmas Day, so he left Omaha to return to Kansas City around 3 P.M. His companions were Ken Pettit (Iowa '41) of Logan, a lineman on the 1939 Iowa football team who had joined the Navy Air Corps with Kinnick, and three cadets from Omaha (see the diary for 24–25 December 1941).

Kinnick's car was now his own, a 1941 Ford sedan. Scrapbook 2 contains several snapshots of Kinnick and fellow cadets taken later at Pensacola wherein the car is frequently visible. When and where he bought it is unknown.

Friday night   Dec. 26, 1941

Dear Family:

I hope you all enjoyed our brief time together as much as I did. For me the grievous world situation dimmed not at all the significance of Christmas day. In fact it made me hold it that much more dear. Our visit was short, but we were all together in good health and happiness which was the important thing. Christmas eve was just as I had hoped it would be, mother. The meal was fine, Bob was there, a fire burned in the fireplace, date bars and candy were plentiful. All in all everything was just right. And before I go further, let me say how much we all are enjoying the box of goodies you put up. It contained many more toothsome tidbits than I had anticipated.

Our trip to Kansas City yesterday afternoon was completed on time although we hit a good deal of snow. Between Omaha and Falls City it was pretty slow going. The highway was covered with five or six inches of wet, slushy snow making it quite slippery going. Fortunately, just as it was getting dark we ran out of the storm and hit clear pavement. We arrived about 9:30 without mishap except that something has happened to my muffler. My engine sounds like it has a cut-out on it. Couldn't help realizing what a luxury a fine car is. The weather was most inclement and yet we sailed along in perfect comfort, dry & warm, listening to fine music over the radio.

A low ceiling kept the right wing from flying this morning, but will probably get to go up tomorrow A.M. Changed my bed linen today. Can hardly believe it myself.

All goes well here. Keep me posted on what Ben does & how George is getting along. I'm betting George gets his competitive urge aroused one of these days and shows all of you some real basketball & some real grades. Only quitters are satisfied with "*floating*."

Love,

Nile

21 ✳ To the Family, 6 February 1942

Kinnick left Kansas City for his second training station, New Orleans, on 3 February 1942 (see the diary for further information on this and the other periods it covers). Merle was Merle McKay, briefly a student at Iowa (her picture is in the 1942 *Hawkeye* among members and pledges of Pi Beta Phi). She is "Murl the purl" and "Moil the Poil" in later references. Kinnick knew her only slightly in Iowa City; their first date was on 11 January, three weeks before his departure. The other cadets from Section 50 who rode with Kinnick and Pettit were Al Agan and Marvin Haugebak.

Friday   Feb. 6, 1942

Dear Folks:

I suppose you will want to hear about our trip down here. It is apt to be a rather uninteresting narrative, but I'll do the best I can.

My last, and very pleasant, date with Merle found me getting in around 3 AM. Nonetheless, in the hope of getting an early start for New Orleans, I piled out of bed at 5:45 with the rest of the boys. It was a vain hope, however. The powers that be kept us waiting around for our traveling orders until 2:45 that afternoon. Finally, all red tape was complied with, and we pulled out for the southland – Pettit, I, and two other boys from our section. We followed #71 to #35 to #13 and into Springfield, Mo. for supper. Out of there we followed #60 to Willow Springs, where we picked up #63. It was on this road that the map shows that innocuous looking strip of gravel 50 miles long. Well, sad to relate, a gravel road in Arkansas is not the same animal it is in Iowa even though a state road. Frankly, it was one of the worst highways I have ever traveled – nothing but a wagon trail, and a poor one at that. It was hilly, winding, poorly marked, and full of chuck holes and boulders. I thought my poor car was going to shake to pieces before we hit concrete again. About midnight we drove into Jonesboro, Ark. where we stayed the night. Although it was a poor bed in a tourist camp, I found it mighty welcome, having had but 3 hours sleep the night before.

The next morning it was raining making it doubly difficult to get up and going. We managed to make it around 8:30 AM, immediately pointing for Memphis, Tenn., not even stopping for breakfast. My impression of Arkansas was anything but good – nothing but poorly marked, poorly surfaced roads, swamps, gullies, sterile looking soil, mules, people who looked like hungry hound-dogs, unpainted one room shacks, and the darkest looking Negroes I have ever seen. At Memphis we hit highway #61 which follows the river south to New Orleans. The land in Mississippi was very level and looked as if it might have been quite fertile at one time. However, it now appears weary – almost sterile looking. None of the fields had fences – the livestock wandered up and down the road at will. The entire countryside was cluttered with small one or two room, unpainted, clapboard shacks – the homes of the Negro farm laborers. Never before have I seen such poverty in the country – in the city, yes, but never before out on the land. Not infrequently we saw a duplex arrangement in which the colored family lived on one side and the domesticated animals on the other. On 1st blush that statement may have a humorous ring, but it most certainly shouldn't. This situation must be an ever increasing social problem to the south. We ate lunch in a little town called Clarksdale in Mississippi. We all remarked how much less prosperous everything looked in comparison to towns up North.

As we came into Vicksburg we had a commanding view of the mighty Miss. R. in all its majesty. High on the surrounding bluffs we drove along drinking in the tremendous vista presented. Not for naught is the Mississip called the Father of Waters. Wasn't it here that Grant gained the victory of the west which turned the tide in favor of the North back in Civil War days? If he had to storm those steep cliffs to gain his objective no wonder he always lost so many men in winning the battle.

I had hoped to see a great many beautiful southern mansions in Natchez, but evidently the highway didn't run near them. We did see a few fine looking homes, but nothing to compare with what I had read existed there.

Around seven oclock we pulled into Baton Rouge, La where we stopped for supper. Our highway ran right by the state capitol so we stopped to have a look around. It is a magnificent looking structure surrounded by well landscaped grounds, and right in the center of everything stood a large bronze statue of Huey Pierce Long proudly basking in the glare of a huge spotlight shining down from the very top of the capitol dome.

At last we were on the last leg of our trip – 83 miles to N. Orleans. We pulled in there about 9:30 or 10 oclock quite weary but determined to have a look around before going to bed. We took a room at the LaSalle hotel, a rather unpretentious looking hostelry whose interior in no wise belied its exterior impression. After shaving and washing up a bit we sallied out. What an interesting city! I wish that we might have had more time to look around before reporting aboard yesterday afternoon at 3:30. As it was we saw just enough to whet our interest. The buildings and general appearance along Canal st, the main drag, is quite modern and clean looking. However, just three or four blocks to the north (I think its north; I can't seem to get my directions straight down here) is the French quarter presenting a picture of a by-gone age. It was in New Orleans that Rhett Butler & Scarlett O'Hara spent their honeymoon, I believe, and this French district corroborates in every detail the scenes shown – right down to the small iron railed balconies on nearly every building. The streets are extremely narrow, being designated as one way for modern traffic. Antique shops, saloons, bars, old eating places abound. I hope to eat at Arnauds & Antoines before being transferred from this base. The latter establishment claims to have been in business continuously for over a hundred years, and to have been host to every president of the U.S. during that period at some time or another. We finally got into bed Wed. night around 1 oclock much to my satisfaction for I drove the entire distance.

We arose quite late on Thursday morning, drove around awhile, then reported aboard out here. Our present base is located on Lake Pontchartrain (sp) a body of water of no small dimensions. There is a great deal of construction work going on preparatory to making this a base of some significance. As a result the whole place is suffering from growing pains and red tape which we, as students, feel indirectly. From all I can gather our liberty is going to be almost nil. In fact the more I see of this base the more I think K. C. was a mighty fine place – and "Murl the purl" enters into the calculations a bit. We had a radio test this morning just to see how much we had forgotten in a week. I didn't do very well, but it was just carelessness. I don't anticipate any particular trouble.

I note by the bulletin board that I have a "dog watch" on Sunday, ie, 12–4 AM, and since it is a holiday (no operations) I shall have to stand twice. I'll be on 4, off 8 hrs, then on 4 again, ie, 12–4 PM, then 12–4 AM. It will be the 1st watch I have stood since entering the service, my student officer rank excused me, heretofore.

This is about all I have time for now. The older students tell us that once we get under weigh here, we'll be lucky to find time to write a postcard home. So if you don't hear from me too regularly you'll know why. Will do the best I can to keep you informed of what is going on. Looks as if I won't have much time to do any Science study – that I don't relish. Perhaps, I won't be as busy as I think I might. Anyway love to all – was awfully glad to see you over the weekend just past.

Good luck to you George and let me hear from me now and then if you feel so inclined.

Yours,
Nile

22 ✳ To the Family, 18 February 1942

Late in this letter Kinnick says he hardly recognized Wyman Hayward. In 1935 Nile and Ben Kinnick drove their father's Model A Ford to Colorado, New Mexico, and the West Coast – from Los Angeles to Seattle – to see the sights and visit family friends and relatives. Kinnick's earliest letter in the collection, 18 July 1935, describes their stay at the New Mexico farm of the elder Kinnick's college roommate, Gene Hayward. Wyman Hayward was his son, whom Kinnick had not seen since. In or around 1935 Kinnick wrote a long account of the entire trip that survives in a fair-copy typescript (box 2). Kinnick's allusion to the AAA is to the controversial Agricultural Adjustment Act, an early New Deal measure that Henry A. Wallace implemented as secretary of agriculture in Roosevelt's first two terms.

Wednesday   Feb. 18, 1942

Dear People,

So much has happened since last I wrote you that I hardly know where to begin. Perhaps, it would be best to first tell you that I am now located at Pensacola, and from what I have seen of it, I like it very much. Now to start back a little farther and bring things up to date.

We spent most of Monday checking out of the New Orleans base. It is always a long and tiresome process and this was no exception. Around three oclock we had complied with all the red tape and our traveling orders were issued – directing us to report at Pensacola not later than Tues. noon. It being only a little over 200 miles distant, we thought there was no necessity of getting started right away. When I say we, I refer to the same boys who rode from K.C. to New Orleans with me – Pettit, Agan, & Haugebak. Although, we weren't going to have a lot of time we still thought it a good idea to see a little more of N.O. before departing. But first we needed a haircut. That being taken care [of] we went to a movie and then down into the French quarter. I wish I had a good ability at descriptive expression, for were it so I could paint a very interesting picture of this section. It has the best and the worst of about everything – from antiques and restaurants, to women and liquor. We were heading for Antoines and a fine meal of which we had heard much. Neither the interior or exterior of this famous place is pretentious – but the food is good – excellent in fact. I started off with oysters on the half shell ala Rockefeller – and ala 60¢ for one half dozen. They were tasty, they were good – but they were also brief! Oh yes, the menu was printed entirely in French. You would have died watching us order – especially Haugebak & Pettit. I helped them as best I could much to the amusement of the waiter, I am sure. Ioway & Nebrasky stuck out all over us. George would have been mortified! Following the oysters I had a small steak, very small in fact, because I had to have enough money left to buy some gas. *Everything* was ala carte so I skipped potatoes & vegetables & settled for a salad ala Antoine which was nothing but a very ordinary looking jumble of lettuce & four leaf clovers. The steak was as well cooked as any meat I have ever eaten. It almost melted in your mouth. But let me tell you about the salad. George will love this! As I was gathering together my last mouthful, I spied a small but quite active worm squirming around in the middle of the plate. Far from being alarmed at such a sight I was quite amused that this could happen in this very famous restaurant. It didn't take much urging from the rest of the fellows, in fact none at all, to persuade me that I should call it to the attention of the waiter – just for the devil of it. With impish glee I beckoned for him, and as he stood at my elbow all poised and ready to please, I said, "Pardonne, garcon, but does this little beastie go with the salad? Is this salad ala Antoine?" Man, did he become apologetic – "so sorry, messieur (sp), etc, etc" – then he scurried away to get me another. After dinner, with no dessert, for obvious reasons, we walked back to have a look at the Mystery Room. It was a very ordinary looking private dining room with cedar shavings on the floor and autographed pictures of famous people on the wall – no more, no less.

At 8:45 we got started for Pensacola, planning to drive as far as Mobile, Ala & spend the night, finishing the trip the next morning. It rained hard most of the way over, but it was a very pleasant drive, nonetheless. Inside the car we enjoyed fine music from the radio and remained dry and comfortable. Intermittent flashes of lightning showed a countryside that I am sure must be very pretty by daylight – especially around Biloxi and Gulfport. We were unable to get a hotel room in Mobile so kept on driving until we hit a cabin camp 7 or 8 miles east of there. Lucky, we were, too, to hit such a fine camp. We got a swell little bungalow with two double beds and a gas heater for 4 bucks. It then being one oclock & still raining we turned in immediately. We were late in getting up, it was so comfortable to lie in bed and listen to the gentle patter of the rain on the roof. About 10:30 we got under weigh again, arriving at Pensacola at 10 minutes before noon. It was an uneventful last 50 miles except for the miles long caravan of army trucks we met and the crossing of a stream named Styx, which brought a brief debate as to whether we were entering or leaving Hell!

The buildings – hangars, barracks, administrative offices, etc – are laid out in much the manner of a college campus. In a great many ways the whole setup reminds me of a university. There is a fine moving picture house, a gym, bowling alleys, just about everything you could devise in the way of recreation & amusement. We live two to a room rather than in one big barracks room as heretofore. My roommate is Jack Wright one of the K.C. boys. Pettit & I weren't able to get together since all assignments were made even before we arrived. Wright is a thin, effeminate sort of guy but quite harmless. He has no more interest in me than I in him, but we will get along quite alright I know. There was a time when anything less than a handpicked roommate would have been a catastrophe for me – but no longer. Will tell you more about the base & the life here in my next letter.

Have run into several boys I knew at Iowa and a good many others who know fellows that I do. Never have any trouble getting acquainted or making friends. Wyman Hayward showed up at my room this afternoon. I didn't recognize him right away – and no wonder. His conversation soon showed how much he has matured since last I saw him. We had a fine visit for 20 minutes or so. He told me many things about what he has been doing & about the rest of the family. It seems Vice-President Wallace's daughter was in a camp near Cimarron last summer & that when Mrs. Wallace was down to see her Mrs. Hayward asked them both out to dinner. Can you beat that? I wonder if Mrs. W. asked Mr. H. if he liked the A.A.A.? Wyman is planning to get married as soon as he gets his commission. Don't know just when that is, but he says he is 2 months behind his class due to an appendix operation.

Thanks so very much for the Valentine goodies, mother. I enjoyed them immensely even though the pckge was pretty well mutilated by the time I got it. Incidentally, the chow here is marvelous – best yet.

Now, mother, if you ever get time I'd like to have you do this for me. Give me references both in the Bible & S. & H. which you think are particularly pertinent to these times. I'm hoping to have more chance to look at my books from now on. I know that the Bible is full of stories of courage & faith that would help a great deal – but, unhappily, I'm not as conversant with them as I would like to be.

So glad Ben made the grade ok – & that he will be able to get his degree before graduating. Sure would like to hear from him.

Haven't gotten the black sox as yet.

Things go well – love to all.

Yours,

Nile

Will be shipping my civilian clothes home one of these days possibly collect – our paychecks haven't come thru for some reason or another.
N.C.K.
Naval Air Base
2nd Battalion
Bldg 653 – Rm 1234
Pensacola
  Florida

23 ✳ To the Family, 4 May 1942

In his diary for 29 April 1942, Kinnick writes that the only Dr. O'Brien he recalls was killed two years earlier but that he must also know the Dr. O'Brien of this letter. The doctor in question was Cecil S. O'Brien, Head of Otolaryngology at University of Iowa Hospital. He need not have known Kinnick to know that he was in Pensacola. That Kinnick did not think of this implies that he was unaware of his continuing local fame.

Bob Hobbs had entered the Navy Air Corps at Fairfax Airport shortly after Kinnick, on 2 January 1942. Ben Kinnick and Eleanor White of Council Bluffs, both 1942 graduates of Iowa State, would marry in New York on 19 July 1943. Eleanor enlisted in the WAVES and was stationed in New York when Kinnick visited her after his transfer to Quonset Point in January 1943.

Kinnick's parents were shocked when they read of his plan to join the marines (Kinnick, Sr., carbon, 6 May 1942). They had not known that there was a marine air branch or that cadets could put in for navy or marine commissions. Kinnick's choice was refused on 4 June. One former Navy Air Corps pilot has said that selection by lot, the explanation given Kinnick, was unlikely. He suggests that the navy wanted to keep Kinnick for publicity purposes.

After Navy Air Corps training, Ben Kinnick would have his choice of the marines approved. He became a marine bomber pilot and was killed in action over the Kavieng Peninsula on New Ireland on 17 September 1944.

Monday   May 4, 1942

Dear People,

I am now satisfactorily by my 33 hour check, as I may already have written you, and will take my final check in primary squadron this afternoon. I wish that I could have a week or two in which to practice all the maneuvers I have learned, but such is not to be. By the end of this week I shall be starting primary formation flying, and just about the time I get the hang of it, something else will be scheduled. And so it goes, as we are hurried toward the sterner task ahead.

On last Wednesday I found a letter in my mail box marked from the Commandants Quarters. It was with great curiosity that I opened it, wondering what in the world could have occasioned it. It turned out to be an invitation and not a disciplinary summons. In short, it said that Dr. & Mrs. O'Brien of Iowa City had informed them that Pettit & I were down here, they would so much like to meet us, and would we please drop in and see them on Friday at 5:30, signed Bess Read, the captains wife. Well, we were flattered naturally, the captain is a 4 striper and we are but lowly cadets. However, it would be no easy matter to get there. Classes don't let out until ten minutes of five and my white uniform, the only suitable dress, was not yet ready. Nonetheless, the invitation of a captains wife is virtually command so we planned to go. I managed to borrow a uniform that fit fairly well and away we went. It turned out to be a cocktail party in the back yard with two and three stripers thicker than the sands of the seas. Mrs. Read introduced us around to a few people, and would say that we were from Iowa, had they ever been there? No? – well, my dear, you should see those *magnificent* farms and the barns SIMPLY BURSTING with grain. It was I who about burst with inward laughter. What a riot. Soon the cocktails made rounds and no one knew whether we were cadets or admirals, and everything was very congenial. When we left we were conventionally urged to come in just anytime, etc. May drop down for an ham sandwich and a glass of milk some Sunday night.

Not having any whites as yet, nor Bob either, we couldn't leave the base over the weekend. Pettit, however, freshly out of the hospital was anxious to get to town, so I loaned him my car for the evening. Bob and I took a stroll, sat on the barrack steps and leisurely talked for awhile, then retired early. We sprawled on the beach Sunday morning for a couple of hours, reveling in the warmth and comfort of sand, sea, and sun. In the afternoon Bob went sailing with 3 other fellows whom he had promised previously, and I took a rather lengthy nap. After supper I read awhile in Carl Sandburg's "Prairie Years" of Lincoln's life, before turning in early. And now another week has begun. The sun is just coming up, and our class is in radio code, but having checked out some time ago, as have a great many, I hastily indite this letter to you.

Last week I had a long letter from Ben saying that he and Ellie were very much that way, and that he was thinking of promises of betrothal, etc. He has written you, I believe, and received counsel of caution and conservatism for the most part. It must be tough for a young fellow to be champing at the bit and get no aggressive encouragement from his family. I must confess, however, that I, too, suggested he watch that he wasn't carried away by the spirit of the moment. However, I also told him that I thought it was a good idea, which I most certainly do, if it can't be worked out properly. She is a grand girl from what I know of her, and it sure is a lonely world without feminine comfort and interest. Well, its really his decision and no one elses. I hope he gets things arranged to his satisfaction.

There goes the bell, I must run. What about my golf clubs and shoes? Things go well. Am thinking seriously of joining the Marines. Better state your objections quickly if you have any.

Love,

Nile

24 ✳ To Nile Kinnick, Sr., 27 May 1942

In April 1942 Kinnick's father spoke before Omaha teenagers being trained for farm work because of the wartime labor shortage. He sent Kinnick a photo clipping from the *Omaha World-Herald* (scrapbook 2) showing him before a blackboard putting a piece of chalk in the tray. On the board he has written in vertical order "Grains," "Forage or *Roughage*," "Silage," and "*Hay*." Kinnick wrote this letter in blue ink, and between "logically" and "(No offense intended)" he inscribed a phrase later canceled in a different ink repeatedly and with such force as to tear the paper fibers and make the canceled matter irrecoverable. From the sense of the context, the placement of the words on the blackboard, the line space involved, and the vigor of the cancellation, an inference of "amount to bullshit" or a similar vernacular expression of equal length is obvious. It is unlikely that Kinnick made the deletion, for he could see that his father or mother would get the drift, and all the more closely the more thoroughly he canceled the passage. The cancellation seems rather the act of his father or mother, done possibly not because either took offense but to shield Kinnick from later readers.

The song Kinnick mentions was "Don't Sit under the Apple Tree," from the 1942 movie *Private Buckaroo*, featuring the Andrews Sisters, whose recording of it was popular for the rest of the war. Bob Hobbs and Kinnick's cousin Elsie Louise Clarke, daughter of Charles F. Clarke, would marry on 26 August 1943. Fred was Uncle Fred Clarke in Seattle.

Wednesday   May 27, 1942

Dear Gus,

Just time for a brief note before "lights out." First let me tell you how much I enjoy your long letters. Knowing how busy you are I cherish them doubly. Wish we could take a weekend trip together – even get stuck in the mud somewhere – and talk long and interestingly about this flying game. I shall never be satisfied if I don't have an opportunity to teach you to fly sometime.

Some of the boys may be living just from day to day with a fatalism precluding plans for the future. Not I – my imagination goes beyond the war to those blessed days of peace which will one day come again. I frequently think of what I shall want to do for a livelihood. Aviation will be a tremendously growing industry then, and it may be that I shall want to stay in it in some capacity or another, but right now do you know what appeals to me? I want to be a flour salesman, if there are such animals. That is, I want to hook up with some good flour company & start out as their sales representative in Iowa. My idea being that such a job would give me an opportunity to travel about the state & among the people I like – farmers & small town inhabitants. The future could hold two alternatives – advancement up the ladder to the home office – or, possibly, a political campaign for senator. Do you see any possibilities in such a setup? What are the best flour companies in the midwest? Would there be *good* money if I was *good*? Just a thought – nothing definite – how does it strike you? I am pretty sure I don't want to go back to law school.

As for Moil the Poil, I still correspond quite frequently with her. Sure wish I could get back up that way for a few days. It may be that I'll get stalled there for awhile when I get leave. As a matter of fact my feminine correspondence has been quite good the past few months. All are nice little chicks whom I hope aren't "spending too much time under the apple tree with someone else but me." (There is a song that goes like that. Get George to give you the whole of it.) Glad to get your slant on Bob & Elsie. I would figure about the same, although Bob is very quiet about the whole thing, and I don't want to frighten him away with too pertinent questioning. They would sure make a dandy couple. Personally I am rather glad that I don't have a serious heart affair right now, but sure would like to be surrounded with the lighter infatuations I have mentioned. K.C., Chicago, D.M., etc. are all too, too far away.

Am sending back the picture of you deftly & precisely replacing the chalk – all a very characteristic gesture in my mind. Trust your talk didn't lead the boys to think that forage, silage & hay logically [amount to bullshit?] (No offense intended)

Enclosed is a letter from Fred I thought you would like to see.

Here is a pretty good one – as the instructor got out of his cockpit after giving a student his last hop before his 33 hr check, he said, – well, you go up this last solo hour, I think you can iron everthing out – if you have enough time & a big enough *iron*!

S. B.

25 ✳ To Arletta G. Clarke, 28 May 1942

Celia Peairs discovered Governor Clarke's inaugural address while doing research for her 1942 master's thesis at the University of Chicago, "Report: Attempts to Secure Aid-to-Dependent Children Legislation in Iowa." Kinnick's quotations of his grandfather err only trivially (see *Inaugural Address of George W. Clarke . . . Delivered January 16, 1913* [Des Moines, 1913]).

The Hemion boys, then in the service, were nephews of Uncle Fred Clarke's wife. When Nile and Ben Kinnick visited the Clarkes on Mercer Island in Washington in 1935, Fred and his son Ted took them along with Whit and Bobby Hemion up to the Sucia Islands in his cruiser. Sumner was Sumner Macomber, a relative of Aunt Kate Macomber Clarke. As a boy, orphaned during the flu epidemic after World War I, he lived for a time with the Clarkes in Adel. When he later lived with his grandmother in Des Moines, he often went out to Adel, where Kinnick and he were playmates. He was in the navy during the war and saw duty in the Pacific. Ben Kinnick was elected to Student Board and Cardinal Key, both select organizations at Iowa State, the latter a scholastic honor society.

Though Kinnick queries his spelling of "hieroglyphics" and "propitious" in the first paragraph, he spelled both words correctly.

Thursday   May 28, 1942

Dear Grandma,

I am writing this out at squadron, using my stationery box for a table, so if it is unusually illegible you will understand why. Under the most propitious (sp) circumstances my hand is difficult to decode, but I fear *these* pages may look like a study in hieroglyphics (sp) before I finish. (I'm not so confident of my spelling without my dictionary for reference).

I carry on a desultory correspondence with a girl by the name of Celia Peairs – she among others, that is!?! Celia, at present, is working on her thesis at Chicago U., dealing with old age pensions, aid to dependent children, etc. A couple of weeks ago she wrote that in her research she had run across the inaugural address of Geo. W. Clarke in 1913. She thought it excellent, and asked if he weren't my grandfather, and had I read it. I was ashamed to admit that I hadn't. Thereupon, she forwarded me a copy in booklet form from the U. library, saying that by all means I should make myself acquainted with it. It happened that it arrived when Bob Hobbs was in the room so we read it over together, both agreeing that in truth it was very excellent. Such addresses of grandpa's should long ago have been brought to my attention. My only memory of grandpa giving a speech was on a fourth of July down at the park. As I recall it, the speakers rostrum was up at the west end near the pavilion and festooned with flags. Betwixt the wind, a poor p.a. system, and some guy piling boards nearby, a good deal of his talk was effectively kept from his listeners. I can see him standing there yet with his hair being intermittently ruffled by the breeze. Unhappily I don't remember anything of what he said, but I do believe that I have depicted the physical picture fairly close. I earnestly hope my reminiscing fills you with proud memories and in no wise makes you sad. I should feel terrible if I have erred in writing you in this vein. But back to the 1913 inaugural address of which I first made mention. His opening remarks particularly appealed to me. Do you remember them? – "I acknowledge my very great indebtedness to the people of Iowa. The obligation of this moment profoundly impresses me. It is not with any sense of triumph that I enter upon the duties of the office into which I am this day inducted, but with a deep sense of its duties, the wide possibilities of its influence, & my inability to approach the ideal of fitness & performance. If I can but be the servant of all, if I can with the help of others contribute something to the common good, if I can assist in making Iowa more distinguished still among the states for the desirableness & wisdom of her laws & the cleanliness of her political life, that will be something." He went on to say that the common good should be the primary aim of the action of that legislature, that human rights should be put above property rights, & that "man should be put above the dollar." He urged the passage of a workmen's compensation act, a public utilities bill, improved roads, county mgn., short ballot, better rural schools, woman suffrage, reform of court procedure, & enlarging & beautifying the capitol grounds. In his peroration he proclaimed that the subjects up for consideration of that general assembly suggested "the loosening of the grasp of human selfishness & the extension of the hand of sympathy & brotherhood." Noble sentiments graciously phrased – and his life exemplified the ideals he spoke, much to the benefit of his progeny and all those with whom he came in contact.

I am now learning to fly by instruments and to orientate myself on a radio range so that in bad weather I will be able to follow a radio beam into an airport. We do most of our flying under an hood precluding the use of the horizon, etc, even of the sense of feel, for under a hood, as in a fog, when surrounding objects can't be seen your senses play you false. You can't tell for sure whether you are turning right or left, climbing or gliding without the use of the instruments. All of this is dual instruction so someone is always on the lookout to see that everything goes well. I wrote the folks in some detail about this training, perhaps, you will get to see that letter.

Had a nice long letter from King the other day. Enjoyed hearing from him a lot and feel quite guilty that I haven't written him since coming into the service. Also received a long letter from Fred about a week ago a copy of which he sent to Bob H, Whit & Austen Hemion, & Sumner. He extended an invitation to all of us to come out for a cruise after the war. Certainly, we'd all be in the mood for something like that. As for U. Charlie not having anything to write about, that shouldn't matter. I enjoy hearing from him regardless. His humor, comments on the general situation, and comparisons of the present with things past always interest me.

Didn't Ben finish up in grand style? He must be the happiest guy alive, what with romance and honor recognition & all that sort of thing.

As for the cookies, grandma, they were excellent even though a little squashed. And don't rob your rationed sugar supply to send me more, grand though it would be.

Your letters of affection and encouragement bring me much comfort. Thank you for taking the time to write.

Things go well with me and hope they do with all of you.

Much love,
Nile

26 ✳ To Nile Kinnick, Sr., 29 June 1942

Kinnick's father could at once identify the hotel from which his son wrote the following letter because Kinnick typed it on letterhead stationery of the Caribbean, on the ocean from Thirty-seventh to Thirty-eighth Street in Miami Beach. His traveling companions had been Marvin Haugebak and "a kid by the name of Carlson from Philadelphia" (diary, 24 June).

The title of the Rosalind Russell and Fred MacMurray picture was *Take a Letter, Darling* (1942). The *Time* article, in the 4 May 1942 issue, concerned navy carrier pilot Edward H. O'Hare, who had recently been awarded the Congressional Medal of Honor for shooting down five Japanese bombers during a single flight. He spoke to the cadets at Pensacola, and his talk in part inspired Kinnick to choose a fighter assignment (diary, 13 May). The Westbrook Pegler piece was a celebration of the American businessman as a patriot (*Reader's Digest*, July 1942). Sandow was the strongman and physical fitness advocate Eugene Sandow (1867–1925), in Kinnick's day still a byword for he-man.

Monday, June 29, 1942

Dear Gus,

I am writing to you from room 421 of this very delightful little hotel in Miami Beach. It fronts on the ocean itself, sports a swimming pool, a nice beach, and every other luxury dear to the leisure class. But more of this later; if this is to be a travelogue of the past few days, I had best start at the beginning.

We got away from the air station in Pensacola about noon on Friday – Haugebak, Carlson, and I. Following route 90 we drove an uneventful trip to Tallahassee where we stayed all night, getting in there about 5:30 PM. There were more road warnings along this particular strip of highway than there were billboards. Warnings for sharp turns, chuck holes, narrow bridges, bridges under repair, men at work, dips in the pavement, detours, and stock at large were as numerous as the fence posts. As to the latter warning, they could hardly overemphasize it. At frequent intervals hogs, sheep, goats, cows, or pickaninnies would clutter up the highway as effectively as fleeing refugees. Once again the landscape brought forceably home the poverty of the southern Negro farmer of which we have heard quite a bit but seen very little. We passed through mile after mile of country dotted with those single room, unpainted huts that serve as shelter for the colored folk. You will remember that my account of our trip through Arkansas, Mississippi, and Louisiana told of the same thing, and, of course, Alabama and Georgia present the same depressing picture. These hovels are not only distressingly small and dingy, but are without even a window. True, there are openings which might loosely be called windows, but in reality they are nothing but barn doors, no glass or shutters or anything like that. Seriously, I doubt if a northern farmer would consent to having his livestock so poorly housed.

In Tallahassee we put up at a very comfortable and reasonably priced cabin camp. It only cost the three of us four dollars total for a well ventilated, clean little cabin with two large double beds, a radio, and bath. While walking around the town looking for a place to eat supper, we found, much to our surprise and amusement, that the soldiers on the streets from a nearby encampment mistook us for naval officers and would snap to and salute as we walked by. It proved to be fun for a little while, and then became quite tiring for there were a great many soldiers in town. After supper we drove out by the campus of Florida State Teachers College for Women, hoping that there would be a full summer session. Sure enough, there was a goodly number of enrollees strolling about, but, also, there were just about as many soldiers. However, we parked the car and started a little patrol work ourselves. We hadn't been on the grounds five minutes, before we met three delovely blondes face to face. There was no awkwardness in getting a conversation started. As a matter of fact they accosted us first, with a "good evening, gentlemen, you look awfully nice and awfully cool in those white uniforms." Rather flattering, and a nice start wouldn't you say? Really sounds good, doesn't it? Are you wondering just how your eldest proceeded from there? Well, rest assured he would have conducted himself with confidence, and, probably, sufficient decorum. However, if you haven't already guessed, these blonde women of the evening dusk were matrons of 50 years or more, at least. My favor with women under 10 and over 50 has been unfailing. It then being about dark and making it impossible to be discriminating, we walked a bit farther and then headed back for the car. Incidentally, the college has a beautiful campus and fine buildings. There was just time left to make a show which we did. Moontide starring Ida Lupino and Jean Gabin wasn't too good, but neither was it real bad. As we came out of the theatre afterwards, I recognized Bob Vernon, a tall, dark southern chap, who used to teach my geology lab. class when I was a freshman at Iowa. We both shook hands with an exclamation of what a small world it is and asked what the other was doing down that way. It turns out that he is now assistant state geologist, has acquired a wife, and, also, about twenty five pounds. Back at our cabin camp we slept well and were glad we weren't in a stuffy hotel.

At nine oclock the next morning we were under weigh again, taking route 500 out of Tallahassee, till we hit number 19, following it to Williston where it joined with route 41. Turning south at this junction we followed that highway into Tampa, then on 541 to Bradenton where we again hit number 41, and so on down the western edge of the state thru Sarasota, Punta Gorda, to Fort Myers where we stayed all night. It was a long hot trip, almost dull. There didn't seem to be much to see, at least not from the highway, and we had no time for side excursions. At Punta Gorda we ran into the heaviest rain I have ever seen. We couldn't see 15 yards ahead of us, necessitating that we creep along at about 25 miles an hour with our headlights on. It let up after about 15 minutes although it continued to drizzle all the way into Fort Myers. Not being able to locate a suitable looking tourist camp we were forced to put up at an hotel. The Franklin Arms sounded high toned and even looked good from the outside, but the five dollar room we got was as free of a breeze as a cedar closet. We piled in rather shortly after eating, but might as well have slept in a Turkish bath. I was wringing wet when I got up the next morning. And oh yes, the head, you will want to hear about it. It was a cubicle about four feet wide and six feet long, housing, nonetheless, a shower, a wash bowl, and a toilet. It was all very intimate when we all started to shave, shower, and "read". In fact the whole layout must have been planned by a New Deal architect, the toilet paper being situated high and directly back of the right shoulder which was already in close contact with the exterior wall, an almost impossible "get" even for an athlete. And so passed our sojourn at Fort Myers.

It was ten oclock before we got started on Sunday morning, Carlson being a bit indisposed and refusing to get out of bed any earlier. While waiting for him to get up I read with interest a Time magazine, and a Readers Digest. From the former I have enclosed an item which I read with much pride and approbation, and from the latter I snipped an article by Pegler which is more than a little pertinent. From Fort Myers we took 41 until we hit 94 which took us right into Miami – arrival about 12:30. En route through the Everglades, which from what we saw is nothing but many square miles of swamp land, we had our only unhappy incident of the whole trip. For some cause I can't ascertain for sure, a large, jagged hole was torn in the rubber of my right hind tire. When it occurred it sounded like a blowout, but the inside casing was still intact, and the inner tube still had its load of air. It didn't take us long to change to the spare, and we were soon on the road again. I am hoping that I shall be able to get the injured tire fixed up so that I can least use it for a spare. Arriving in Miami, we drove north a ways looking over the town, then turned east across the causeway into Miami Beach. Starting south down the Beach we drove by block after block of fine looking hotels all situated right down next to the ocean. Things not being quite what they used to be down this way we decided to find out if it would cost too much for us to stay at one of them. Pulling up in front of the Caribbean Haugebak went in to inquire, and came out with the news that [the] three of us could get a room for five dollars, plenty satisfactory to us.

We found our room to contain three single beds, two dressers, a swell shower, and a large, roomy closet. Depositing our luggage we took the elevator into the basement where the mens locker room was located. Changing into our swimming trunks we strolled out for a swim, either in the pool, or in the ocean. The layout was just as you see in the movies. Around the pool were many tables and chairs occupied by men and women sipping their drinks and sucking at their weeds.

On the beach, and, also, around the pool were several small, square shaped tents with a marquee where the "vets" lolled in the shade. For the moment I thought I had stumbled into a Zionist convention, but closer observation revealed a few other Aryans in the neighborhood. Man, what a parasitic existence; such artificiality, such boredom, etc, etc., but, also, what a fine setup for three Naval Cadets to take it easy before reporting in at the station. We swam a little, tossed some quoits, and just sat soaking up the sun and watching the hard looking businessmen and tired looking women enjoy their luxury. I wish George might have been along. He would have expressively described it all as being "plenty neat". For his benefit I must relate one other incident. There were some weights on the beach and some of the dandies were struggling without much success to get the heaviest above their heads. So old Sandow, just for the hell of it, strolled over and waited until he got the all clear signal, then spat on his hands, rustic that he is, and seized that 155 lbs and snatched it aloft with precision and dispatch. Of course, now that young Hero is "rasslin" 100 lbs sacks of sugar, I presume that such a feat would be ducksoup for him also. About 5:30 we went over to Miami proper for something to eat and a show. In every block would be two or three stands selling fresh fruit juice of all kinds – pineapple, orange, cocoanut, papaya, lime, lemon, etc. You can guess that I didn't pass up very many of them. After supper we saw Fred MacMurray and Rosalind Russell in "Take a Letter" or something like that. Found it quite good. Everything is dimmed out down here after eight oclock. Only every other street light on one side is lit, and that quite dimly, and cars must drive with only their parking lights on. I found it somewhat difficult to pick my way back to the hotel, not being too familiar with the streets and buildings. After reading a little while I strolled out behind the hotel by myself. It was a grand night. The moon was full and bright, the palm trees around the swimming pool swayed in the fresh sea breeze; I walked down to the edge of the beach, stood with one foot up on the concrete wall, and drank it all in. It was wonderful, the wind, cool and invigorating, the waves running endlessly up the sand, here and there a light blinking down south a mile or so. It was a night for romance, love and affection, and I had a pleasant longing for a woman full and fair, but it was not to be, so I slowly wandered back to the hotel and up to bed. Our room was on the lee side and didn't benefit from the breeze off the ocean, but it was quite comfortable sleeping anyhow. We are due to report in at the air station at Opa Locka sometime tonight. Then it will be a rigorous schedule again, but not without its interest and fun.

I have addressed this letter to you because of the things that I am going to say from here on. They will be of interest to the whole family, yes, but only you will be able to understand completely and share with me my feelings. All the while that I was driving down here, my mind was thinking of what I might do when this war is over. Almost entirely my thoughts were of a farm and how much the soil and sun and crops appeal to me. My imagination ran rampant; my enthusiasm was so keen the first day that I nearly took time out at Tallahassee to write you. Oh for the farm where a man is truly independent, and where he deals with fundamentals, where the changing seasons brings changed work, and a man is out of doors all the time. It is on the farm that a man can devote his life to his investment and see the improvement and growth from year to year. The orchard will soon be in maturity, now, the windbreak will really be a protection in a few years, the kids are growing up in an ideal atmosphere – out in the open where the air is clean and pure, and under the discipline of their daily chores. Yes sir, on the farm a man could own a Piper cub and not have to worry about where to land it or where to keep it. I really don't know much about farming, I don't have enough money to get started, nor the prospects thereof, and possibly I wouldn't like it as well as I think. Certainly, not unless it was a good farm and things went reasonably well, but that is true of anything I might attempt. Anyway I enjoy thinking of such things and there is no doubt that I am a mid-westerner through and through. All this may be a bit distressing to mother, but it will strike a responsive chord in your heart I know.

Must close now. It is about time for us to get out of this hostelry. Have a hunch that I will be pretty busy for the next 8 weeks or so. May not be able to write as often as usual, but will get off a postcard or note now and then.

Bought another stamp for my car the other day. Automobiles are really a luxury these days.

Yours,

SB

Much love to all and let me hear from you whenever you can get around to it.

Things are going well, and I feel fine.

27 ✳ To the Family, 31 July 1942

Marvin Haugebak was restricted for a few days because he refused to obey a waveoff signal (Kinnick to the family, 26 July). Kinnick's reference to another earlier letter is to one of 20 July, in which he grants that Roosevelt has been an "outstanding president" but complains that he has compromised his courage and integrity. He goes on to lament the government's failure to control inflation and to do something about the rubber shortage. There is no form prescribed by Mary Baker Eddy for the passage from John 8:32.

Friday   July 31, 1942

Dear Family,

How much better it is to have my after supper hours free for reading, writing, and lounging. Here I sit leisurely pounding my typewriter and listening to my newly purchased radio. In truth I must be a rustic for I am keenly enjoying the barn dance music that is coming in over the air, and in the morning while dressing I can get the best cowboy music you ever heard. George would be sorely distressed with me I fear. . . . which brings to mind a postcard I rec'd the other day signed by one Geo. K. who casually stated that he was anxious to get back to school! Really should save that communication as marking the beginning of an epoch. What is it that makes him eager to return to school – young lassies, football, or classes. I hope that it is a combination of all three, for they all have their place.

I believe that my last letter was hastily indited late last Monday afternoon just before I left on liberty. Marvin was restricted as I have already told you, and I found myself quite content to enjoy my freedom all by myself. I stopped on the way downtown for a sandwich and a glass of milk, then went to a movie out on the Beach. It is strange how hungry I am for something I haven't yet been able to define. Regardless of what I order – steak, fish, fruit plate, hamburger, malted milks, etc. – that indefinite longing persists. Quite frankly I think nothing short of the home table will fill the bill. After the movie I warily herded my auto through the blacked-out streets to the Patrician where Marvin and I have put up on previous liberty nights. After registering I took my stuff up to the room, and then strolled out behind for a breath of fresh air before retiring. It was the most beautiful night you can imagine; perhaps, you folks marveled at it and thought of me as I did of you. I found a wicker chair out near the edge of the beach, and pulling it over near a palm tree and swinging it around so that it faced the ocean, I sat down and tried to absorb all that I felt and saw. The wind that rattled the fronds above me was fresh and invigorating in a measure that only an evening sea breeze can be. I took off my cap, breathed deeply again and again, lay back in perfect comfort, listening to the unbroken rhythm of the waves rushing up the sands. But the moon was the greatest wonder of it all. Round and full no clouds contested her light, even the stars kept a respectful distance. She was queen of the night, lovely, pure, unapproachable, undisputed sovereign of the celestial realm. Soft and silvery was her light, bathing all below in gentle benediction. I closed my eyes and gave myself over to quiet reverie, dreaming now of home and family, now of Iowa friends and unrestrained laughter, and mostly of the missing complement to such a wonderful evening. Shortly, thereafter I went to bed.

Well, I guess I am going to be a fighter pilot. When they asked me to indicate my choice I could no more refrain from saying fighters than I could refuse a second dipper of ice cream, and of course there was no reason why I should, but for a while there I thought I didn't know what I wanted. This means that my training period will be a little longer, but also a little better, I think. All going on schedule I should get leave about the end of August or the first of Sept. The nearer it gets the more anxious I become. Marvin had the most hits in our group and, of course, also got fighters. Last night the whole flight, twelve of us, went down to the officers club for supper. It was a gay and festive evening, with much laughter and repartee, terminating only when the lights were turned out and we had to return to the barracks. Bob had his first gunnery run today and got six hits, which is pretty good for the first time. He very likely will get fighters also. A good many of the boys who have finished up within the last three or four weeks have received orders directing them to transitional training at Norfolk or S. Diego then to active squadron out of Seattle, mostly escort duty flying off converted freighters, I believe. I can guess that Bob and I would welcome some such duty.

Your fine letters of the past few days have brought me much enjoyment. Father's indictment of the administration, and subsequent description of the country side as you drove back from Adel were most appealing. Incidentally, I wrote you folks a letter from the Patrician a week ago expressing rather strongly my feelings about the general situation in the gov't and can't tell from what you have written whether you ever received it. The rather poor mail connections throws our correspondence off schedule somewhat. It might be a good idea to indicate briefly what letter was last received just so we will know where we stand. Thanks so much, mother, for the Readers Digest, the Sentinel, and the cookies. The latter arrived in fine condition and were completely palatable. Your remarks concerning the happy times we used to have at grandma's struck a most responsive chord in my heart. I have priceless memories of those days.

Mother would you tell me the exact capitalization that Mrs. Eddy gives to the following Biblical statement: "Know the truth and the truth shall make you free."

It is only lack of space and time that keeps me from telling in detail how much I enjoy the stories, anecdotes, comments, that your letters contain in abundance. Must pile in now. Goodnight and much love.

Nile

My uniforms arrived today – $217 worth – what a racket – don't fit too well either. Perhaps I can get them altered a little while I'm home – can't get much satisfaction out of the uniform tailors.

28 ✳ To the Family, 25 September 1942

Kinnick received his orders for advanced carrier training on 25 August 1942, more than a week before he took his commission in Miami on 3 September. He was to report at Norfolk, Virginia, and join Fighter Squadron 16, and already he knew he would be assigned to a carrier not yet commissioned (Kinnick to his parents, 25 August). The orders were disappointing because Kinnick had repeatedly requested assignment to San Diego, by all accounts he heard a more agreeable place than Norfolk. But he looked forward to the three weeks between his departure from Miami and his arrival at Norfolk. He was to drive with Marvin Haugebak to St. Louis, where they would part company, Haugebak going on by train and Kinnick driving over to Kansas City to see Merle McKay on his way to Omaha. He spent more than a week with the family in Omaha and Adel. He left the 1941 Ford in Adel, where it was stored in Uncle Charles's garage or barn, and his father took him on to Des Moines to catch the Rock Island Rocket for his last visit to Iowa City, where this letter begins.

Annotations follow the letter in order of relevance to the text. Discussion has not been provided for several people, such as Jim Kearns and Tait Cummins, for whom the text gives adequate identification.

Friday   Sept 25, 1942

Dear Folks,

It has only been a week since I left you in Adel but much has happened which you will want to hear about. When I got off the train at Iowa City I found Glenn Devine and Jim Kearns waiting to meet me. You will remember Jim as the sportswriter from the Daily News who was so generous to me in 1939. In fact he was quite instrumental in getting me the big time publicity necessary for All-American recognition. He is now with Marshall Field's Chicago Sun and was assigned to cover the Iowa Pre-Flight School's game with Kansas. Their train left shortly after I arrived so I didn't get to talk to him for very long. He had a column in the Sunday paper in which he made reference to me in the kindest terms. I cut it out and enclosed it in a letter which I forgot to mail before leaving Iowa City. I believe I left it lying on Bill Stuart's desk, or somewhere around the room. Perhaps, he has forwarded it to you by now. Glenn was good enough to haul my two large pieces of baggage out to the temporary residence of the Fiddle-de-Fees and then drive me over to the fieldhouse. Football practice was just about to get under weigh and the usual gang was hanging around outside the dressing room door – the coaches, Frank, Eddie, and Jim; the sportswriters, Bert McGrane of the D.M. Register, Eddie Munzel of the Daily News, Charlie Bartlett of the Chicago Tribune, and others; and then, of course, there was Karl Leib and Dr. Alcock – practice wouldn't have been complete without those two. It was wonderfully good to see everyone again and heartwarming to realize how sincere each was in his greeting. Eddie suggested I take a little workout which sounded good to me, so I donned a pair of sweatpants and a quarter sleeve and kicked a few with Frank. Didn't do badly either; I was surprised. After practice I phoned Bibba for a date and then went down to supper with the boys at the Union. It was just like old times – eager appetite, good food, lusty, happy companionship, the prospect of a game the next day; I enjoyed every minute of it. That night Billy and I took our dates out to the Mayflower and then to Tiffin, a couple of the well known joints, where I ran into a great many more old friends. And so ended my first day in Iowa City.

On Saturday I arose pretty late, took some dirty clothes to the laundry, and then went out to the Phi Psi house for lunch. Most of the old bunch are gone, of course, but I did find a few whom I could call by name. Mrs. Post, the housemother, Ma Messner, the cook, and her portly daughter, Mabel, who helps in the kitchen and makes the beds, were all on hand looking much the same. The boys were proud to announce that they had a full house and that they had won the scholarship trophy last semester, all of which sounded pretty good to an ardent alumnus like me.

On the way over to the game I ran into Sgt. Buckley and Sgt. Lemmais who used to drill me in ROTC. Several of the other sergeants saluted me, but not these two old friends; they just shook hands in their bluff, hearty way, free from all formality and military etiquette. In the dressing room I found Judge McKinley – old faithful himself. Up in the press box I ran into Tait Cummins of the C.R. Gazette, Leo Kautz of the Davenport Times, and several others. Just outside in the stands I exchanged greetings with Dick Plock of Burlington (partner of Carl Pryor & youngest member of the Ia. board of Education). Pres. Hancher, Craven Shuttleworth, Rollie Williams, Mr. Wienecke, ad infinitum. Immediately at the end of the first half I submitted to a radio interview, which I fear went off rather poorly – perhaps, you heard it. Shortly afterwards while conversing up in the press box someone told me that the crowd was yelling, "We want Kinnick." I was hesitant to believe it, for I couldn't hear them, but when reassured I walked to the door and sure enough they were yelling just that. Wasn't it wonderful! Such a fine, spontaneous gesture! Certainly the people of Iowa have been good to me. I wanted to go down front to the microphone and tell them what a grand crowd they were, but by that time the teams were coming back on the field, and I thought it best just to acknowledge their tribute by stepping outside the press box and waving my cap. Wish that I had heard them sooner. Iowa won their game quite handily, using only straight football. However, I am still doubtful of their leadership and quarterbacking. The game against Nebraska this week will tell the story.

Tom Louden, from Fairfield, who is in V-7 training at Abbott Hall in Chicago, got into town late in the afternoon Sat., so the boys put on a little party for both of us out at Tiffin that night. Sunday morning I went to church in Iowa City, greeting Mrs. Wienecke, Mrs. Bradley, et al, then after dinner I took the trolley to C. Rapids. Clarke met me at the station and drove me back to his bungalow where Mary and the kids were just finishing their noon repast. Mike has grown quite a bit, but Portia even more so – and both of them are cuter than you can imagine. Truly, they have a fine little family. I always enjoy visiting them. Sunday night we left the kids with some lady and went to see "Pride of the Yankees." Found it quite good, and now have a keener appreciation of George's remark, "Don't be like Mrs. Gehrig, Mom." Mon. morning I visited a couple of hours with Tait at the Gazette office and then walked over to the Bupane Gas Co. hoping to see Otto. He was out, however, and wasn't expected back that afternoon, so I pulled out for Iowa City on that 2 o clock trolley.

Before going over to the Iowa practice field I stopped in the Navy Pre-Flight School's dressing room at the north end of the stadium to say hello to Mertes, Frye, Couppee, and Brady. After watching them work out a little while and considering their score against Kansas I don't see how they can miss. Anderson put his lads through a little scrimmage late in the afternoon just for my benefit. He is going to use the T formation almost exclusively this fall and thinks he really has some pretty fancy stuff all cooked up. Unhappily, it was about the poorest exhibition I've ever seen. Nobody could do anything right, Anderson was fit to be tied. However, Mon. night scrimmages are never any good, and I *did* see enough to convince me he has quite an offense if he gets some good quarterbacking and the boys all pull together. After supper at the training table and saying goodbye to all the coaches and players I went to see "Talk of the Town." I must have been expecting too much for I thought it very mediocre.

About ten o clock the next morning I dropped into the bank for a long chat with Frank Williams and Mr. Farrell. Just before noon I strolled over to the law school and briefly greeted those professors whom I could find – Mr. Sayre, Mr. Updegraff, Dean Ladd and Mr. Perkins. The latter man is really a favorite of mine. He volunteered during the last war even though he had a wife and two small children, he has since become one of the outstanding authorities in the field of criminal law, he is an excellent teacher, thoroughly human, an outdoor enthusiast, in short, a grand good guy. I thought him especially glad to see me which made me very happy. After lunch I picked up my laundry, packed, and persuaded one of the boys to haul my bags down to the station and then take me up town. While strolling around I ran into Harry Bremer with whom I share a pretty good friendship. We stopped in at Racines #1 across from the Jefferson for a glass of orange juice and a lot of conversation. Shortly before 3:30 he drove me down to the R.R. station so I could catch my train. I left Iowa City secretly happy over the manner in which she had welcomed me back. However, there were some things I saw or heard which saddened me. Dean Jones, my old filling station friend, heads the salvage drive for that area and he says he is getting very little cooperation because the farmers and others are afraid the Jewish junk dealers will make some money. I sensed that the old jealousies and rivalries between the two banks, and between the different business houses were running deeper than ever. I saw more big cars around the fraternities & sororities than ever before. Frank Williams & Flave Hamborg blithely told me of *driving* clear up into Canada for a fishing trip this summer, and how they were going to *drive up* to Mitchell, So. Dak. for some pheasant hunting this weekend. The college is full of young men more anxious to finish their education than to serve in the armed forces. Every incident I have mentioned is quite understandable and in no way maliciously unpatriotic, but it doesn't indicate a spirit dedicated to winning the war. I hated to see & feel all this in my favorite town among my closest friends. Had I actually been on the firing line instead of having it comparatively easy in a training center I would have been contemptuous of what I saw. No wonder Clare Boothe Luce proclaims that we "talk a tough war but fight a soft one."

My train got into the La Salle St. station at 8:30. I took a cab to the Morrison Hotel and was fortunate enough to get a fine room with bath on the 12th floor for $2/75, mainly because Jim Harris had wired the chief clerk for me. This fellow always took care of the team when we stopped there while I was in school, and he never fails to call me by name whenever I put up there. The lobby was crowded, everybody trying to get a room, so I felt highly thankful for the service. I took a stroll before going to bed. Am always interested in watching the people. Had an ice cream sundae with nuts at a Walgreen Drug store, then turned in.

In the morning, following a protracted sleep, I called Aunt Mary, dashed off a note to you folks, and took a cab to the station an hour beforehand. Like a true farmer I took no chances on missing my train.

I left Chicago at 1:45 PM Wed & got into Norfolk at 5 PM on Thurs, an half hour late. The trip was long and slow but not entirely uneventful. I found myself in a pullman full of men in the coffee business headed for a convention in Covington, Va. My judgment would be that most of those laddies were pretty much amateurs at drinking and gambling but of course that didn't deter their enthusiasm, nor confidence, one minute. After a couple of hours of such company I decided to try the club car. There I had the misfortune to sit down beside an army major who was already pretty tight and still ordering. He started off by calling me lieutenant, and ended by proclaiming he had been with Stillwell in Burma. In between he had spouted enough tall tales full of inconsistencies & contradictions to convince me that he was mostly wind – a veritable Major Hoople. When he got started on Burma I returned to the coffee convention. After awhile I struck up a conversation with the only sober man in the pullman who turned out to be the Chicago representative of a Costa Rican coffee firm. He had been in charge of the Costa Rican exhibit at the Worlds Fair in 1933 and hadn't been back since. We had a thoroughly enjoyable talk the gist of which I would set down were not my pen hand tiring so rapidly. Suffice it to say that Costa Rica has been a Republic for a couple of hundred years remarkably free from dictatorship, that she is very much pro-American, and that it is the dream of all her young men to come to the U.S. sometime. In response to my inquiry about size he said he thought C.R. was about as large as Lake Michigan, an estimate which I scouted. What are the facts?

I don't know how long it had been since I had slept in an upper, but that was the only pullman berth I could get on that train. Dressing and undressing in such quarters is a feat for a contortionist. However, I managed it and slept quite well despite the revelry of the coffee merchants when they finally retired.

The next morning I went to breakfast with a lt. senior grade in the Naval Reserve. He was from Los Angeles and also headed for Norfolk. He was almost as bad as the major. If he had been every place he said he had, known everyone he said he knew, and did everything in the last war he said he did, he would have had to have been 75 instead of 45. I finally managed to get away and settle down with a Time magazine. We passed through Richmond, Williamsburg, and at last drew into Newport News. There we had to take a ferry over to Norfolk – a one hour ride on a boat about like the "Dawn." On the way over I made the error of asking a small, bespectacled individual about the location of the Naval Air Station. He declined to inform me in that particular, saying that he had no way of knowing whether I was a spy or not – which was ok. However, he was tight and anxious to talk so he fanned the breeze for 45 minutes without a letup, saying he was with the U.S.O. but only as a patriotic duty, that he had spent most of his life on Wall St, had a town house & a country house out on Long Island, etc. etc., I was glad when the boat docked.

After getting a bite to eat the aforementioned Navy lt., another guy, & myself took a cab out to the base, arriving about 8 oclock. The air station is right next to the operating base, comprising an area terrifically large in extent. I finally located the officer of the day & was sent down to barracks SP64. I asked without success if Bob & I could room together, but next best, I find myself with Haugebak again.

This morning I started checking in, but since they aren't too "eager" about this I am going to procrastinate in the hope that Bob will get here in time to check in with me. The rumor is that we are all going to be transferred to Jacksonville in a couple of weeks to finish our training. All the planes here – 1st line aircraft – are to be ferried down. The why & wherefore I don't know, but that is the way the story goes. Also, the uncorroborated rumor is that fighter 16 is going on the New Lexington (formerly Cabot) to be launched tomorrow, but not ready for duty for two or three months. I urgently suggest you keep this to yourself.

At lunch today I bumped into Russ Luerssen. He is in port for a few days, but Betty has a lecture in K.C. & can't make it. He came up to the room for awhile, and we had quite an interesting chat. This brings you up to date, I believe – and has almost exhausted me in the process. Just a couple of more lines then I must close.

Father, in this same letter or under separate cover I shall send my gov't insurance policy which I would like for you to file for me. Incidentally, I note that it *is* term insurance and will have to be converted at a later date. Also, if it won't cost too much send me some coat hangers (12 or 15.) There are absolutely none around the base, & the boys say they cost 29¢ a piece in town. If it costs over a buck don't send them.

Mother, I have purchased for you a pair of large gold wings & another set of small ones. Neither is very fancy looking, but about the best available. Will send them along whenever I can manage to get them wrapped.

All goes well with me.

Much love,
Nile

P:S: This is my best address:

Ensign _____

ACTS. Fighter 16

U. S. Naval Air Station

Norfolk, Va.

What address did you use in sending my winter flight equipment, Gus. Would appreciate a quick reply & quick action on the hangers.

Glenn Devine: In 1942 assistant athletic director at Iowa; in the early 1920s a football teammate of his more famous brother, Aubrey Devine.

Iowa Pre-Flight School's game: The Pre-Flight School at Iowa, established early in the war, stressed athletics and physical conditioning to an extraordinary degree. In a letter of 5 January 1943 Kinnick would warn Stuart against "those physical culture maniacs" (letter donated to the collection by William C. Stuart). The Iowa Pre-Flight and other training-station teams were strong during the war, for they had access to recent college players of experience and quality.

I left it lying on Bill Stuart's desk: The note was sent on to Omaha. It is in the collection, and the Kearns column is in scrapbook 2.

the temporary residence of the Fiddle-de-Fees: In 1942 the Phi Psis rented their chapter house on Riverside Drive to the Army Air Corps premeteorological program and moved to a large eastside house at 505 Iowa Avenue until 1944.

Karl Leib and Dr. Alcock: Karl Leib of the College of Commerce was chairman of the Board in Control of Athletics. Nathaniel G. Alcock was the head of urology at the University of Iowa Hospital.

a couple of the well known joints: The Mayflower was a large Victorian mansion on the east bank of the Iowa River at 1110 North Dubuque Street, site of the present Mayflower Apartments. The Mayflower had become a roadhouse and a facility that rented rooms for large and small parties. The "joint" in Tiffin, five miles west of Iowa City, was Ken and Fern's, a smaller place with a jukebox and a dance floor. It sold beer and soft drinks. A supper club, much expanded, is now in that location.

Judge McKinley: Michael L. McKinley (Iowa '95) of Chicago, a judge in the Superior Court of Illinois and an Iowa football loyalist for decades. A song was written in his honor and played by the university band at the homecoming game in 1940.

Pres. Hancher . . .: In 1940 Virgil M. Hancher succeeded Eugene A. Gilmore as university president. Craven Shuttleworth, a Cedar Rapids attorney, was an Iowa football player in the 1920s. Rollie Williams was the head basketball coach (see letter 2). Mr. Wienecke was Charles Wienecke, husband of Louise Wienecke. She was a Christian Science journalist practitioner in Iowa City. Mrs. Bradley was another Iowa City Christian Scientist whom Kinnick knew from his church attendance.

the crowd was yelling, "We want Kinnick": The game Kinnick attended was a nonconference game with Washington University of St. Louis, won by Iowa, 27–7. There were 8,000 present. The following week Iowa would defeat Nebraska, 27–0.

Abbott Hall: At Northwestern University, given over to the V-7 program early in the war.

Clarke . . . Mary: Cousin Clarke Van Meter and his wife. He was the manager of the Bupane Gas Company in Cedar Rapids.

"Don't be like Mrs. Gehrig, Mom": In *Pride of the Yankees* Lou Gehrig's mother is characterized as at first strongly opposed to his playing professional baseball. She wants him to become an engineer like his uncle, though eventually she becomes a knowledgeable fan. Frances Kinnick may have objected to George's many athletic involvements as detrimental to his schoolwork.

hoping to see Otto: Otto Kohl, one of Kinnick's football coaches in Adel, moved to Cedar Rapids in the early 1930s and became the owner of the Bupane Gas Company.

Mertes, Frye, Couppee, and Brady: Bus Mertes, George Frye, Al Couppee, and Charles Brady – all former Iowa football players, then on the Pre-Flight team.

Frank Williams and Mr. Farrell: Williams was the president of the First Capitol National Bank (see letter 6). Farrell was the vice-president.

Mr. Sayre . . .: Paul Sayre, C. M. Updegraff, Mason Ladd, and Rollin M. Perkins. Perkins was also a Phi Psi and a member of the Board in Control of Athletics.

Harry Bremer: Former owner of Bremer's, a men's clothing store in downtown Iowa City. He sold his interest in 1941 and spent much of his time in travel, including a southern swing in early 1942 (see the diary). Several years earlier he had returned from a trip to Africa with two lions that he kept in a pen down by Ralston Creek, behind his house on Woodlawn Circle. Because of neighbors' complaints, he donated the lions to the city park zoo. When they died they were stuffed and put on display in Macbride Hall, where they remain.

Racines #1: On the northwest corner of Washington and Dubuque streets, one of three Racine's locations in Iowa City. All were tobacco shops that sold soft drinks. Besides being also a short-order restaurant, Racine's #1 posted the latest baseball scores, and betting on games could be found there. In the basement there was high-stakes poker day and night, and if the floating crap game was not going on at Racine's, one could get its hotel room number there.

Dean Jones: Dean Jones operated the Standard Oil station at the corner of Dubuque and Market streets.

Flave Hamborg: The University of Iowa treasurer.

Clare Boothe Luce: Kinnick adapts a passage from an article on Luce in *Time*, 21 September 1942, p. 19. She was attacking the Roosevelt Administration, not the American public, in her keynote address before the Connecticut Republican Convention.

Major Hoople: A humorous braggart and liar in Eugene Ahern's comic feature *Our Boarding House*. It had been nationally syndicated in newspapers for many years.

the "Dawn": A Seattle area ferryboat. It made landings at Fred Clarke's dock on Mercer Island in Lake Washington.

the New Lexington (formerly Cabot): The new carrier had been authorized on 19 July 1940 under the name *Cabot*. After the sinking of the USS *Lexington* at the Battle of the Coral Sea in May 1942, the ship under construction was given the commemorative name. It was launched on 26 September 1942 and commissioned on 17 February 1943.

Russ Luerssen: Husband of Kinnick's cousin Betty Bice Luerssen, daughter of Don and Ruth (Kinnick) Bice of Atlantic (see letter 2). A home economist based in Chicago, Betty gave lectures and conducted cooking schools in surrounding states.

29 ✳ To the Family, 17 December 1942

Kinnick wrote this letter in Greensboro, North Carolina, during a return trip to Norfolk. He was staying at the King Cotton Hotel and used its letterhead stationery. Shortly after reporting at Norfolk in September, he had been sent to Jacksonville, where he received training in the F4F, the Grumman Wildcat. That completed, he was given until midnight on 18 December to report again at Norfolk. In a letter from Greensboro on the sixteenth, he explained to his parents that he wanted to report no sooner than he had to, so he had accepted a ride from an unnamed pilot on his way to Chicago who was stopping over in Greensboro to visit his girlfriend. The girlfriend arranged a date for Kinnick on the sixteenth with a woman later identified as Anne Kanoy (diary, 9 May 1943). In his 5 January 1943 letter to Stuart, Kinnick would write that the girlfriend "fixed me up with the slickest little number you ever ran an eye over or put an arm around. It was so good, I stayed around an extra day," evidently into the eighteenth. In a letter of 20 December, without mentioning a second date, Kinnick writes the family that he checked in at Norfolk with only five minutes to spare.

Thursday – Dec. 17, 1942

Dear Folks,

When I wrote you yesterday morning fog and rain hung in around my window blotting out all light and warmth. Around eleven A.M. it got colder and began to snow. A brisk wind was blowing out of the North, swirling the damp, white flakes around the building corners and up and down the street. Most of the shoppers cringed against the wet and cold, and huddled up against the store fronts for protection against the wind. However, for me it was invigorating and sharply reminiscent of the winter weather I used to know. I belted my great blue coat around me and strode face up against the snow, breathing deeply, strongly. It was wonderful to feel my ears tingle and my nose grow damp and moist. Really, the weather was mild, I suppose, but it smacked faintly of the December element in the midwest, and I loved it.

Right after lunch I browsed around looking for a Xmas gift for Grandma. Finally decided on a piece of English silver, a sugar dredger – or sugar shaker, as I would call it. It is nothing very fine, but I think she'll be able to find use for it on her breakfast table – and it does have an interesting history. It is supposed to be part of a shipment received since the war composed of silver contributed or sold by British families to further the war effort. I want you to urge her, mother, to accept it without any great expostulation or any hurried attempt to get something for me.

I got something for you in Jacksonville a couple of weeks ago and mailed it just today. You will find that it is much like some other jewelry I have given you, but better looking, in my view. In any event you may get some enjoyment in choosing among them for a particular occasion. Can you make any suggestion for George or shall I just send him some lettuce?

Last night the girl friend of the boy who drove me up here got me a date, and we all went out to the Embassy club for dining and dancing. It was an highly satisfactory evening – the best blind date I ever had, and the Embassy was certainly a desirable setting. Get the picture – a large, log-built, rich man's hunting lodge, now a road house, located about ten miles out from town, nestled in among the hills and snow covered pine trees; a huge fireplace of burning logs, trophies on the wall, juicy steak with french fries, soft music, a pretty girl – well I'm running out of paper.

Much love,
Nile

30　✳︎　To the Family, 25 December 1942

Kinnick grew up with Joe Kubasek, one of three sons of a poor widow in Adel. A family album (box 3) contains a glossy print of the Adel Junior High School basketball team of 1930–31, where Nile and Ben Kinnick appear along with Joe Kubasek and other early friends Kinnick mentions in his correspondence. (The *Des Moines Tribune* for 8 April 1931 printed the same photograph and identified all the persons; clipping courtesy of Jim Mitchell, son of Golden Mitchell; see annotation to letter 14. The *Tribune* spelling "Kubasek" is preferred over Kinnick's "Kubacek.") The Schwartz and Schwartz pond references are now obscure.

The *Charger* was a ship designated to train pilots and ships' crews in carrier procedures (see *Dictionary of American Naval Fighting Ships* [Washington, D.C., 1963], 2:71). The *Charger*'s return to port led to everyone's being secured because pilots went through their procedures only when the ship was out in Chesapeake Bay, its area of operation throughout the war.

Lee was cousin Ted Clarke's wife (see letter 37, postscript). Kinnick often joked about Uncle Fred Clarke's letters. In June 1939, on his mother's advice, he had apologized to his grandmother for a recent remark about them (Kinnick to Arletta G. Clarke, 13 June 1939).

Dear Folks,

This is Christmas day, and I must have a talk with you even though we are half a continent apart. Sitting here all alone in my room my thought constantly turns to the holiday seasons we used to enjoy in Adel, particularly before Ben and I started high school. What happy, happy memories I have of those days. Remember how we used to go coasting morning and afternoon, and, sometimes, even after supper? And Schwartz's pond, the first body of water to freeze solid enough for skating each winter – do you suppose there is anyone in Adel who hasn't skated on that pond at sometime or another? Now that I think back on it the Schwartz family was awfully good to all us kids, asking us in to get warm, feeding us popcorn and fudge, showing every concern for our comfort and happiness. Well do I recall the first sled you folks gave me for Xmas; it was to replace the little "firefly" which I had outgrown. All eager for my pleasure you suggested that I look out the south window and see what old Santa had brought. I hastily climbed up onto the davenport anxious to verify my hope. I remember the scene as if it were yesterday. Mother was on one side of me and father on the other, both smiling and all aglow with the spirit of giving. But alas little Junior didn't appreciate the sled at all. He wanted to, and tried, but hell, it was only an old Luther and not a Flexible Flyer. How could a fellow keep up without a Flex? And then I think there were tears – probably all the way around. Do you recall all this? I daresay you do. Ultimately Ben & I both got nice big Flexible Flyers and the Luther was given to Joe Kubasek. Those were the days when stockings were hung from the mantle, when wreaths of holly were placed in the windows and on the door; a huge Xmas tree stood in the corner all lighted and surrounded by gifts. No happy novel, no idyllic little story could have improved the picture. How little I appreciated the peace and beauty of those times. If I were home this very day I could not possibly hope to recapture those experiences. But I know one thing I would do for certain. I would read out loud that delightful little poem, The Night Before Xmas, and also Dickens Christmas Carol. Then I'd sit back and enjoy the traditional Xmas music, either over the radio or from a record – Silent Night, Little Town of Bethlehem, Round yon Virgin, and the gay favorite, Jingle Bells. Have you done all these things today? If you haven't, I'm disappointed. That kind of Xmas seems rather important to me now.

The Charger came into port Tuesday night, and we were all secured until Saturday morning. Nearly everyone lit out for New York or Washington, but I elected to stick around and read. Am just finishing a book entitled The Destiny of Western Man by W. T. Stace which I want purchased for me out of my funds. It provides some secular vocabulary and phraseology in support of the relationship between democracy and Christianity which I have been looking for. As I have said rather frequently during the past year I am enjoying reading more than ever before in my life.

Your long letter with the enclosed clippings reached me here ok, mother, also Georges short effort. However, I haven't as yet gotten the letter which was to be the follow-up on the telegram. Did I acknowledge the candy you sent me in Jacksonville? It was very good. A letter from grandma brought $5 for a Xmas gift. One from Fred discloses that Ted expects a baby in March. The wording is Fred's; it would seem that Lee expects the baby – don't you agree?

Am enclosing grandma's check which I would like to have father endorse and cash for me.

I'll probably be here until the 1st of the year the way things look right now. Anyway address my mail to this station, and it will be forwarded if I have gone.

Things go well. Merry Xmas and Happy New Year to you all.

Much love,

Nile

31 ✳ To the Family, 3 January 1943

In this letter Kinnick has arrived at Quonset Point, Rhode Island, not far from the Bethlehem yards at Quincy, Massachusetts, where the *Lexington* had been built and was then located. Most of his stay at Quonset consisted of gunnery practice and additional carrier training, some of it possibly make-work to occupy the time while the *Lexington* readied for sailing. In late April and early May, he flew three plane-ferry missions between Quonset and Norfolk (see the diary), and these took up his time to a little more than a week before he went to sea. He had several weekend leaves during this period, and four of the remaining letters discuss these interludes. Annotations follow the letter in order of relevance to the text.

Dear Folks,

This is the first Sunday in 1943. How different the prospect from a year ago at this time! If things were to break just right, and there is every reason to hope that they will, the Allies may have Hitler pretty much on the run by spring. The magnificent armies of Stalin are knocking hell out of the Hun on the eastern front, and if we can win a decisive battle in Tunisia, particularly in the air, the end should be in sight. Any invasion of the continent will be awfully rough, but once we get a foothold and start to move in, Nazi resistance should crumble rather quickly. The whole dastardly regime is founded on fraud and monstrous lie. Confronted with impending doom its leaders will turn on each other and hasten the finish. That job done we can direct the full force of our might against Japan. If we strike at her upper body from China, Russia, Alaska, and the sea our task might not be as long as some would have us believe. The surprise and brilliance of the African blow would indicate our strategists won't be content with the long way home in the Pacific.

I checked in here last night just 5 minutes before midnight – again not very much to spare. This morning's daylight discloses a huge base with most of the buildings made of red brick. The BOQ (bachelor officers quarters) is a fine big building with comfortable rooms, spacious lounges and recreational parlors, and an high ceilinged mess hall. Coming in the front door the lobby and attendant desk reminded me of a college union edifice. This mornings breakfast gave promise of very good chow, but I'll keep my fingers crossed for a few days. There is one disturbing possibility, however – supposedly all of squadron 16 is going to be moved into the annex part of the building where the rooms are not nearly so nice.

Getting in and out of the Naval station at Norfolk is a nightmare. The base itself is immense, the buses and streetcars are always crowded, the cabs almost extinct – and there I was with a duffel bag, a fortnighter, and a small navy issue bag. Happily, a couple of us managed to get a station wagon which took us out to the main gate where we finally hailed a taxi. This was at one oclock Thursday afternoon and we were trying to catch an one-thirty train. Although it was 15 or 20 miles into town and the driver had "snailitis" we did manage to pile aboard just as the train was pulling out. We were due into Washington at six-forty, but didn't make it until ten minutes after nine. You can imagine what a delightful trip that was! We were held up an hour and a half in some little place called Petersburg. The next train out of Washington for New York didn't leave until 11 PM, so we had time to get a bite to eat and look around the station. The traffic in and out of there is terrific, but very efficiently handled it seemed to me. I wanted to phone Sid but couldn't remember the name of the family with whom she is staying. You should have seen the mob waiting to catch that eleven oclock train, mostly soldiers. When the gates were opened it was every man for himself in the mad scramble for seats. As I plopped down in a dirty coach seat just ahead of another guy, I recalled the leisurely manner in which I climbed aboard my Pullman in the winter of 1940. It hardly seems possible that three years have passed, does it? At midnight, as the old year yielded to the new, everybody was about half asleep, too tired for hilarity and the usual shouting. A few minutes later there was some excitement, however. I happened to be awake and saw it all happen. A huge, heavily muscled Negro soldier, well under the influence of liquor, stepped inside the door, took a look around, then drew a deep breath and let out the wildest, loudest, most blood curdling Tarzan yell I have *ever* heard. Everybody jumped half out of their seat, women gasped, children cried – and then all gave way to laughter as the large colored boy apologetically explained that it was New Years and nobody should be asleep. I might add that he repeated his little act several times before getting to New York, and each time it was equally effective.

At 3:30 an ensign named Burckhalter and myself dragged from the Penn station to the Penn hotel via the connecting tunnel. Dodging the lingering revelers we signed for the 3rd to last room available and rolled in for some sleep. The next morning Burck went out to see his girl who lives on Long Island, and I perused the paper at breakfast trying to decide what shows or plays to see. Before walking over to the Commodore Hotel where officers can get play tickets at half price, I sat down in the lobby of the Penn to reminisce a bit. The last time I had been there was in June 1940, on my way from the $\phi\psi$ convention in New Jersey to the Worlds Fair. Chuck West met me, and some very pretty girl whose name I [have] wished very much I could remember. I recalled happening on to Hobie Mulock of Des Moines, one of Jim Hoak's good friends. He has since been killed in an auto accident, I believe.

After picking up a ticket for "Life with Father" (evening performance) I decided to see the movie "In Which We Serve." It was excellent and deserving of all the fine things which have been said about it. I guess I'm a sucker for depictions of courage, honor, duty, devotion to home and country – my eyes were wet half the time. Incidentally, it was playing at the same theatre in which Sec Taylor and I saw "Raffles," or something like that, in the winter of 1940. Sec covered the banquet in Philadelphia and Savold's fight in the garden, graciously getting tickets for Anderson and me for the latter. On my way back to the hotel following the movie I had quite an unusual experience. As I stepped off the curb at the corner of 48th st. & 7 Ave, just a few blocks north of Times Square, I heard someone speak my name. Turning around I was confronted by two coast-guardsmen one of whom I recognized as Gordon Alt an old B.H.S. product. The other boy's name was Snyder and said he knew Ben at Iowa State. While we were talking a chap in civilian clothes standing nearby asked if he could get in on all the handshaking. His name turned out to be Miller and a fraternity brother of Ben's at college. Some coincidence wasn't it? New York didn't seem quite so big to me this time, perhaps, because I didn't have to use the subways. I stopped for a moment at 42nd & Broadway and gazed at the Times building from which the score Iowa 7 – Notre Dame 6 was flashed time and again in neon lights on the night of Nov. 11, 1939. It was Chuck West who told me that as we stood on that same corner the night of the Heisman Award.

I took a leisurely dinner in the Cafe Rouge of the Penn Hotel. Too bad George couldn't have been my guest, for I was all alone and Charlie Spivak was giving forth in a most enjoyable manner. According to all reports he is supposed to have some outfit. Is that right, George? Afterwards I laughed continually at Howard Lindsay & Dorothy Stickney in "Life with Father." It was so very good, so very funny throughout. (Pet peeve: – those vacant minded patrons who laugh so loudly, and long, that you miss the immediately succeeding lines; those who maintain a whispered commentary throughout the play.)

On Friday I thought that I would see "Random Harvest" playing at Radio City. On my way up there – 50th st, the Penn Hotel is on 33rd – I paused at Rockefeller Center to watch the skaters on the artificially maintained ice rink. It would be a rather novel experience to cavort there, I suppose, but give me the good old Coon River every time. The line at the ticket office discouraged me from seeing Greer Garson, that

From left: Ken Pettit, Bob Hobbs, "Ice Cube" (otherwise unidentified), Jim George (see letter 9), Art Manush (Iowa '39; co-captain, with George, of the Iowa baseball team), Nola (otherwise unidentified), and J. D. Garrett (otherwise unidentified). This photograph was taken at the Little Club at the U. S. Grant Hotel in San Diego on 11 January 1943. Pettit and Hobbs ran into each other early in the evening, just after Hobbs arrived in San Diego, and around ten that night they came upon their old friends George and Manush together with the others at the Little Club. The group posed for a club photographer, signed their names beneath their pictures, and added witty sentences on the back. Pettit explained the situation to Kinnick, who received the picture and folder at Quonset Point. In a letter to his parents of 21 January he wrote, "Golly, how I would like to have been there too!" Print, Kinnick Collection.

winsome lady of much charm – and lovely legs – so I went to see Noel Coward's "Blithe Spirit" instead. It was very clever and kept me chuckling for two hours. Having previously taken my bags from the Penn station to the Grand Central in a cab, I now hustled to make my six oclock train. Hurrying east on 43rd I passed the Columbia University Club where Anderson and I stayed for the Iowa Alumnae dinner, and a little farther down the Christian Science Church where I attended services the next morning. Bagatelle – Arthur Murray's dance studio is right next door. The trip from New York to Providence, R.I. was uneventful and accomplished in four hours. The train made quick stops in New Haven the home of Yale and in New London the location of Connecticut College for Women. Isn't that where Sarah Guiou (sp) went to school? From Providence I caught a bus out to Quonset Pt 20 miles distant. As per usual the bus service between the air station and town is inadequate. It was terribly crowded and many enlisted men had to wait for another vehicle. And so I have come to my final station before shoving off to sea.

Glad to learn that George is getting along well in basketball. Power to him and keep me posted.

Much love,

Nile

Please send me a quarterly if you have not already done so.

> *I wanted to phone Sid:* Sid was a nickname for Kinnick's cousin Elizabeth Van Meter, who was working in Washington.
> *Chuck West:* A Phi Psi (Iowa '38) who lived in New York and in the 1939–40 period worked for United Airlines. He attended the Heisman Award ceremony in addition to at least one other Iowa City Phi Psi, Ed McCollister (Iowa '39). The "very pretty girl" is unidentified.
> *Hobie Mulock . . . one of Jim Hoak's good friends:* Jim Hoak (Iowa '40) was a Phi Psi from Des Moines. Mulock was a student at Dartmouth; he died in an auto accident in 1941.
> *"In Which We Serve":* Kinnick misrecalls the theater. *Raffles* played at the Roxy when Kinnick saw it in January 1940. *In Which We Serve* was at the Capitol in early January 1943.
> *Coon River:* The Raccoon River, which passes through Adel.
> *Sarah Guiou:* Kinnick's inscription of the surname is ambiguous, but "Guiou" may have been what he wrote, for a "Sarah Guiou" turns up in a clipping from an undated and unnamed newspaper pasted among the late 1939 items in scrapbook 2. The clipping is a humorous account of her impatience while Kinnick, her escort, is surrounded by autograph seekers at a "Christmas tide" spinsters' ball. Kinnick's fame was recent and in its lionizing phase, and he went home for the Christmas holiday in 1939. The best inference is that Sarah Guiou was an Omaha resident.

32　✳　To Don Fish, Bob Stacy, and Kingsley Clarke, 24 February 1943

Kinnick's three correspondents were several years older than he – Fish by about ten years, Stacy and Clarke by five. Don Fish worked for the Farm Bureau and lived near Adel. Bob Stacy had been a deputy auditor for Dallas County before entering the navy. He was stationed in San Diego and in December 1942 spend a furlough in Adel, where a picture of him in uniform appeared in the *Dallas County News* (clipping in scrapbook 2; compare Kinnick's "You looked very 'salty,' matey"). Cousin Kingsley, then in the army and stationed in Florida, was married to Mary Jane Stacy, sister of Bob Stacy (the "M. J." of this letter). Annotations follow the letter.

Wednesday　Feb. 24, 1943

Dear Gents,

Today I received your letters forwarded from Omaha. Much appreciate your including me in your round robin correspondence, but fear that the next swing of the circuit may find me out at sea. Supposedly, we are due to board our carrier the latter part of March. Have been in training for over a year now, and the prospect of action sounds good.

Don, it sure has been a long time since I have seen you; don't know whether it was two or three children ago? The family picture you enclosed is a dandy, and, as you say, "brings me up to date." I am entitling it "A Proclamation of Virility" or "Malthus Defied" and sending it along to King and Bob as a challenge. All joking aside, it is good to see you and yours looking so well and happy and to learn that things are going along for the better. Can't refrain from noting how pretty and charming Mrs. Fish appears – and what lovely legs – tsk, tsk. Don, do you remember the time you and Nig Garoutte took me along in your model T Ford to watch a football game at Guthrie Center? And how R. Mortimer and I used to cycle out to your grandad's farm and play tennis on that old dirt court? You were quite a big shot to me in those days – and still are, now that I have been "brought up to date." We almost parted friendship, however, the night in grandma's yard when you showed me the punishing qualities of the figure four scissors. You daggone near killed me; my innards still hurt when I think of it. Thought I would bust laughing the time we were playing water tag in the Winterset pool, and you became so tired you could hardly wiggle.

And then there were the days of the Farm Bureau picnic when you were County agent – ice cream at Wilburs – and all that sort of thing – including the watermelon stealing episode starring R. Stacy and K. Clarke. Man, what times we used to have.

For your benefit, perhaps a brief recital of my activities the past year would not be out of order. Three days after reporting at Kansas City for elimination training the Japs jumped on Pearl Harbor completely un-awed by the Navy's new recruit with the AA sweater. By the first of February I had learned to solo with some degree of safety, and had just begun to log a little dual time with a beautiful creature out on Pawnee Road, when I was ordered to the pilots pool at New Orleans. For about ten days I endured the most rigorous ground school schedule (no fly-ing) plus a 4 hour watch every third night. At the end of this most dis-agreeable period a big batch of us were unexpectedly hurried on to Pensacola. My training there – and it was pretty daggone inten-sive – lasted until the latter part of June. Flew several different types of training planes – N3N, Stearman, Vultee, SNJ, and one service type, an OS2U on wheels. In accordance with my choice, which sel-dom happens in the Navy, I was sent to Miami for fighter training around the first of July. Operated in SNJs most of the time, known in the army as the Harvard, and finished up with 20 hours in the F2A or Brewster Buffalo. Received my wings and commission on Sep't 3rd, and raced home on 15 days leave. Found most of my girl friends mar-ried, pledged, or disaffected, and the majority of my male buddies away in the service. Spent a quiet week with the folks in Omaha, and di-vided the remaining days between Adel, Iowa City, and Cedar Rapids. Reported at Norfolk on Sep't 24th under the impression that I would be at sea in 5 weeks. And now here it is 5 months later, and I am still on the beach. From October to January I was in operational training at Jacksonville flying the good old Grumman Wildcat. It was by far the best training yet. Most of the instructors were veterans of Midway or AVG pilots. Enroute to Quonset Pt to join my permanent squadron I was detained in Norfolk a few days for carrier landing & takeoff qualifi-cation. Since coming here we have concentrated mostly on gunnery. Inasmuch as the war is being fought with guns I find myself in hearty accord with the squadron training policy. Have been down to New York a few times and once up to Boston on liberty. Have seen some good plays and raced around a lot on a minor scale. A few years ago, the spring of 1940 to be exact, I sat beside brother Edward Everett

Horton at a banquet tendered in his honor by the Phi Psi group in Cedar Rapids; he was playing a two night stand in "Springtime for Henry." We became pretty well acquainted, and he asked me to bring a date and watch the performance from the wings, which I did. Well, when in Boston I chanced to notice the same billing at the Colonial Theatre. Just for the devil of it I decided to drop backstage after the play and say hello. Happily, he remembered me and even seemed pleased. At any rate it wasn't two minutes before he had asked me to join a little party he was giving at the Copley-Plaza. It was a novel and enjoyable evening for me. Met some top drama critics (so what!), Paul Draper, the dancer, a lovely, leggy la femme from the cast, and dined on lobster Newburg for the first time. Hardly know how I'll be able to stand Adel or Dallas Center again!! Ah me.

Kingsley, since you share my admiration for Winston Churchill you'll be interested in the new book I recently bought. "The Unrelenting Struggle" is a compilation of his speeches from Nov. 12, 1940 to Dec. 31, 1941, and is a powerful sequel to "Blood, Sweat & Tears." Whenever my enthusiasm for the war flags I just sit down and read a few pages and in a few minutes I'm all keyed and raring to go. Wish I had the time to set down for you a few of the paragraphs which especially appeal to me. By the way, be sure and see the movie "Young Mr. Pitt" if you have an opportunity. You will recall that he was the son of the Earl of Chatham, who championed the cause of the American colonies and all personal liberty, proclaiming that a man was secure in his home no matter how humble and "that all the forces of the Crown could not enter in." Pitt the Younger became prime minister of England at 24! Think of that! At the close of the Napoleonic Wars he said, "England has saved herself by her exertions, and will, I hope, save Europe by her example." Old Winnie is of the same breed and will rank in history with them, trumpeting his call of battle to all free men, and declaring to his people that "we shall not fail mankind."

The war goes on and the Allied cause is improving. Believe Germany will try one last, big offensive somewhere, then dig and try to hold what she has; perhaps, sue for peace! We mustn't even consider letting up for a moment under any circumstances. They will be a tough nut to crack, but we can do it. My opinion would be that 1944 will see the end of the European side of it. Realistically, and yet free from all hatred, I think it would be a good idea to let the Russians walk in on the German homeland for awhile. Imagine you could get a favorable vote on that from Joe's boys. How long it will take to whip the Japs depends on how much aid we send China in the meantime, which, of course, is contingent on retaking Burma. With all due respect to Halsey, I'm a little skeptical of his optimism. Don't want to be, but I recall how the Navy men were sure all along before the war that they could step on Japan in 6 weeks at the most. Perhaps, 1946 will see the end of the whole business and the termination of my four year hitch. Naval aviation is *good* money, interesting, fun, and a good life if you like it, but not for this chicken. I am coming back to the midwest and fast.

How to implement our noble & pious generalities, domestically and internationally, after the war is going to be really tough. In broad outline I am for America & Britain maintaining a sea and air force that will dominate both oceans. The hope of world order lies in the cooperation of these two countries with China and Russia both of whom will maintain large land armies, I presume. It seems to me that a decent agreement is possible among these four powers. But whatever happens, if the U. S. ever permits any country to exceed her air & sea strength she is a damn fool. Frankly, I don't believe I am in favor of all this disarmament stuff, anymore than I am in favor of cancelling my insurance when I quit flying. Rickenbacker declares that the armistice will send home the most intense individualists the country has ever seen; that they aren't going to stand for all this "politicking" and bureaucracy. On the other hand Henry AGARD Wallace says the men will demand that the gov't guarantee jobs & security; that if there can be total employment during war why can't there be in peace. From what I have observed in the service I fear Henry is closer to being right. There are too many Americans who don't yet appreciate the real value of liberty & freedom of enterprise. If the gov't continues to "take over" more & more who is going to be the arbiter in any complaints and disputes which arise? The tyranny and abuses of business and labor will then be present in the government itself and doubly hard to correct. In the interest of justice and public welfare I agree that a gov't should stand by as a benevolent sheriff, alert and on the job, but I am suspicious of any extension of that power. Whenever this administration, or some other, becomes more impartial as between labor and capital this union mess will begin to clear up. The union movement has been attended with the same growing pains and abuses as the early history of the corporations. When Congress passes a law demanding judicial settlement of disputes between labor and its bosses as well as between labor and capital, we shall have started on the right road. As long as an administration is definitely prejudiced in favor of labor regardless of the circumstances of the case, business has little opportunity to prove that it could solve the unemployment problem. In my mind any extension of gov't control in this country is particularly bad, for the simple reason that we, as a people, do not yet take pride in government positions; they are almost positions of contempt in our eyes. That psychology doesn't augur well for the efficiency and integrity of our gov't service. The Republican party makes me so damn mad I almost give up. If they would just get together they could oust the New Deal next time, do the country an immeasurable service, and set in motion a positive, productive, economy, (rather than negative) once again. As things stand now Franklin will again turn the trick. Willkie has been a good minority voice, has a long run, international viewpoint, but he is impolitic, foolishly so, in his statements, and I'm afraid he lacks something in the popular mind. Truly the next few years will be critical.

Well, I have sounded off at too great a length I fear, and with an assumed profundity all out of proportion to my experience and wisdom. Beg your tolerance, gentlemen. Will be briefer and restrict the scope of my remarks next time.

Bob, I didn't intend that this should sound as if it were directed mostly to Don & King, but your letter didn't give me much to work on. Glad to learn that things are going along ok. Someone sent me your picture clipped from the Dallas County News. You looked very "salty," matey.

Well good luck and best wishes all the way round. See you again one day.

Yours,

Nile

1166-N.A.S.

Quonset Pt. – R.I.

King:

Inasmuch as so much of this is directed to Don maybe it would be best to forward it to him next & let him send it on to Bob. Use your own judgment. Rec'd your letter some time ago, and will let this serve as a response. Give my best to M. J. Did you know that Bob H. is now in Hawaii, Ben at Corpus Christi? Along with all the rest of the boys back from the Pacific Sum was in an enviable position while on leave.

Would like to have talked with him. We have a pilot in our squadron who was at Midway & later 3 weeks on Guadalcanal. What stories he has to tell! If I get back I'll feed that Adel Rotary the wildest tales they ever heard – John Snyder included.

Nig Garoutte: Loren Garoutte, an Adel man about ten years older than Kinnick.

R. Mortimer: Randall Mortimer was on Kinnick's junior high school football and basketball teams (see headnote to letter 30).

ice cream at Wilburs: Wilbur Van Meter, Kinnick's uncle, father of Clarke and Elizabeth Van Meter. He farmed near Adel.

a beautiful creature out on Pawnee Road: Merle McKay, whose family lived on Pawnee Road, about four miles south of Fairfax Airport in Kansas City, Kansas.

N3N . . . an OS2U on wheels: These trainers were the N3N, made by the Navy Aircraft Company; the Stearman N2S, an open-cockpit biplane known among pilots as the Yellow Peril; the SNV, or Vultee Vibrator; the SNJ, an advanced trainer with retractable landing gear made by North American; and the OS2U, an observation plane made by Vought that could be rigged with floats or wheels. The OS2U also operated off battleships (see the diary for 19 February 1942).

AVG pilots: The American Volunteer Group – better known to the public as the Flying Tigers – were pilots who volunteered to serve under Claire Chennault in China before the United States went to war with Japan.

Edward Everett Horton: An undated clipping from the *Cedar Rapids Gazette* (scrapbook 2) shows Horton, Kinnick, and three other Phi Psis posed in conversation at the Cedar Rapids Country Club in the spring of 1940.

"Young Mr. Pitt": A 1942 picture starring Robert Donat that Kinnick praised the day before in a letter to his parents. There too he exclaimed at Pitt's becoming prime minister at twenty-four, Kinnick's own age.

a man was secure . . . could not enter in: The inclusive words cover an adaptation and approximate quotation of the elder Pitt, the earl of Chatham, in Bartlett, *Familiar Quotations*, p. 230 (see headnote to letter 16).

"England has saved . . . by her example": Nearly verbatim quotation from the younger Pitt's speech at the Guildhall in 1805. Kinnick's immediate source is unknown.

"we shall not fail mankind": In *The Unrelenting Struggle* (Boston,

1942), which Kinnick says in this letter he has just bought, the title of a 1941 speech in Glasgow is "We Will Not Fail Mankind" (p.22).

Rickenbacker: Captain Eddie Rickenbacker, an American flying ace of World War I, from 1935 president of Eastern Air Lines, during World War II a traveling assistant to the secretary of war.

Henry AGARD *Wallace:* The point of Kinnick's emphasis on the middle name is unclear. Possibly he was mimicking an oratorical stress he had heard or distinguishing Henry A. Wallace from his father, Henry Cantwell Wallace (1866–1924), who was secretary of agriculture in the Harding and Coolidge administrations. Henry A. Wallace became vice-president in Roosevelt's third term.

Ben at Corpus Christi: Ben Kinnick had begun Navy Air Corps training in July 1942 at St. Mary's College in California.

Sum was in an enviable position: Sumner Macomber (see headnote to letter 25).

John Snyder: Nephew of Scott Snyder, editor-manager of the *Dallas County News* in Adel.

33 ✳ To the Family, 13 March 1943

This letter reports on Kinnick's second trip to Boston. The first trip included the Edward Everett Horton party described in letter 32. He would go there again on 26 March with Frank Rogers, a pilot in his squadron and one of his two roommates on the *Lexington*. In a 27 March letter to his parents, speaking of that third and last visit to Boston, Kinnick recognizes that "in the absence of my very closest friends I believe I would rather spend my leisure time alone. It sounds a little selfish and . . . peculiar, but that is the way of it." The trip reported in the present letter was one of those solitary enjoyments. Annotations follow the letter.

Saturday night   March 13, 1943

Dear Folks,

Yesterday I went to Boston-town again. A dense, dripping fog hung in all morning giving little prospect for flight operations the rest of the day, so those of us due for liberty were secured early in the afternoon. I got into Boston around five oclock and registered at the Statler. Before eating I decided to take in a movie. The bill at the RKO theatre proved to be highly entertaining. Jack Benny in "The Meanest Man in the

World" was funny enough, but a short featuring Leon Errol left me weak. Gus, would have choked with repressed mirth and rolled into the aisle. On the stage Bob Allen and his band shared the spotlight with Beatrice Kay from the Gay Nineties radio program. They played an arrangement of "Jingle Bells" that was marvelous. It had to be to get such a fine reception out of season. Evidently Allen had had so much success with it during the holidays he was loathe to shelve it. Miss Kay brought down the house with her lusty, gusty rendition of favorite songs, old and new. Her voice was coarse, unpleasant, and she sang in a rude, boisterous manner, but she brought laughter, gaiety, relaxation to all of us.

Shortly after eight I sat down to dinner in the Terrace Dining Room of the Hotel Statler. Starting with clam chowder, filling on Lobster Newburg and green peas, finishing with apple pie and cheese, I dined leisurely and comfortably. Someday I want to take mother to dinner at such a place. We will chat, dance a waltz or two, linger over our desserts, and then go to the theatre or the opera. Buying a Time, Life and Sentinel I retired to my room fairly early, read until sleepy, then dropped off in peaceful slumber.

This morning I wakened rather late, stayed in bed reading until 11 AM, finally hitting the street about noon. At a nearby bookstore I bought the gov't issued document "Peace & War," revealing intimate U.S.-Japanese relations from 1931–41. Also I bought a text on Gregg Shorthand, thinking this time I might persevere until I mastered it.

Dinty Moore's, by self-admission a "famous Boston eating place," had been recommended to me, so I took lunch there. It is located at the end of a dirty little alley off Washington St, but for all its unfavorable exterior appearance it is a delightful little dining establishment. The atmosphere is quiet, unhurried, the prices reasonable, the food excellent. Much to my surprise, and pleasure, I noted murals reproduced from three of Grant Wood's paintings. If my memory serves rightly, they were, to wit, "Springtime in Town," "President's Birthplace," and "Stone City." After my filet mignon (emphasis on mignon) and deep dish apple pie had been consumed I proceeded leisurely up to the Wilbur Theatre.

"Kiss and Tell" was uproariously good entertainment. Jesse Royce Landis and Robert Keith had the leads, neither of whom had I heard, which, of course, is a confession of ignorance and not a reflection on their popularity. It was extremely funny throughout, and in some places was a riot. Toward the end the audience almost expired en masse. I love to laugh. There is nothing which appeals to me more, and this filled the bill in 4.0 fashion.

I returned to Providence early, because I have the duty tomorrow and a security watch that night. The weather is miserable out right now. A wet snow is underfoot and a chilly rain falls intermittently. I'm glad to be inside with my pen and books.

Enclosed are a couple of clippings, one from Time and one from the Providence paper, which touch on scenes dear to me for reasons hard to set down in words, but which I know you folks can readily appreciate. However, a second reading of the article on the Iowa farmer discloses a minor error of description, I believe. The writer speaks of the icy wind sweeping out of Nebraska and a few lines later of the "riderless horse" swinging to the east. But perhaps I misinterpret that type of weather vane. Anyway Time paints a fine word picture of early morning farm life. By the way is that Van Devender one of the Dallas County men we know? I am also sending a bit of poetical expression written by our colored mess boy at the squadron. The form and structure may be faulty, the spelling poor, but the theme and sentiment are good, very good. He trys his hand at poetry quite frequently, but this is far the best. He called me aside and asked me to read and comment on it. My criticism was favorable, yet he didn't seem to want it back so I kept it. Now I am wondering if it is really original with him. I believe it could be, but I am not too sure.

Keep me posted on how B.H.S. makes out at Lincoln. Am pulling for them all the way. George I'm proud of the way you are leading your team, the unselfish way in which you speak of the first team all-city recognition given to Mulvaney & Rose. Good boy! Shall answer your last letter as soon as I can. Ditto, grandma's.

Much love,

Nile

P:S: Without foreboding but as a matter of common sense I want to make a specific request concerning my will. Should its exercise ever be necessary I desire that *mother* have the lady's wrist watch and *father* the New York Sun pocket watch. This is more than a request; it amounts to a codicil to my first testament. All other of my possessions and assets I want used for the general benefit and happiness of the Kinnick family as mother & father may see fit, George's college education being of prime importance.

"Peace & War": The book was *Peace and War: United States Foreign Policy, 1931–1941* (Washington, D.C., 1942). In a letter to his parents of 23 March, Kinnick says he has finished reading it.

Gregg Shorthand: See letter 18, where Kinnick also thought he would take up shorthand.

three of Grant Wood's paintings: Kinnick gives the correct title of *Stone City;* the others were *Spring in Town* and *The Birthplace of President Hoover.*

a couple of clippings: The item in the "Providence paper" has not been located. The *Providence Journal* for 1–13 March contains nothing that Kinnick would find especially evocative. The *Time* article, in the issue for 15 March, describes a sow giving birth on a cold morning in western Iowa. In a letter of 11 April Kinnick's father identified the Van Devender of the article as John Van Devender of Dallas County. He also wrote that the "riderless horse would constitute the vane and therefore would hang to the lee side."

a bit of poetical expression: The poem does not survive in the collection, nor any information about the messboy.

the New York Sun pocket watch: On 22 January 1940, after Kinnick's two eastern trips, the *Iowa City Press-Citizen* listed a watch from the *New York Sun* among his awards and trophies (clipping in scrapbook 2).

34 ✻ To the Family, 5 April 1943

On Kinnick's assignment to Fighter Squadron 16 (VF-16), see the headnote to letter 28. Bill Reiter, mentioned here, was Kinnick's other roommate on the *Lexington* besides Frank Rogers. Reiter too would die in 1943, during a 5 October raid on Wake Island. The suffix "F" in navy code meant planes manufactured by Grumman. The model Kinnick and Reiter were retrieving was the Wildcat, a fighter. The new F6F was the Hellcat, a fighter. The other and largest of the three in Kinnick's comparison, the TBF, was the Avenger, a torpedo bomber.

Monday   April 5, 1943

Dear Folks,

Not so long ago a couple of Navy fighters – not from our squadron – were crash landed near Newburgh, N.Y. Lost in the fog and low on gas the pilots made a belly landing in a farmer's field, that is to say, they brought their craft in wheels up to avoid the possibility of nosing over. The feat was neatly accomplished – no injuries to personnel and apart from bent propellers the planes suffered only minor damage. Men from the carrier aircraft service unit (CASU) located here at Quonset hauled the planes into an Army field at Newburgh and made the necessary repairs. Then CASU having no pilots qualified in an F4F-4 asked for two fliers from VF-16 to ferry them back. Bill Reiter and I were designated.

Lt. Com'dr Sherrill, skipper of Casu, flew us over in the GB-2, which in Navy code means a personnel transport made by Beechcraft. You will find a picture of it among the Beechcraft advertising photographs on page 206 of the Feb. issue of Flying. It is a five place, single engine, bi-plane – a neat little job, just right for the family after the war? We left Quonset about 10:30 AM, flew west to Hartford, on to Poughkeepsie, then dropped into Stewart field at Newburgh about 11:30 AM. It was contact all the way, though halfway between Hartford and Poughkeepsie it closed down to about 1500' with poor visibility. Providing the weather at your destination doesn't get below 500', normal instrument conditions in a two place plane wouldn't be too bad – or rather skillful cooperation should produce a safe landing. Handling a fighter under such conditions, however, is quite another story. As a general rule, regardless of good or bad weather, we use our radio facilities to check our dead reckoning and as a matter of practice to meet a more difficult situation. This trip was particularly easy. The Providence, Hartford, & Poughkeepsie ranges all overlap, and we passed from one to the other by simply changing frequencies. The magic of radio provides invisible but well marked highways across the sky. The future of this marvelous technology is fascinatingly unlimited.

After lunch at the Army officer's club Bill and I began a thorough inspection of the repaired planes before taking them up for a test hop. We made careful inquiry concerning the type & success of the crash landing, the nature of the damage and just exactly what had been done for remedy. The opinion of the chief aviation machinists mate and the officer supervising the repair held that the propellers were the only serious damage and that the stoppage had not been sudden enough to hurt the prop shaft or crankshaft. Of course portions of the under engine cowling and wheel fairing were bent, but not badly enough to prevent flight. No structural damage was reported, yet we quite properly made our own inspection. Next we turned up the engines on the ground for one hour, checking the prop control in all positions and testing the magnetos carefully. Bill decided that his plane was ready for flight, but I found that my "rpm's" fell off about 200 at takeoff manifold pressure in full low pitch, indicating that something was wrong with the governor; also my oleos needed pumping up. A check of the prop control mechanism revealed that a small triangular support for the governor control rod had not been properly fastened. Now with that fixed and the oleos up I felt all set for the test hop. The pitot tube was badly bent which would throw my air speed indicator considerably off, but knowing the proper manifold pressure and ship attitude necessary for climbing, gliding, and landing I was not apprehensive about that. (Am relating this as a matter of interest and not in any pride of ability. Any of the boys could, & would, do the same.) Down from our check flights I pronounced my craft ok and ready for the trip back. However, Bill wasn't satisfied with the way his acted – it vibrated unduly and shuddered terribly at speeds over 150 knots. Reluctantly, but according to his best judgment, he gave it a down. At first the mechs thought the prop must be improperly balanced. Not having the proper instruments and tools on hand for remedying such a trouble, a new one would have to be brought up from New York. Further examination by a civilian mech employed by the Army disclosed that one of the blades was 5/16″ out of line (the Navy only allows 1/8″) and 8 degrees out of pitch. Evidently the men who had installed the new props had gotten it "out of tooth" – in fine, not properly aligned with certain markings on the hub and blade. The time necessary to fix it would make it too late to leave for Quonset, so we decided to stay all night.

You will note that Newburgh is just a few miles above West Point and just a little below Hyde Park. Whenever the President spends a few days at home a squadron of P-47s from Mitchell Field flies up and stands by at Stewart Field as a precautionary measure. The latter field is being used mainly for the training of a portion of the West Point Cadets who will graduate right into the Air Corps. It is beautiful country, this Dutchess County and Upper Hudson area. It has a settled, peaceful appearance, and the wooded hills and grassy glens look like something out of Washington Irving (I wonder if I have used a proper simile?)

Sunday morning dawned bright and clear, a wonderful sunshiny day in the spring of the year. We got up around nine oclock, leisurely took breakfast, just as leisurely filed our flight plan while the men warmed up our planes, and finally about 10:30 AM we were ready to go. What a joy to taxi into the wind, give her the gun, race down the runway, and lift into the air, climbing swiftly out of the valley over the hills and eastward into the risen sun. With a favorable tail wind it only took us 40 minutes to make Quonset. We circled Bill's house once just to let his wife know he was back ok, tailed in over the Jamestown bridge, joined the traffic circle and landed. Would have given anything to have you all along. It was an exhilarating, thoroughly enjoyable hop.

While eating supper Sat. night in Newburgh I noted by the calendar that it was April 3rd – and I thought of you Gus. Happy birthday, sonny boy, and lots of them.

We were informed today that we are to get F6Fs after our shake-down cruise. You probably haven't heard much about this plane, and it would be best if you keep circumspectly quiet about what I might say concerning it; also about the P-47s and the squire of Dutchess County. The F6F is made by Grumman and stands in size between an F4F and a TBF. It has a 2000 hp Pratt-Whitney engine and is just about the best aircraft yet to come out of the US – or at least so we hear. Naturally, the squadron is pretty happy over the prospect.

Pappy, I wish you would save the Fortune magazines and mark any articles of particular interest and import. Also pick up for me a volume or two on Wilson and the League of Nations. Do you know who are the main guns in the farm bloc in Washington? Whoever they are, they are just as bad as John L. Lewis. It really pains me to see the farm interests making every effort to crack the existing price structure, for farmers mean Iowa to me, and I want always to be proud of her and what she stands for.

Let me know what decision is taken at the business meeting of the church members concerning the full payment of the mortgage.

Must sign now – things go well.

Yours,

Nile

P:S: The part of this letter dealing with checking and ferrying aircraft may be of interest to Ben. Why don't you send it along to him plus this additional counsel:

– Always take off in *full low* pitch and have your prop in FULL LOW when landing, so if you have to take a waveoff you can get full power. This is IMPERATIVE! If you are using a Curtiss Electric prop make sure the generator is giving full voltage before taking off – also check the increase, decrease controls and the vernier.

35 ✳ To the Family, 14 April 1943

Kinnick's first paragraph adequately sets the circumstances of this letter, except that his departure was not so imminent as he thought. Annotations follow the letter.

Wednesday   April 14, 1943

Dear Folks,

The imminence of our departure date has prompted the skipper to grant three day leave for each of us at scheduled intervals. I debated quite some time on how I should spend mine. Much as I wanted to get home I decided the uncertainty of air travel and the length of time necessary by train weighed too heavily on the negative side. Your earlier suggestion that one of you might come out here was given full consideration, but, frankly, I felt that if I couldn't see the whole family around the home hearth I'd rather pass the idea entirely. Consequently, I accepted the alternative of three care-free days in New York City, getting back just last night.

I had a fine time, but I was alone; and happiness unshared is like a picture without those colors which give it warmth and meaning. Give a man one close friend, tried and true, and he is fortified against the world; make that friend a woman and there are no heights he cannot scale.

Sunday afternoon I heard Marian Anderson at the Metropolitan opera house. I was lucky to get a ticket, for they were all sold out, except for standing room, when I presented myself at the window. However, as I stepped out onto the sidewalk again, a small, furtive figure in a ragged, gray coat directed me across the street to a little cleaning establishment. There a character by the name of Joe was getting scalper's prices for ducats which he had purchased in anticipation of a sell-out. I paid $3 for a seat in the Grand Tier and was glad to get it. The Met from outside is a huge, dirty, unimpressive looking building, but within it is just as you have imagined it. The halls and lobbys of each floor are spacious, high ceilinged. The auditorium itself is immense flanked all the way round by a succession of five balconies, called Parterre tier, Grand tier, Dress circle, Family circle, and Balcony. The walls, carpets, upholstering, everything is a deep, luxurious maroon color. Miss Anderson was dressed in a beautiful, full length, velvet gown of quiet green with a splash of silver extending diagonally across the front from waist to hem. She is a large, well proportioned woman, with plain features. Her entrance was poised, graceful, and I thought she appeared profoundly conscious of her responsibility to her people as well as to her audience immediately out front. Most of the program was confined to classical pieces by the old masters – Handel, Schubert, Bach, etc – which she sang with great beauty and feeling. From where I sat she seemed to close her eyes and slightly knit her brows with intense concentration. Classical music I can't truly appreciate, but the old Negro spirituals and "Comin' thru the Rye," which she sang especially for three rows of service men seated on the stage behind her, were right down my alley. Her powerful, heartfelt rendition of "Sometimes I Feel Like a Motherless Child" was marvelous. I could hear the moan and wail of the Negro soul echoing through the centuries. By urgent request from out front, quite in violation of Met decorum, I presume, she sang Ave Maria for an encore number. The perfection of her tone and interpretation swelled out over her listeners, and we all closed our eyes and felt as if we were in church. It was wonderful, mother! How I wish you might have been there, and grandma, too.

Of equal interest and enjoyment to me was a study of the audience. There were very nearly as many colored people present as there were white. And what a justifiable pride they took in Miss Anderson. In my row of 12 or 14 seats your sonny boy was the only pale face. From my observation and brief conversation with some of them during intermission I would say that they were a well groomed, well conducted lot. Evidently they represented the upper crust from Harlem, and they were a distinct credit to their race. It was a hopeful example of the American faith in democratic equality.

Going from the sublime to the ridiculous, I took Ellie to see Sons of Fun starring Olsen and Johnson Sunday night. It is a second edition of Hellzapoppin', rough-house comedy from start to finish, uproarious, hilarious, episodic, crazy, wild, exhausting. I wish Gus and Uncle

Chas could have been on hand to see the fun. Frank Libuse put on his little act with the piano and female singer which I saw at Billy Rose's Diamond Horseshoe in the winter of 1940 and again in the summer at the World's Fair. There were better shows in town, but I couldn't get tickets. The stage really does a booming, land-office business during war time.

At the Paramount Theatre I saw Saroyan's "The Human Comedy," an appealing, heart-tugging little story of a family which experienced both joy and grief and met them equally well. Mickey Rooney was good, but mostly he needed a haircut. Frank Morgan is always delightful, but Jackie Jenkins stole the show. His wistful, freckled little face, his tears and smiles, his disconnected questions pictured the emotions and thought of a childhood we all knew at one time or another. Les Brown's orchestra held forth on stage, and it was good – much better than when I last heard him at the Blackhawk in Chicago. Vaughn Monroe was playing in the Century room of the Commodore Hotel where I was staying, and I saw Jan Savitt at the Strand Theatre – all of this primarily of interest to George. Big, lovable Ethel Waters was making a local appearance with the latter. I really enjoyed her rendition of "Stormy Weather." The Berry brothers, whom you may have seen in the movies, were also on the bill. Keep an eye out for Bob Dupont should he ever appear at the Orpheum in Omaha. He is the best juggler I have ever seen. Gus, would really have gone for him.

"The Patriots" a play about Washington, Hamilton, and Jefferson during the early days of our country, I saw one afternoon. It showed the incomparable, impetuous Hamilton in a more unfavorable light than Jefferson, just as Atherton's biography of the former pictured Jefferson to a disadvantage. Certainly, these two great men stood for diametrically opposite philosophys of government. Happily, Washington, that venerable man, was in between exercising his genius for compromise. The complete triumph of either of these powerful ideas would not have been good. Their reconciliation guaranteed to this country a sound body and a great soul. In looking for books on Jefferson don't neglect Bowers' "Hamilton and Jefferson," for they really should be read and studied together.

Monday night I saw the stage performance of "Star and Garter" with G. R. Lee and Billy Clark – without the *e* you'll be glad to note. It was full of earthy wit, ribald songs, scantily clad girls, slapstick comedy. But it was harmless and gay, and I laughed and had a good time.

Afterwards I took a cab over to the Waldorf-Astoria where I had reserved a table in the Wedgwood room for the supper hour. As a boy, dinner was at noon, supper at six oclock. Later I learned that dinner, more properly, was in the evening, lunch was the mid-day meal, and supper came only as a snack on Sunday night. Now I find that the supper hour is around mid-night after all the shows are out. My sole purpose in going to the Waldorf was to hear Alec Templeton, the blind pianist, who plays each night at 12:15. I was not disappointed. He gave me the most enjoyable forty minutes I have spent in a long time. There in the beautiful Wedgwood room with its soft purple walls, its lovely curtains in mild green pastels, its ceiling the color of rich white leather, I sat over my plate of delicious Lobster Newburg and heard a master at his work. Mr. Templeton has a pleasant, alert, clean-lined face and is as poised and gracious as any artist I have ever watched. For the entertainment of dilettantes like myself he has devised a program which we can enjoy and appreciate. He takes popular songs and plays them in a classic manner, and the classics he modernizes or swings. It is a marvelous talent, and he does it delightfully. I almost fell out of my chair when right off the bat, he said that first he would play the Iowa corn song then depict how he thought de Bussy would have arranged it. And believe it or not, there it came, the *Iowa Corn Song* dressed up in the silk and satin of cultured music – from overalls to full dress in a twinkling of the eye. Of course, in deference to his professional pride he must play some classical stuff – Rachmoninoff's "Prelude C Sharp Minor" and one of his own compositions "Trout Streams." During the latter I could clearly see the bubbling, laughing streams bouncing down Long's Peak and the speckled trout splashing over rocks, down the cataract, and into the quiet pools below. Toward the finish of his program he asked the patrons to suggest any four songs or musical compositions at random. The four suggested were Greek Concerto, Girl with the Flaxen Hair, As Time Goes By, Taboo. He then improvised as he went along, without a hesitation, without a falter, playing the most beautiful medley you can imagine. The only thing I knew was "As Time Goes By," but I could hear that melody in the background like a tower bell in the distance. He did the same thing with Hungarian Rhapsody, Brazil, Old Black Joe, and "You'd Be So Nice to Come Home To." It was marvelous, mother! Wish you could have been there. He took my breath away and left me enchanted.

Enclosed is a column which appealed to my sense of humor and which by changing a few names and the title of the piece from Narcissus to Pink Elephant's Waltz could aptly apply to my early days as a pianist.

There is much I would like to say in answer to the fine letters just received from father, but it is now way late, and I must get to bed. So I shall just acknowledge the enclosures and say thanks to you all for your faithful correspondence.

Hope you can understand my decision to spend my short leave in N.Y. City.

Much love,

Nile

P:S: Gus – an *oleo is* a shock absorber.

Grandma this letter is to you too – every time. Perhaps Ben would like to see this letter and get some idea of what he would like to do when on leave in N.Y. – he & Ellie.

Marian Anderson: Tickets for the recital were difficult to find, partly because Anderson's engagement was for only one performance.

Sons of Fun: Chic Johnson had left the cast when Kinnick took Ben's fiancée, Eleanor White, to see the show at the 46th Street Theater. Frank Libuse's "female singer" was his wife and stage partner, Margot Libuse.

Les Brown's orchestra: Compare Kinnick's discomfort at the Blackhawk in letter 19.

I saw Jan Savitt: This means that Kinnick also saw *Edge of Darkness*, starring Errol Flynn, part of a movie–stage show bill at the Strand Theater. Kinnick usually told his parents about the movies he saw. He may have kept silent here because of Flynn's recent sexual scandal (see the diary for 18 May 1943 and accompanying note).

"The Patriots": A play by Sidney Kingsley at the National. Reviews were lukewarm.

Billy Clark: Kinnick confuses Billy and Bobby Clark, two veteran stage comedians. Bobby Clark, the performer in *Star and Garter* at the Music Box, was a baggy-pants comedian and tumbler. The *New Yorker* favorably noted the show as "rough but stimulating" (17 April 1943). Kinnick's "without the *e*" distinguishes the performer's name from the Clarke family name.

Long's Peak: Kinnick's account of his 1935 trip to Colorado, New Mexico, and the West Coast gives a detailed description of his climbing Long's Peak (box 2).

Enclosed is a column: The column is not in the scrapbooks and cannot be identified. Kinnick's training in piano was early, rudimentary, and brief. In his own opinion he could not play at all (see the diary for 1 June 1943).

an oleo is *a shock absorber:* In a letter of 11 April, Kinnick's father guessed that he was referring to shock absorbers in letter 34, in which he said that his "oleos needed pumping up." An oleo or oleo strut was a hydraulic and compressed-air shock absorber in the landing gear.

36 ✳ To Nile Kinnick, Sr., 15 April 1943

This is the last letter in the collection in which Kinnick speculates about his future career. Over time his letters show a bias toward a career in elective politics at the state and national levels. Toward this end, he was willing to do whatever additional legal study would be useful, but he was more enthusiastic even about becoming a flour salesman to foster a political career than he was about going the conventional route from law practice to public office. Annotations follow the letter.

Thursday noon   April 15, 1943

Dear Gus,

Your well written letters are a source of much enjoyment – and much pride – to me. Time and again I have regretted not saving them. I trust you are filing a copy of each to which we may make future reference. Together with the letters Ben and I have written home they should provide an interesting record of this period of family experience. George could profit much by studying their thought and style. Lest your modesty deter you from making the suggestion, I hereby urge him to take a lesson from the old man in the art of written correspondence.

Your response to my thought that we might some day combine our talents for mutual profit and enjoyment made me very happy. You as farm production manager and I as a warrior in the political field, frequently returning to the country homestead for encouragement and strength has the most appeal. However, let's keep our minds and eyes open for any opportunity of whatever nature – and which could include the whole family. Among the five of us we have a good combination of health, energy, ambition, brains, talent, industry. It would be so much fun to capitalize on it to the happiness and benefit of all. Well, its an idea – and not at all impossible. For me specifically, Gus, I wish you would cagily and unobtrusively sound the political opinion of the men and women in different areas with whom you come in contact. In Iowa find out what they think of Hickenlooper, Wilson, Gillette, et al. Why they do or do not like them. What they think should be done for public benefit within the state borders, etc. Nationally, try to determine what are their convictions and hopes for the post war world. What they think of the different political candidates and so on. Store up your observations and answers for the day when once again we can sit down and discuss them face to face. Would suggest you give NO indications of your son's possible intentions.

Had a letter by V mail from Bob the other day. It was quite short and didn't say much. Rather think, however, that he is land based for the present somewhere in the South Pacific. Didn't sound as if he had seen any action.

Enclosed is a money order for $60 which I want used for war bonds in addition to the monthly purchase I have previously directed. Starting this month my allotment should be sent to you folks, so keep an eye out.

Appreciated the comment on my poetical interests and also your effort along this line. Its a lot of fun to try one's hand don't you think?

Had seen Lippmann's article on Willkie and thought his point well taken. In N.Y. I bought a copy of Wendell's new book, "One World." The parts that I have read are very good. If he could speak as well as he can write he would be a cinch.

Give my best to Reese for the butter. Very generous of him.

Am anxious to hear the latest flood news. Hope they were able to keep it in check.

While in N.Y. I bought, rather belatedly, a birthday present for you consisting of three books. Knowing your interest in geography and passion for exact detail I purchased a leather-bound, current edition of Rand-McNally Atlas. Our other one is pretty old by now. I thought I remembered you expressing an interest in Currier and Ives lithographs, hence that book. But it may [be] I have confused my desire with yours. The book on American paintings I got primarily because of the pictures by Curry, Benton, Grant Wood, and especially because of the painting,

Coney Island by Cadmus. I can still see you laughing at the guy pinching the little boys behind when first you saw it in the paper one Sunday morning. They should arrive about Mon. or Tues.

Note by the paper that Tom Harmon is missing. Sounds tough, but he may turn up one of these days.

Must race back to squadron now.

Love,

Nile

the comment on my poetical interests: On 21 March Kinnick closed a letter to his parents with eight quatrains of comic doggerel he called "State Finals," about Benson High School's recent losing effort in the Nebraska high school basketball tournament, to which his father replied appreciatively on 8 April. George Kinnick was a member of the Benson team. This and Kinnick's other attempts at verse were usually meant to be jokes, humorously inept.

Lippmann's article: The article, in the *Des Moines Register* of 9 April 1943, was a long and very favorable review of Willkie's new book *One World.*

Give my best to Reese for the butter: In view of the wartime scarcity of butter, the gift to the Kinnicks of a pound from their friend Reese Hastain was a noteworthy gesture (Kinnick, Sr., carbon, 8 April).

Currier and Ives: An edition of these works available to Kinnick was Harry T. Peters, *Currier and Ives: Printmakers to the American People* (Garden City, N.J., 1942).

The book on American paintings: A book available to Kinnick that contained Paul Cadmus's *Coney Island* and works by John Steuart Curry, Thomas Hart Benton, and Grant Wood was Peyton Boswell, Jr., *Modern American Painting* (New York, 1940).

Tom Harmon is missing: On 15 April, the *New York Times* announced that Army Air Corps Lt. Tom Harmon – Michigan All-American, Heisman runner-up in 1939, and winner in 1940 – had been missing over Dutch Guiana since 8 April. On 18 April the *Times* announced his rescue, and on 22 April it published his account of the incident. He and a crew of five were negotiating an army bomber through a heavy storm, but when he put the plane into a spiral to fly contact below the overcast, something cracked in the right wing and right engine, and the plane became uncontrollable. Harmon ordered everyone to bail out, but two men died in the crash and the others were not found. Harmon survived after walking through jungle and swamp for days until he found local people, who took him to the base of the Antilles Air Task Force. Later that year Harmon went down over China and was rescued by Chinese guerrillas (*New York Times*, 7 and 30 November 1943).

37 ✴ To the Family, 24 April 1943

Kinnick's reference here to his "last letter" evidently means his last letter to his parents (letter 35), as distinguished from the letter to his father of 15 April (letter 36). The close of this letter indicates that Kinnick still believed that the *Lexington* was about to leave, but it did not sail until 11 May, a month later than he had estimated in a letter of 19 March. This 24 April letter stands as his only farewell, though he would write again before sailing. That letter, of 3 May, is a note to wish Frances a happy Mother's Day on the ninth and to state that he encloses his social security card, driver's license, and a money order for deposit. There are only three further Kinnick letters in the collection, all written after the ship left port. The first, of 22 May, is a note to tell his parents that all is well and to comment briefly on war news and family doings. Near the end he apparently gave a date when the *Lexington* would return; this portion was cut out by the naval censor. The second letter, of 30 May, was also to his parents, who received it after the telegram announcing his death. The letter comments on the recent sale of the family home in Omaha, on news of Ben Kinnick, Ken Pettit, and Mike Enich, and on passing the time playing bridge and reading. The last letter, possibly the last he wrote, is letter 39, below. Kinnick signed himself "Nile C. Kinnick" in the letters he wrote after sailing. A full name may have been policy for mail passing through censors. Annotations follow the letter.

Saturday April 24, 1943

Dear Folks,

Mother's acknowledgment of the books from Scribners made no mention of my last letter. I hope that by now it has come into your hands, for it tells at some length and detail of a few days I spent in New York. However, it didn't speak of my girl friend [I] met on the way back to Quonset, and of her you really should hear.

I caught the three o'clock train from Grand Central, and as always it was very crowded. Happily, I was able to get the last available seat in my coach. Right next to me sat a little old lady in a faded, well worn, blue coat, holding in her lap a scuffed and slightly battered leather pocketbook bearing the metal initials L. M. Underneath her feet which didn't quite reach the floor was a small black suitcase. Out in the open away from the station the sun shone in our window warm and comfortable. I helped her off with her coat, and she shyly asked if I would prefer sitting in her seat where I could watch the passing countryside better. I declined as graciously as I could and turned to my magazine. In a little while she asked in a quiet, diffident voice if I were in the Air Corps? had I been across yet? she hoped I wouldn't have to. Every few paragraphs she called my attention to certain landmarks, spoke of the town we had just passed and of the next to come, pridefully mentioned the Merritt Parkway which lay just out of sight, behind the hill – and then apologetically, regretfully observed "but you want to read your magazine?" It was true that I did – baldly put, I suppose I was annoyed at her interruptions. But she was so sweet and good – and lonely – that I was ashamed of my selfish indifference to her friendliness. I closed my magazine and tucked it under my leg for the rest of the trip. We talked of many things, just simple, everyday things, but I was glad that I hadn't stubbornly stuck to my reading. The dull gray smoke from the engine billowed back past the window, drifted in among the trees and underbrush, momentarily hanging there like a dense, dirty fog, then dissipating and disappearing in the clean country air. I bought two small packets of cashew nuts from the Union News candy butcher who intermittently passed through calling his merchandise in a weary, belligerent voice – one for her and one for me. She remonstrated in a most sweet and gentle manner, fumbled with the snap to her pocketbook declaring firmly that it was she who should be buying for me, the man in uniform. (All of which reminded me of another dear and noble lady, loving matriarch of the happy clan of Clarke – whose last letter I still have not answered!) My companion spoke of her nephew in the Marine Corps, of her people in Hartford, lamented the late spring and sagely observed that nothing would grow when its feet were cold and wet. It developed that she was a spinster and lived all by herself in a small cottage near the sea just outside of New London. It was lonely, yes, but she usually had someone renting all but the one room she occupied, and in any event she preferred it to living in the city, especially New York where she had been visiting. (Now grandma, if this gives you any ideas about returning to Adel, I shall never forgive myself for writing this little story!) From her window she was wont to watch the airplanes passing overhead and diving through their various bombing exercises. They provided a certain, strange companionship, and would even more so now that she knew me. Just before we pulled into New London she asked if she might have my name and address. Under the circumstances it seemed an odd request, but her simple sincerity quashed my condescension, and I wrote it out for her. In a neat, legible hand she did the same for me, and in a way so gentle and good that I felt ashamed I had not made it easier for her by asking her to do it. As the train rolled on I saw her walking off across the station platform with her small black suitcase in one hand and the battered pocketbook in the other. But that is not the end of the story as at that time I thought it undoubtedly was. A few days later, when I had all but forgotten the incident, I received a sturdy little package mailed from Niantic, Conn. It was a full pound box of delicious cashew nuts of which I am extremely fond. I find it difficult to say exactly what this experience has meant to me, so pregnant with kindness, generosity, love, and sacrifice. Surely it is such thoughts and deeds which flicker from out the night of hatred and strife that promise the certainty of mankind's true brotherhood. God bless Louise Miller!

I now know the exact date when we are to leave this station and where our ship will be when we board her. You will understand that I cannot in good conscience divulge these details, however, this will probably be the last long letter you will receive from me which should indicate something: It is my guess that we will spend from three to four weeks on a shakedown cruise then return to the mainland for F6Fs. Between now and the 1st of June I would suggest that you address my mail NCK, VF-16, Commandant, 5th Naval District, Norfolk, Va. Always indicate my rank, but *never* use the name of my carrier. After June 1st the chances of any mail reaching me before I return is pretty small, but unless otherwise directed send it in care of Postmaster Atlantic Fleet, N.Y.C. You are at liberty to speculate on my whereabouts if you keep it *strictly* within the family. All correspondence will be censored hence forward, so use your head. I expressed my large suitcase home today, and the key will be enclosed in this letter. It is coming C.O.D. which expense should be met from my account. Inside the Willkie booklet will be found a squadron picture of all but two or three of the pilots.

Should it develop when Ben is home on leave that he needs more money to cover the ring, travel, and entertainment expense, please advance him liberally from my savings. There is no reason why he should demur, for he soon will be making more money than he knows what to do with.

I owe letters to A. Kate, grandma, Elsie Louise, Geo., Kingsley, and Elizabeth. Hope that, directly or indirectly, you will express my regret for failing to answer – apart from you people I have been sadly delinquent in my correspondence the past month or so.

Gus, I think a good history of Iowa should be added to my library. Hasn't the gov't sponsored writer's project gotten out something pretty good along this line? Hope you will keep tucked away in your mind the chronological order of the important events happening this coming year, I am apt to fall behind. Particularly, listen and learn all you can of the political forces loose in the land.

The next presidential nominating conventions are only 14 months away, the election itself, only a year and half. It is vitally important that everyone, from electorate through the political parties up to the nominees themselves, measure up to the highest concepts of statesmanship. Roosevelt has been a great president, doing the country immeasurably more good than he has harm. However, the damage he has done is of an insidious, long range nature, unappreciable to the great mass of people who think in terms only of the immediate present, and ergo all the more dangerous. In fine I think his wild, unrestricted schemes of finance, his willing employment of political expediency at every turn, his ever-growing, irresponsible, burdensome, inefficient governmental bureaucracy, his flippant attitude toward the importance of private initiative and enterprise, his reluctance to surround himself with the best possible men, his promotion of class jealousies and disrespect, have definitely undermined the moral fibre of this country. If the old time virtues of private resourcefulness and thrift, adherence to principle, governmental economy, intellectual & political honesty are of no importance, then Franklin has had scarcely any fault as a president. It is extremely difficult to wage a successful campaign of opposition on these points, as he well knows, but it is all the more reason he should be gotten out. However, the all important thing right now is to win the war and win the peace. It is absolutely essential that the U.S. assume her responsibilities of international cooperation and security after this war. In my mind there is only one man on the political front who could do as good a job as Roosevelt and that is Willkie.

Bricker is sitting tight and trying to sneak in the back door. These are times when a man must stand up and be counted for what he believes on the international scene. Furthermore, I don't trust the old-line Republicans surrounding him. Much as I dislike a good many of Roosevelt's methods and regret to support an indispensable-man philosophy I take him over Bricker. What we need is men of greater stature & character in Congress!!!!

This task which lies ahead is adventure as well as duty, and I am anxious to get at it. I feel better in mind and body than I have for ten years, and am quite certain that I can meet the foe confident and unfraid. "I have set the Lord always before me; because he is at my right hand, I shall not be moved." Our home and family life has been grand and fruitful, and it will be even better after this war is all over. All that we have been or shall be we boys owe to your affection, discipline, and guidance. Wherever we go, whatever we do, I know that our minds shall frequently flood with tender memories of the hearthside and with happy plans for the day when law and peace shall reign once again. Truly, we have shared to the full life, love, and laughter. Comforted in the knowledge that your thought and prayer go with us every minute, and sure that your faith and courage will never falter no matter the outcome, I bid you au revoir.

Much love,

Nile

P.S. Mother's & grandma's good letters came in this afternoon's mail before I mailed this. Glad to learn of Ted & Lee's baby, also, John & Jerry's – and Anne's, too, tsk, tsk. You write a beautiful letter, grandma, I always enjoy them so much. Letters from all you people have meant a great deal to me, and I have taken pride in their excellent form and content. Regret keenly that I have not saved them all.

George:

You are just beginning to come into your own physically and mentally. Don't fail to make the most of these next few years, they count for much. Continually strive for improvement in writing and speaking, enlarge your vocabulary, discipline your thinking processes, develop your *memory powers*, try for at least *twos* in your schoolwork, and without turning thought in on the physique develop your muscles until you are strong as an *ox*. All this will be easy, even that which you don't care for particularly, if you maintain & broaden your sense of hu-

mor and stick by your BOOKS. It is important that every member of
the family grow and look forward *all* the time.

> "Not enjoyment, not sorrow
> Is our destined end or way.
> But to act that each tomorrow
> Find us farther than today."

Merritt Parkway: In southwest Connecticut.

a squadron picture: On the reverse of the glossy print (box 3) Kinnick wrote the names of the squadron members. The Willkie booklet is unidentified.

a good history of Iowa: Kinnick was thinking of *Iowa: A Guide to the Hawkeye State* (New York, 1938), compiled by the Federal Writers' Project of the Works Progress Administration.

Bricker: John W. Bricker, then governor of Ohio and in 1944 the Republican candidate for vice-president. Later he was a U.S. senator from Ohio and an isolationist even after the war.

I have set the Lord: Psalms 16:8.

Ted & Lee's baby . . . John & Jerry's – and Anne's: On Ted and Lee, see letter 30. John and Jerry were John and Geraldine Kinnick of Berkeley, California. John was Kinnick's cousin, son of his uncle Butler Kinnick. Anne is unidentified, and so the point of Kinnick's "tsk, tsk" – usually a sign of pretended and humorous dismay – is unclear.

Not enjoyment, not sorrow: From Longfellow, "A Psalm of Life."

38 ✳ Paul Buie to Mr. and Mrs. Nile Kinnick, Sr., 6 June 1943

FIGHTING SQUADRON SIXTEEN
℅ Fleet Post Office
New York, New York
June 6, 1943

My dear Mr. and Mrs. Kinnick,

It is with deepest regret and sympathy that I inform you of the loss of your son, Nile, in an airplane crash on the second of June 1943. Nile was engaged in a practice flight that took off from the U.S.S. LEXINGTON about eight-thirty on the morning of the second of June and

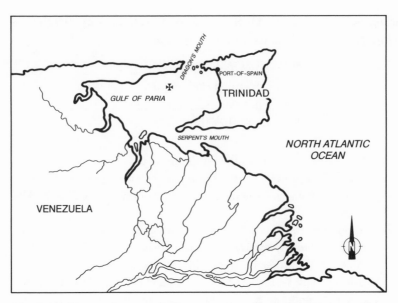

The Gulf of Paria, showing the location where Kinnick crash-landed his plane.

remained with his flight until he was forced to land in the water about an hour and twenty minutes later. His plane developed a serious oil leak about ten minutes before he landed. Having lost all oil the engine, without lubrication, failed, forcing Nile to land in the water. Nile made a normal unhurried water landing in calm water about four miles ahead and in full view of the ship. He was seen by one of his team mates to get clear of the plane. Both the Lexington and the plane guard boat proceeded directly to the scene of the landing, which had been kept under constant observation, both from the air and from the ship, and was further definitely identified as being the exact location by gasoline and paint chips in the water, arriving at the spot about eight minutes later. A diligent and immediate search of the exact location of the landing and the adjacent waters, by both planes and ships, failed to reveal any trace whatever of Nile. Since Nile was definitely not on the surface of the water eight minutes after he landed and at no time for the next hour and a half, it must be assumed that he drowned. Knowing Nile to be a very good swimmer, an excellent athlete, and in wonderful physical condition, it is inconceivable that he could have failed to remain afloat for the short period of time required for the crash boat to arrive unless he had been seriously hurt in the landing itself.

I would like to emphasise the fact that there can be no doubt whatever that the exact spot of Nile's landing was very thoroughly searched both by ships and planes immediately following the landing. A water landing is normally a relatively safe landing, especially under conditions of calm water. There is small probability of serious physical injury in such a landing. It is very difficult to understand just what could have gone wrong. The best guess, and it is nothing more than a guess, is that his safety belt broke on landing allowing Nile to lurch forward upon impact probably striking his head on the structure of the airplane and injuring him to the extent that he could neither maintain himself afloat nor remember to inflate his life jacket.

Nile was an outstanding man in every respect. His calm and determined manner, his quick grin, his sound common sense, and his outstanding all around abilities made him a wonderful asset to the squadron and a man that we were all proud to call our friend. His loss was a terrible blow to all of us and a serious loss to the country he so ably served.

Again let me extend my deepest sympathy to you for your great loss. Should there be any service that I can render, either now or later, please do not hesitate to call on me.

> Sincerely yours,
> Paul Buie
> Lieutenant Commander, U.S. Navy
> Fighting Squadron Sixteen

Mr. and Mrs. N. C. Kinnick
1114 – South 79th Street
Omaha, Nebraska

39 ✳ To Celia Peairs, 31 May 1943

In Des Moines on the evening of 4 June 1943, Celia Peairs had just read in the paper of Kinnick's death when the mailman came to the door with this letter, which he had overlooked on an earlier round. At some point Celia removed her name from the greeting, the close above the signature (in letters to her this was usually "Love"), and an uncertain amount of Kinnick's prose after each of the text paragraphs, which she left intact. She destroyed all the deleted material and may have sent the excerpt to the *Des Moines Register* or the *Des Moines Tribune*. But the first known publication of the letter, a white on black photofacsimile of Kinnick's handwritten text, was in the *Daily Iowan* of 13 October 1943 (clippings, boxes 1 and 2), where the caption said the letter had been sent to a "friend . . . in Des Moines." Dorothy Klein Ray, at that time the managing editor of the *Daily Iowan*, recalls that Eric Wilson, the news editor for the University Publicity Department, showed her the original letter before the paper printed it. The *Daily Iowan* staff and stringers for the Des Moines and other out-of-town papers were all housed in East Hall, so the letter may have passed to Wilson from someone at the *Register* or *Tribune* desk. Other papers quickly printed the excerpt in type, making further changes. In the absence of the closing as well as the name in the greeting, grammatical convention induced some writers to write as though the "friend" was a man. The original is lost; the text here is a transcription of the facsimile as printed in the *Daily Iowan*, but it restores "Celia" to the greeting.

Some of the imagery and idiom was resonant for Kinnick. Over a year earlier, in a letter to Ben of 21 March 1942, he had written: "Soon the countryside will be green . . . and, yes, the grass will be a grab and a half high, and picnics will displace the afternoon schedule."

Monday   May 31, 1943

Dear Celia,

Your welcome letter reached me last night here in this far away place of which I am permitted to tell you nothing. Carrier life is interesting and adventurous, but after a time it begins to drag. Word from you boosted my spirits no end.

Am so glad you could speak enthusiastically of your visit in Iowa City. That little town means so much to me – the scene of growth and development during vital years – joy and melancholy, struggle and triumph. It is almost like home. I love the people, the campus, the trees, everything about it. And it *is* beautiful in the spring. Ah, for those days of laughter and picnics when the grass was newly green and about a grab and a half high. I hope your friend showed you through the Union, the Fine Arts Bldg., the Little Theatre of which we are so proud. And I hope you strolled off across the golf course just at twilight and felt the peace and quiet of an Iowa evening, just as I used to do.

Nile C. Kinnick
Ensign U.S.N.R.

The Diary

INTRODUCTION TO THE DIARY

Kinnick's diary occupies all or part of three spiral-bound composition books. The leaves are the typical ruled white paper measuring 8 x 10½ inches; the covers are black leatherette stamped in gold. The first notebook – "Vol I" in Kinnick's later numbering – begins with prefatory matter on both sides of the first leaf. The recto of the second leaf begins the diary proper, and on this page another individual, possibly Kinnick's father, began numbering the pages in pencil (the diary is in blue ink throughout). The pagination runs from 1 to 133; the verso of the last leaf is blank.

The second notebook – "Vol II" – begins with a repetition of the formal identification. At the lower left of that unnumbered page Kinnick's father inscribed the inclusive dates covered in the notebook. The pencil numbering again begins with the diary proper and runs from 1 to 113; the verso of page 113 and the remaining eleven leaves are blank.

After the eight months following his last entry in the second notebook, Kinnick turned to a third notebook, possibly because he had left the first two in Omaha in September 1942. He had already begun using this third notebook to list books he wanted and at least one he had already read, *War and Peace*. His letters early in 1943 often instruct his parents as to titles and kinds of books he wanted to be purchased for his postwar library, and the list probably dates from that period. There are two blank leaves after the book list; then the pencil numbering starts with his recapitulation of his activities from the first of the year, done when he decided to resume the diary in May. The pagination runs from 1 to 30; the remaining leaves are blank. At the bottom of page 30 Kinnick's father wrote: "6/2 – Wednesday 09.52 Nile crashed 4 mi off Stbd. bow 105° | plane F4F #7 USS Lexington. Gulf of Paria. S.A." He wrote this much later, after seeing the *Lexington*'s log.

The entries in all three notebooks usually follow one another without extra space breaks (see illustration with entry for 15 May 1943). For the reader's convenience, such breaks are introduced here throughout. In the May 1943 diary, Kinnick indicated dates by numerals only, such as "5/9"; this styling is kept. For ease of recognition, his earlier use of both roman and italic styling for dates has been changed to italic throughout, and the numerals in the May diary are set in **boldface.**

Annotations follow the diary in chronological order of the entries. Many names in the diary refer to people Kinnick knew only in passing; for the most part they are not identifiable and are not discussed in the annotations. Other names not identified are of people the reader may be expected to recognize, such as Sally Rand, Mel Ott, and Gene Tunney, or people sufficiently identified in context. Others, such as Marvin Haugebak, Bob Hobbs, Kingsley Clarke, and Ken Pettit, should be familiar to readers coming to the diary from the letters. I have identified people mentioned only rarely in the letters or referred to in the diary only by first names if the reader's recognition seems questionable, and I have tried to identify people Kinnick knew outside the navy but did not mention in the letters, such as Francis Heydt and Kilmer Bortz. I have identified quotations or stated that I have not, but several items in the May 1943 entries are problematic, such as "restless as the sea," "as easily heard as your name," and "pay with the ring of my money for the smell of your roasting goose." These and other such items are ignored, for even whether they had external sources is not apparent, much less the nature of the source.

The terminology of the Navy Air Corps is explained only when the context would be confusing without clarification. Aircraft are regularly identified, as are acronyms that seldom or never appear in specialized dictionaries. For information on aerobatic maneuvers (such as the Immelmann and the slow roll) and for further data on ships, aircraft, training procedures, and the flying experience, the following titles are useful: *Dictionary of American Naval Fighting Ships* (Washington, D.C., 1963), vol. 2; the magazine *Flying*, especially vols. 38–42; Samuel Hynes, *Flights of Passage: Reflections of a World War II Aviator* (Annapolis, 1988); *Jane's All the World's Aircraft* (New York, 1909–); and *The United States Air Force Dictionary*, ed. Woodford Agee Heflin (Princeton, N.J., 1956).

Vol I – Dec. 3, 1941 – Feb. 25, 1942

Herein is contained a record of my service in the

U.S. Naval Reserve Air Corps beginning on Dec. 4, 1941 –

    Nile Kinnick jr. – age 23.

    5024 Hamilton St.

    Omaha,

    Nebraska

Wednesday, Dec. 3, 1941

Tomorrow I report at Kansas City for elimination training in the U.S. Naval Reserve Air Corps. I am looking forward with enthusiasm to this new experience. I am fully aware that this country is on the brink of a shooting war in two oceans, and that I might, in a very short while, find myself in the thick of very serious combat work. But what should be done, can be done, and the best way is always through not around. Every man whom I have admired in history has willingly and courageously served in his country's armed forces in times of danger. It is not only a duty, but an honor, to follow their example as best I know how. May God give me the courage and ability to so conduct myself in every situation that my country, my family, and my friends will be proud of me.

Thursday – Dec. 4, 1941
Kansas City – Kans.
Fairfax Airport.

Ken Pettit stayed all night with me last night in Omaha and rode down here with me today. We left Omaha about 7:15 AM and arrived at Fairfax Airport about noon. Our conversation en route bespoke a mutual enthusiasm for this new experience. Getting situated here was very similar to registration day at the University. We had to report to the Chief Petty Officer with our orders and get a student check-off list, which was nothing but a list of things which we had to do before attending class. Unhappily, we will be living out of our suitcases until next Tuesday. It seems the graduating class won't leave for the Southland until that time which means no lockers for some of us for a few days. As a matter of fact, we won't have regular bunks until Tuesday either. At present we lay our carcass on temporary cots. You should see my uniform! The pants were five inches too long, and the shirt sleeves were two inches unnecessary. As for my shorts, they hang down to my knees like the conservative 1890 bathing suits. However, apart from the fit, the clothing is very good. It is excellent quality and durable.

Shortly after our arrival several boys came up and introduced themselves. Among them were, Rickert of Bankers Life in D.M., Lyle Roberts of Tecumseh, Nebr, Hartzell of Albia, Ia, Bob Hayes, a Sig Chi from Iowa U, B. Runyan of Omaha, Carey, a brother Phi Psi from K.U.

(we exchanged grips, huzzah!) and several others. There seem to be some pretty good gents around here. And oh yes, I ran into Pete Moeller of Detroit who was a fellow law student at Iowa last year.

After supper Ken and I drove over to town and saw "Sundown," a just-fair movie.

Friday, Dec. 5, 1941

This morning we all took a bunch of written tests, to wit, an intellectual aptitude test, a mechanical aptitude test, at which I'm afraid I did not shine, and a biographical inventory question and answer sheet.

In the afternoon we marched over to the South hangar and heard some beetle browed old rascal lecture on the danger of carelessness around a propeller blade. It was well and humorously presented. We, also, learned a *little* about the construction and operation of a plane. Following this we lined up in the sick bay for typhoid shots and vaccination for small pox. I guess we get "shots" about every Friday. Reminds me of the way we used to herd the pigs together for vaccination when we were still farming.

Commander Wright phoned up from the office of the Flight Selection Board over in town and asked Ken & me to attend the final meeting of the K.C. quarterback club at the Continental Hotel tomorrow night. Francis Heydt also phoned to say hello & ask me out to dinner as soon as I get settled. Larry Winn called to ask if I would make a recorded interview for his sports broadcast to which I consented.

After supper Ken & I again went to town – and once again saw a rather punk movie. Following the show we dropped into the Drum Room of the President for refreshment, then ambled over to the Town Royale. Whom should we run into there but Donnie Allen, Sid Brody, & Homer Bradshaw all of D. Moines and stationed at Ft. Leavenworth with the observation corps. Said meeting augurs a bit of revelry when we can get together again in the not too distant future.

Finally, we got back to the barracks, getting in ahead of the mob by about an hour and half, of whose arrival we were all too audibly aware about 2:30 AM. Barrack life is quite tolerable, but hardly a place in which I would want to bring up young Lord Fauntleroy.

I should have mentioned that I ran into Lou Rich of the D.M. Reg. & Trib. in the lobby of the President Hotel; also, that I called Katie

Smith for a date next Thurs. night. Paul Wolfe gave me her number and recommended her quite highly. Certainly, she sounded good over the phone.

Saturday, Dec. 6, 1941

Spent about an hour & a half in the Christian Science reading room this morning. It is located in the Waldheim building and provides an atmosphere most conducive to effective study. It will be about the only place where I can find the peace & quiet requisite for decent Science study.

Wrote several letters in the forepart of the afternoon, then Ken & I went to another punk show. We met Commander Wright, Dr. Robinson, & Ensign Jones in the lobby of the Continental Hotel about 7 oclock. The banquet turned out to be a much larger affair than I had anticipated. It was given for the second successive year in honor of the most outstanding player in the Missouri Valley & Big Six Conference. This year the trophy went to Bob Stueber of Missouri U. The rules committee was meeting this weekend, also, so there were coaches, officials, newspaper & radio men from all over this area. I saw many, many old acquaintances and met almost as many more new men. There is no better group than a gathering of men connected with college athletics.

Sunday, Dec. 7, 1941

Attended services at 1st church at 9th & Forest on the East side.

News of Japan's unprovoked attack on Pearl Harbor came over the radio about three oclock. About a third of us were lounging around the barracks. Everybody accepted it quite unemotionally, seemingly more interested in whether liberties would be curtailed than whether the U.S. could retaliate effectively. Must confess that my own feelings were somewhat similar to the rest. However, I wish my training were already over, & I was ready to go. I am torn between a desire not to miss out on anything, and a feeling that I am better off here.

We saw Sally Rand put on her bubble & fan dance at the Towers Theatre tonight. Can't recommend it very highly. Doesn't begin to compare with Gypsy Rose Lee's performance at the Worlds Fair in

New York. The latter's act bordered on the artistic it was so cleverly done. That is heresy coming from a moral man, but, nonetheless, true.

Monday, Dec. 8, 1941

I was assigned to barrack patrol duty this morning. It is the easiest detail possible; gave me an opportunity to read Life's report on the Navy & to write a long letter to Bill Stuart. Between 9 & 10 I was relieved by another man while my section heard a lecture on the use & care of a parachute. Very completely, & humorously, presented by an enlisted man. In the afternoon we drilled for an hour, then went to radio class, next to trig class, & finally heard a lecture on radio instruments. Enjoyed it all immensely. Very glad that I enlisted when I did. Played some touch football around five o'clock. It felt good to get some exercise again. Tonight I drove over to town & made a recorded interview for brother Larry Winn's sports broadcast.

It was interesting to watch the reaction of the different men as we all sat around listening to President Roosevelt's request that Congress declare war on Japan. Nearly everyone accepted the situation quite matter-of-factly and made little comment. Some, of course, feel that, perhaps, they would have done better not to have enlisted in a service bound to see immediate action. The rest are resigned to their unavoidable duty. One man said he had already become a sort of fatalist about the whole matter. This is a quite common, & normal, feeling in all branches of the service, I believe. In speaking in behalf of our declaration of war isolationist Ham Fish said on the floor of Congress "that at the proper time he would report for active duty, preferably with colored troops; that *no sacrifice* was too great in the present emergency": It was the most thoughtless & impolitic remark I have ever heard!! Heard over the radio tonight that 500 unidentified planes were over San Francisco. Seems incredible that the Japanese would come so far. Really don't believe the report can be authentic.

As for my own feelings now that the U.S. & Japan are at war I shall say this. I expected it but not quite so soon. I expected to be faced with the prospect of serious combat action when I joined up. I am ready for whatever it may be my duty to do. I feel much as I used to when the football season started & I knew Minnesota was on the schedule. That is, I realize what is coming up but probably won't be appreciably keyed up until actually moving onto the firing line.

Tuesday, Dec. 9, 1941

Apart from picking up around the grounds we did almost nothing at all during the morning. This base is pretty crowded now which makes it difficult to keep everyone busy with the limited facilities available. It is rumored that three new instructors are coming aboard; if so the flying tempo will be stepped up even more.

Rec'd several letters on the 1st delivery which had been forwarded from Omaha. Among them was a short letter from President Hancher of the U. of Iowa. A reprint of an editorial in the Mason City Globe Gazette by the Daily Iowan prompted his note of counsel & encouragement. The editorial dealt with my short Armistice Day speech delivered in front of Old Capitol. Earl Hall was most generous in his remarks & made me most happy. I had hoped that that particular talk would get some recognition, & the fact that it did just as I was leaving for the service was extraordinarily nice for me. Also received news through a letter from the folks that B. Hobbs may soon be at this base. How wonderful that would be! I have written Gus urging him to try to get Bob to enter this present class a week or so late if at all possible.

Ken & I have now attended two classes of radio & trig. I think the former is apt to prove the more troublesome.

How ridiculously shortsighted this sudden war has made the isolationists look. How must Lindbergh, Wheeler, Nye, etc, feel now that enemy war planes have actually flown over San Francisco. Even Hoover was off the beam, I'm afraid. He was so interested in our danger to the east that he forgot Japan almost completely. It seems quite evident that this war, now spread to every corner of the earth, is being engineered in its grand strategy directly from Berlin. The Axis powers are, in truth, attempting to march around the seas. If Germany gets control of the French Navy the situation will be truly serious. Oh, that this country & England had had the courage to forestall all this when Japan 1st went into Manchukuo, & Italy into Abyssinia. Sacrificing principle to temporary expediency is always costly in the long run. There is no correct road except straight ahead.

Quiet descended on these barracks about 9 PM as we all gathered around to listen to Pres. Roosevelts fireside chat. He was all too right when he said that in fighting Japan we were fighting Germany, and that a defeat for Russia in the Caucasus was a blow against us.

I cannot help but apostrophize here and commend Willkie on his stand since he was defeated for the presidency in the fall of 1940. He spoke & acted as I believe the whole Republican party should have. He showed courage, foresight, & patriotism in the highest sense. Power to him! And lastly, what irreparable harm John L. Lewis did to the prestige of labor by his selfish action in the captive-mine disputes – & this even though the mediation board granted his point.

Wednesday – Dec.10

This day started in no uncertain manner. Some bay-bellied sailor jarred us to consciousness at 6 this morning with a "hit the deck, men" that echoed & reechoed across the barracks. We piled out to uncomfortably realize the temperature had dropped to about 15 above during the night. In fact, I discovered that I had been shivering all night. The guy next to me said my bed-legs shook like a castanet from four on. The crowning climax to all this came when some delightfully dispositioned officer decreed we should take our calisthenics in our shirt-sleeves. Now, if you have never stood on the concrete runway of a flying field in the early hours of a December morn with a stiff wind from the north bawling by your ears, you can't appreciate what I am saying. The only thing I know that can compare to this frigid experience is sitting in a duck blind facing a north wind on a similar morning.

I cannot refrain from making this little observation: We have six toilets, arranged so that three face each other, for about 110 men. Now, it seems to be common for man to feel it necessary to relieve himself right after breakfast. At that time most of the men have not yet combed their hair, but ARE having their first cigarette of the day. I do not have many aristocratic leanings, but, for some reason or another, I do like privacy when assuming the undignified position necessary for a bowel movement. However, with no other alternative available I consistently find myself sitting on a cold stool opposite some lugubrious faced co-student & surrounded by waiting aspirants. If I have painted a relatively clear picture you will agree with me that such a situation is the epitome of the lowest form of democratic relationship among men.

This morning we did very little. We helped push airplanes from the runway back into the hangar, and that is about all. The afternoon was taken up with about the same routine as yesterday p.m. It is interesting to note my enthusiasm for common military drill as compared with my complete distaste for R.O.T.C. my first two years at Iowa. Radio went much better today. Should get the hang of it before long.

Finished up my first article for the Register & Tribune at noon today. Took it in to Col. Peters for censoring about 4 oclock. He expressed satisfaction with it, saying it was well written. My hope now is that MacDonald, managing editor of the Register, will see fit to print it.

Inspection of base personnel is scheduled for tomorrow so Ken & I went to town for [a] haircut. As a matter of economy we headed for the barber college on 9th & Main. It was some experience. I never saw or felt, such laborious indecision. He, the barber, reminded me of my early days in the school carpenter shop trying to plane a walnut board down level. Just as I would get one end to looking pretty good I would discover that I had neglected the other end. So it was with this young student in the barber college. I hardly need add that he didn't come out even. I wear my cap whenever possible although it is far from a flattering top-piece. When he started to shave over my ears & down the sides of my neck I almost froze in the chair. I didn't suppose anyone could do so much damage to my tonsorial appearance in twenty minutes – and I was no Rob't Taylor when I went in. It was the 1st time I ever risked severance of my neck from my shoulders for two bits.

You know, at best, eating is an ungraceful activity. But when 8 or 10 men are rapidly partaking of their sustenance at the same table it is some sight. Usually 4 men or so are facing each other as they eat. It brings back memories of my days on the farm as I watched the porkers get their feeding. I have noted that some of the most dignified officers lose all semblance of superior rank or excellency of movement while eating. Knowing my own shortcoming in this art, I grieve to think of the impression I must give.

Thursday, Dec 11, 1941

There are only about two gripes that I have about the life here thus far. One is the long time you usually have to wait in line before you can get anything to eat, and the other is the mad scramble for wash bowls in the head each morning. There are only 12 wash bowls for over 100 men – and they are all in the same head. I can't get over what a peculiar name they give to the toilet around here – it is known as the "head."

During the morning some vacant headed sailor assigned Pettit, Tamisiea, & me to wash windows outside. The temperature stood at about 15° above. Not exactly a desirable work detail.

The regular routine of classes took our time in the afternoon followed by personnel inspection at 1515. Inspection remarks by Ensign Adams & a mimeographed sheet of delinquencies calling for demerits handed out afterward augurs for more rigid discipline around here from now on.

At seven oclock Ken & I called at the Penn-Marshall ap'ts on the south side for our dates. Katie Smith, the girl I escorted, was very much alright. Had a good time but it was a ten oclock night which made it all too brief. Have another date for Sun. night. Pettit didn't fare quite so well. I feel a bit guilty for the subtle ribbing I gave him back at the barracks afterward.

Discovered that Pettit's flight instructor, Don Carney, is from Rockhurst & was on the All-Star squad in Chicago at the same time I was. He, evidently, is a much better flyer than football player.

While eating at the Hereford Grill prior to calling for Katie & her roommate I ran into Vern Anderson of the Register & Tribune. This is the second R & T. man I have seen down here during the past week. I wonder what their business is down this way.

Snowed intermittently throughout the day accompanied by a high wind.

Friday – Dec 12, 1941

Spent most of the morning swabbing decks & cleaning woodwork. It was field day, which comes once a month and calls for complete cleaning of everything.

Col. Peters appointed me section leader for section 50 which is one half of the boys in the new class. It is an appointment of no great distinction but will be good experience. I was glad to get it. There is a swell group of fellows in this section.

At 11 AM I was in the Link trainer, an artificial device which simulates the control necessary for an airplane. I did not do too well, but feel that the second opportunity will see a big improvement.

Ken received sad news today. His uncle, John Green, a young officer, stationed at Hickham field in Hawaii, was killed by the 1st Japanese bombing attack. Such unhappy incidents as this are bringing this war close to home clear out here in the midwest.

Ken & I saw another poor show last night, & then dropped up to the Town Royale. A bunch of the fellows were in there, and we had a fine time. On the way out I was stopped by a Mr. Barrett who said he knew the folks when he lived in Adel.

Received a letter & a clipping from Bob Hogan. The clipping was an article he had written about me when I entered the service. It is as nice a piece as has ever been written about me – thanks Bob.

Saturday – Dec. 13, 1941

Heretofore, we have had Sat. & Sun. free but starting today we are flying & going to school seven days a week. Under the circumstances that is as it should be.

Ken & I went to a movie after supper. Finally saw a pretty decent bill. About 11 oclock we dropped in on the dance thrown by the Navy Mothers for the service men every Sat. night. I'm afraid there wasn't enough attraction there to draw me again.

Hard to realize that we are at war.

Sunday, Dec. 14.

Followed our regular weekday routine. Hard to realize that it was Sunday – no extra sleep in the morning, no paper, no time for church. Will plan to attend Sunday evening services from now on if it can be worked out.

Had a date with Katie Smith last night. Fairly enjoyable evening considering it was a ten oclock night.

Monday, Dec. 15.

Followed regular routine. Classes are in the morning this week for our wing, and flying in the p.m.

This base is taking on a more military aspect each day. The colonel has decreed that there shall be a student watch from 1600 till 800 – which is from 4 PM till 8 AM. The students are to alternate two hour watches throughout the night. He must pace the barracks from one end to the other, both below and topside. Our weekday liberties have been cut to every other night, and ten oclock seems to be the curfew even on weekends now.

Still haven't heard from the D. Moines Register. Sure would like to know whether they used my articles. Can't imagine what happened to Bob's letter that mother said she forwarded. Bob is probably wondering why in the hell I don't answer.

Ken and I accepted an invitation to attend an Iowa alumnae gathering at Rockheath Inn for dinner at 7:15 P.M. There was quite a group on hand and rather full of Xmas cheer. We had a fine time and regretted leaving so early. The meal was excellent – fried chicken, sweet potatoes, green peas, biscuits, etc. – it was wonderful. When I finished my plate was so full of chicken bones they could hardly carry it away. On the way back we got on the wrong road discovering it only after we were quite aways out of K.C. going the wrong way. Rockheath Inn was on the far eastern outskirts of town to begin with so that left us about 40 minutes to get back to the base on time. Feverishly we inquired directions, finally getting on the road that would take us downtown. I never engineered such a wild ride in my life. We were fortunate not to get pinched. We were exceeding the speed limit by far, running the lights, & everything else. Happily, we sneaked in just under the wire.

Tuesday, Dec. 16.

Ken went up for his 1st period of actual flight instruction today. He came back thoroughly enthused and feeling that he could master the art of flying alright. Two other boys in my section also were up today. I felt just a bit left-out. It was a feeling similar to that when everybody gets to scrimmage except you. You champ at the bit, anxious for a chance to show your stuff.

This afternoon a medium sized Navy flying boat sailed in for refueling. It was a beautiful ship and gave me a very definite thrill. How I hope that one of these days I can qualify to fly such planes. Several enlisted men rushed out to help the pilots out of their gear and to carry in their duffel bags. Half the base personnel crowded around to see the ship & the pilots. It reminded me for all the world of the way the redcaps & interested fans gather around the football heroes as they get off the train in Chicago. A man must have patience around here. Everything is extremely impersonal. It will be a real test for my character &

temperament. It is the first time in a good long time that I haven't had an immediate opportunity to show my full ability. I must qualify that – law school presented a similar situation, but the service tops even that experience for difficulty of recognition.

Lolled around the barracks during the evening for about the first time this year. If I could find some place suitable for a half hour or so of quiet reading & study each day I would have no major complaint, whatsoever, concerning this life.

Expecting to hear from Bob Hobbs tomorrow. It would be grand if he could enter with the class coming in on Thursday.

Wednesday, Dec 17.

I was scheduled for my last 30 minutes in the Link trainer this morning, but, unhappily, I was scratched because Thatcher was sick. Thatcher is my instructor, and a good one from what everybody says. Ken was up again today. His enthusiastic reports make me eager to have a try at it.

Navy & Army bombers come through here quite frequently. They are beautiful & adventurous looking ships. How I would like to climb into one of them and head for the Pacific area!!

Didn't see anything of B. Hobbs today. Possibly he will show tomorrow. It will be great to see him again.

All goes well – this is a fine experience – and it will get "FINER."

Thursday – Dec. 18

Getting quite impatient to fly. I have never suffered from such periods of enforced idleness as when I am out on the *line*. It is a bit difficult to reconcile myself to the petty detail to which I am assigned all too frequently. Here I have had 4 years of regular college work & a year of law, and yet today I was picking up cigarette butts around the ad building like a common snipe hunter. I do not actually rebel at such duty, but now & then a bit of humorous cynicism sneaks into my thought.

Bob Hobbs took his final physical in Kansas City today. He came out to the base about five oclock, and we had a fine talk together. He hasn't changed a bit since I last saw him in Denver in the summer of 1940. It wasn't possible for him to get into the class that came aboard today, but he will be on hand when the Jan. 2nd class comes in.

Gene Tunney, head of the physical ed. program for the Navy, came on to the base this morning. Cap't. Tomlinson mustered the entire base personnel in the south hangar at 12:30 to listen to a short talk by Tunney. The reactions of the boys to what he said varied considerably, but most of them, including myself, weren't too impressed. His points were pretty well taken, but he sermonized a little too much. In short, he bluntly told everyone to cut down on the smoking, avoid liquor, and shun the prostitutes. Naturally, I agree with his beliefs but moralizing to service men is pretty hard for anyone to get away with. Judging from what Cap't. Tomlinson said after Tunney finished, I gathered that he believed one of the reasons the Navy was caught napping at Pearl Harbor was because they were spending too much time on liquor & women and not enough on naval business. I should add that Tunney certainly makes a fine appearance. He is tall, broad, and handsome with a very erect bearing.

It is against my nature & inclination to indict a service with such a fine tradition as the U.S. Navy. But, by golly, I'm getting pretty disgusted with the red tape, inefficiency, and disorganization around this base. I am quite aware that it is a difficult situation, that the facilities are overcrowded, and that several of the officers are products of 90 day training and therefore aren't "up" on everything they should be. However, nobody around here seems to know what the hell is going on. I have never seen so many orders & counter-mands in my life. It seems to me we spend more time on inspections, swabbing the decks, and cleanup detail than we do on anything else. I have been here two weeks and the highest in the air I have been is a top bunk. At the beginning of one [of] our manuals is Kiplings poem "If" with the following line underscored – "if you can wait without being tired by waiting." Well, brother Kipling I can't; not anymore – I'm plenty tired with waiting – and if you wouldn't be "you are a better man than I, Gunga Din!!"

Last night Ken & I saw Walt Disney's new movie starring Dumbo, the elephant with the large ears. It was extremely entertaining. What they can do with these animated cartoons is marvelous! I found myself sympathizing and exulting with Dumbo's changing fortunes just as if he were an human acquaintance.

Ken McDonald, managing editor of the R. & Tribune, wrote to say he hadn't used either of the two articles I sent in. He explained they weren't far off, but were just a little "thin"; they needed a little more "meat" & punch. He did, however, enclose a token payment of $2.50 and encouraged me to try again. Frankly, I thought what I had sent in was quite printable. I don't know yet whether I shall try again. It shouldn't be too hard to write a little more seriously, but I have so little time when I can type that I don't know whether it is worth it.

Saturday, Dec. 20.

For two weeks I did everything around here but fly. The highest I ever got into the air was a top bunk. But today, happy date, I had my first hour of instruction. For my first experience in handling a plane I think I got along pretty well. We did 90, 180, & 360° turns, S turns along a road, climbing & descending spirals – just simple maneuvers, but, nonetheless, requiring close attention for proper execution. My instructor's name is Thatcher (Lt. J.G.). He seems to be a mighty fine fellow. Thus far he has been soft spoken both in giving encouragement and in dealing out his criticism. I can tell that he is going to insist on precision and exactness. That is fair enough. It should be easier to check for the other instructors if I can satisfy him.

Only solo students are flying tomorrow. Will give me a chance to take it easy, read, and get to church.

Am looking forward to getting home for Xmas day.

Sunday – Dec. 21.

Spent a rather leisurely day which was much to my liking. Lyle Roberts, Jerry Rickert, Ken & I went up town for supper and then to a movie. We picked up a friend of Lyle's named Ross Miller who used to be on the faculty at Nebraska and is now connected with the Hereford Cattle Breeding Association. Roberts & Rickert are two of the better boys down here.

Monday – Dec. 22.

Had my second & last shot at the Link trainer this morning. My performance was much, much better than the first time.

Went into Col. Peters office about 1100 to see about going home for

Xmas. Made the mistake of leaning on his desk. Believe you me that won't happen again.

Ray Sharp, a boy who bunks next to me, and who is a fine sort of guy, had a minor accident along about 1600. While taxiing into position for his takeoff his plane hit a mudhole and nosed over on its propeller. The way the crash siren screamed out you would have thought he had nosedived from 1500'!

Tuesday – Dec. 23.

Not much doing apart from the regular routine.

In the evening we went into Kansas City for awhile. Ran into the D. Moines boys stationed at Ft. Leavenworth at the Town Royale about 8 oclock. From the T. Royale we drifted to the Pink Elephant and finally to the College Inn. Not the best evening in the world but there isn't much else to do around K.C.

Wednesday – Dec. 24.

Went up for my second hour of instruction. This time we did spins, stalls, and spirals in for landings with a cut-gun from 1000'. I found that spins gave me quite a thrill. Once again I think that I did quite well. If I were to get an hours work on landings and takeoffs I think I could solo without too much trouble. Perhaps, I am getting too cocky – the next couple of hours will tell.

Left Fairfax for Omaha about 1200. We only got leave until 2200 Xmas night, but it was apt to be the last chance I would have to get home for a good long time so I took it. K Pettit and three Omaha boys, Jack Tamisiea, Carleton Knowles, & Christiansen rode up with me.

How good it was to get home for awhile. Mother had a fine dinner for us Wednesday night and included Bob Hobbs in. Everyone was well and happy although Ben looked a bit peaked. I guess he had a very busy & strenuous quarter at school. I rather think he will be enlisting in the Navy Air Corps one of these days. If so, they will permit him to get his degree in June before calling him for training. I don't know of any better opportunity under the circumstances.

What a significant thing is the meeting now taking place between Prime Minister Churchill & President Roosevelt at the White House! Henceforward, the U.S. & Gt. Britain should work hand in hand for the freedom & security of the world. In my mind it can't be otherwise. Destiny will decree that the English speaking people shoulder this responsibility; I am sure of it. What a career Churchill has had! I have had few heroes in my short life experience, but he definitely commands my admiration & respect. He has been a man of action and of resolution. He has spoken and acted in accordance with a long run principle. He has not kowtowed to tyranny nor sacrificed fundamental truths to expediency. He does not yield! He epitomizes the staying power of the British. And what a speaker! Every word he utters makes my spine tingle.

In the nature of military service it is very difficult to keep posted on the news. But I gather that things aren't going too well in the Pacific. Frankly, I am wondering what our Navy, of which I have heard so much, is doing.

What a magnificent job the Russians are doing! It now looks, however, as if they will undoubtedly have an army intact when all this ends. What is to keep them from overrunning all of Europe? If Russia continues to build her world prestige with military victories, what a problem the U.S. will have with Communists in this country! Must England & the U.S. end up fighting that outfit, too? It looks like a pretty rough & rocky road ahead.

Thursday, Dec. 25

Christmas day 1941 – peace on earth, good will toward men is having a hard go of it these days. However, I am sure that this present world war which has engulfed the U.S. these past few weeks did not spoil the Kinnick family's enjoyment of this holy day. I think the world situation only caused us to hold it that much more dear.

Happily enough our whole family, individually & collectively, faces troublesome situations without any display of emotion or self-pity. I could not help noticing, however, that father was more serious than I had ever seen him before, and that mother had tears in her eyes, when I bid them goodbye about 3 P.M. When I shall be able to get home again, I don't know. It will be interesting to see where I am located next Dec. 25th.

We had to drive pretty slowly part of the way back to Kansas City. The highway between Omaha & Falls City, Nebr. was covered with four or five inches of slush & snow making it very slippery going.

About dusk we hit clear pavement and proceeded at a faster pace the rest of the way.

And so ended my brief Xmas leave.

Friday, Dec. 26.

Was scheduled for instruction the third hour during the morning, but heavy weather prevented my going up.

Took part in the delightful custom known around here as "field day," to wit, clean & scrub the entire barracks. Very dreary pastime, and a once a week demand, instead of monthly, as I previously thought.

Practiced some radio after supper. Am not picking that up as quickly as I would like to.

Saturday – Dec. 27

Finished my third hour of instruction this A.M. We spent the entire time spiraling in for landings from 1000'. I was no star this trip, but feel that next time I will be able to handle them alright.

Had an excited letter from Bob saying that his orders had arrived and that they directed him to report Jan 24th instead of the second. I phoned Comm'd'r Wright about it, and he assured me it was all a mistake – that Bob would be in the Jan. 2d class ok.

Saw the screen version of "Louisiana Purchase" after supper. It was not as good as the stage production, but still very entertaining.

There was a good deal of excitement around here about 11 AM. Boyd Klopfenstein, one of the students, fell out of his airplane as his instructor was circling the field for a landing. It seems he forgot to fasten his safety belt and when the pilot nosed the plane down suddenly Boyd was left stranded in midair. Fortunately, he had the presence of mind to pull his rip cord immediately – which was absolutely necessary since they were only 600' up. Some experience for the 5th hour of flying.

Sunday – Dec. 28

Just solo students were flying today. The rest of us were secure at 8 oclock this morning. Went to church in the morning, wrote letters in the afternoon, and saw the movie "Corsican Bros" in the evening. They staged one of the best duels I have ever seen.

Monday – Dec. 29.

A low ceiling forced cancellation of my scheduled instruction flight. Kind of a dull day when there is no flying.

For some unknown reason the battery in my car was dead today. That means a battery and a muffler that must be fixed. It is a good thing a dividend on my stock came in today. Incidentally, that stock has gone down 5 or 6 points since I bought it. I'd just as soon see it recover one of these days.

Tuesday – Dec. 30

Finished up my fourth hour of instruction today. Thoroughly enjoyed it and did pretty well. Even Thatcher said I had a good hour. Practiced my first landings toward the end of the hour. Believe that next hour I should get the hang of them pretty well.

Served as student officer of the day this 24 hours. Not a very interesting job but good practice for future officer responsibility.

I was disappointed that the Register didn't carry a full text of Churchill's speech before the U.S. Congress a few days ago. Judging from the excerpts he did his usual masterful job. In my estimation he and Lincoln outrank all other statesmen in the art of expression in the English language.

Wednesday – Dec. 31

Foggy weather prohibited flying both in the morning and in the afternoon. In a five word radio test I managed to get the full five the second time it was given. In fact, somehow or another, I managed to take 36 characters in a row without an error.

The new year went out with a bang here in K. City last night. At 12 midnight the downtown streets were packed with a milling crowd of inebriates celebrating in the customary American way. It was a miserable night – it began raining about 9 oclock and in the course of an hour it turned to sleet and snow. Ken and I stayed downtown just long enough to see the New Year in then went back to the base.

It has been interesting to note the reaction of the movie audiences when the U.S. flag or service men appear in the newsreels. Spontaneous and prolonged applause always is given now that war has been declared. A shot of Churchill & Roosevelt received the same approbation. Old Winnie has done a fine job of selling himself – and England – to the American people.

Thursday – Jan. 1st, 1942

New Years Day 1942 – it dawned cold and blustery, increasing in severity throughout the day. Such weather is prophetic of the times, I fear. The year 1942 will be a critical period for the democracies. Wishful thinking, unfounded optimism won't meet the test. Individually and collectively we must face the future with grim determination and courageous staying power born of a confident faith in God and in the destiny of freedom loving nations. Ours must be a daily resolve to fight through to complete victory whatever the sacrifice must needs be.

Saw a movie again tonight, and the newsreel showed Churchill giving his address before a joint session of Congress. I have said much concerning his incomparable ability of expression, but I have not said enough about his natural flare for the dramatic. He is a colorful figure in his every move and utterance. But what completely wins you over is his boyish, genuine smile. He loves crowds and the crowds love him. Each to the other is a happy complement.

A few quotations that appeal to me follow: "I would rather fail in a cause that is bound to triumph than to triumph in a cause that was sure to lose."

> – ?
> "If you can talk with crowds & keep your virtue,
> Or walk with Kings – nor lose the common touch"
> – R. Kipling.
> "In war, Resolution, in victory, Magnanimity,
> in defeat, Defiance, in peace, [Goodwill]"
> – W. Churchill.

Friday – Jan 2.

The storm of the last day and a half left our flying field completely covered with a sheet of ice. There was no flying in the morning, and in the afternoon only those flew who had checks coming up.

Am beginning to get the hang of radio, I believe. It will be a lot of fun as soon as I can take it rapidly.

Bob Hobbs got in about four oclock. Thanks to a whispered word to one of the boys in the ground school office, he will be bunking in the same wing as Ken & I. Bob & I went to a movie in K.C., Mo. which caused me to miss a board talk by Lt. Thatcher, my instructor. I was aware that he was going to give one the next time he had the watch, but I neglected to find out when that would be. It was an excellent lecture, the boys say.

Had my car towed in for battery and muffler repair. Should be able to pick it up tomorrow night. I trust the bill won't look like the nat'l debt.

Saturday – Jan 3.

Our section drilled with rifles for the first time this morning. Man, how heavy those babies get. I can now understand how a twenty mile march carrying a gun and pack would be quite a workout. Never realized before how funny a man's hip action looks while marching – at least when wearing a tight fitting pair of military pants and viewed from behind. I couldn't help noticing how the motion of each man's buttocks differed even though all were executing the same maneuver. In fact viewed from a posterior angle I found that most of the fellows presented a personality entirely at variance with that shown from the front. He who from a normal angle of observation appeared virile and determined was apt to seem quite effeminate and prissy when his walking movement was studied from the rear; he who looked relaxed and at ease from the front looked taut and strained from behind; and he who looked firm and strong was apt to appear weak and dissipated to the man walking directly behind him. Rather a bourgeoise observation, but interesting, don't you think?

The first bomber turned out of the North American plant across the road was given a trial run yesterday. It was a twin motored, medium sized job with tricycle landing gear. It presented a magnificent sight as it roared north down the runway for its maiden takeoff. The entire personnel of both the plant and this training base gathered along the edge of the field to watch. The huge gray goose circled for altitude and then thundered back over the middle of the field at about 800 feet. Man, how it did move along, growling out a prophetic warning to our enemies. This Navy base is to be moved out to Gardner(?), Kans. in the spring, I believe, so that the bomber plant may have full use of this field for testing purposes when its production line rolls into high gear.

Had my fifth hour of instruction this afternoon. It was bitter cold, the thermometer hanging around zero, so I wore a face mask which covered everything except my eyes. I looked like the Masked Marvel or the Sky Devil with this protective covering over my facial features, but it very effectively kept me warm. I did a miserable job the forepart of the hour. My goggles fogged over badly right after I took off, and after trying unsuccessfully to adjust them so they would stay clear I lifted them up on my forehead and finished the hour without them. Didn't think I had done very well, but in talking with my instructor afterwards he indicated that I was coming along quite well. Perhaps, in this experience as in most others previous to this my judgement of my performance will be under the evaluation given to it by others. It is nice to have it that way – fewer disappointments arise.

Bob and I took in Duke Ellingtons stage show at the Mainstreet after supper. Not a very good entertainment and the movie with it was worse. It was getting colder & colder when we returned to the base.

Sunday – Jan 4.

It was even colder yet this morning – 5 below according to reports. I started off to church about ten oclock, but unhappily the battery in my car was dead once again. It must be shot because I just had it charged up yesterday. Decided to take the bus and trolley car in lieu of a car. Rather a long, cold trip to the east side of the downtown district in K.C. Mo. There may be dirtier and poorer street cars than the ones I rode, but I don't know where they are. Stayed in town for lunch, read the D.M. Register until 2 oclock, then went up to the Reading Room for an hour. Finally got back to the base about 3:30 in the afternoon.

Bob and I saw the movie "One Foot in Heaven" after supper. It was a thoroughly fine show – enjoyed it very much.

Monday – Jan 5.

The new phys. ed instructors who came aboard a few days ago inaugurated their program this morning. We now arise at 5:45 AM, endure a half hour of calisthenics, and muster at 7:30 & 7:45 instead of 7:30 & 8:00 oclock. Finished my sixth hour of instruction this morning. Spent the entire period on landings. Believe that I mastered them pretty well. Landing is one of the most interesting phases of flying – as well as highly important.

Had my car hauled in again to find out why the battery goes down so quickly. Made the mistake of leaving my locker keys with the car keys. Couldn't get into my locker for shaving material, pajamas, etc – bit of an inconvenience.

Discovered that Walt Rissmiller, another fellow law student at Iowa, is in the new class. Pretty good guy – will be one of the few fellows that Bob should enjoy. His class seems to include an inordinate number of "sad apples."

Tuesday – Jan 6

Am getting pretty close to a check – seven hours of instruction have now been completed – only two to go. Flew to Sherman field at Leavenworth this morning. Made several landings cross wind which was fine practice.

The garage brought my car back tonight with the good news that the battery was ok – just a loose wire or connection, I guess. Will know for sure tomorrow when I try to start it after it has been standing all night.

The female reporter of shapely proportions who took my picture yesterday morning in full winter flight gear left several prints at the base tonight for me. Am well pleased with both the shots she took. Will be interested to see what she says in her article which appears in the Kansan tomorrow.

Called Merle McKay tonight, a gal of comely appearance and interesting figure who used to go to Iowa. Unhappily, she wasn't in, but I shall call again.

The cold weather continues. True, it doesn't make for comfortable flying, but, nonetheless, I like it – if it doesn't continue for too long.

The changing seasons of the midwest – the intense heat in summer, bitter cold in winter, and unsurpassable beauty and invigorating weather of fall & spring – is what makes it an interesting place to live. Only robust and virile people can live in such a climate and enjoy it.

Section 45 & 46 left for the pool at New Orleans today. What a happy, enthusiastic group they were! May a like lot be mine during the forepart of February. I hope I have the pleasure of running into Sharp, Wright, Roberts, Rickert, and several others again sometime. They are all fine fellows.

Pettit soloed today. How relieved & carefree he feels tonight. He presents quite a contrast to his temperament last night when the pressure was on. I am glad for him. He wants to make the grade intensely.

Wednesday – Jan 7

What a jolt I received this morning! My instructor, Mr. Thatcher, was grounded for running into the tail end of an army plane up at Sherman Field. This means that I will be assigned a new instructor, probably Mr. Bergen, who has something of a reputation as a tough customer – at least a very profane talker. However, I like his looks and believe that I will get along ok even though the change is coming at the end of my seventh hour. I regret very much Mr. Thatcher's plight. He is a fine fellow, and a man under whom I enjoyed working. Everyone seems to agree that he is a fine flyer and instructor, but has been plagued by hard luck ever since he came on the base. I guess he washed out a plane last July, has hit barrels along the runway several times, and now this last accident brought the axe. My most urgent hope now is that I'll get the rest of my hours very soon. Sure do want to solo within the next few days. About half of my section is now safely past its flight requirements.

As a matter of fact this has been a kind of disappointing day all the way around. My car, once again, would not start because of a weak battery. I am about ready to sell the car here in Kansas City and be free of the difficulty. Second thought prompts me to take a deep breath, stick out my chin and persevere until the skies clear again.

Still extremely cold – the forecast is for ten below tomorrow morning. Don't mind it so much during the day, but I haven't slept warmly for three successive nights. Two blankets isn't enough when some of these fresh air fiends in the top bunks open wide the windows. Nothing is more acutely uncomfortable than to wake up at three in the morning shivering like a hairless puppy with no more cover within reach.

Thursday, Jan 8

Thatcher is grounded for sure, and it looks like Bergen will be my new instructor. Hope he gives me a few emergencies – haven't had any as yet.

Finally had to buy a new battery for my car. The expense was rather painful, but it is a relief to have it in good running order again.

Things continue to go along pretty well. In a short while now we'll be heading south – and warm weather; light breezes, etc.

Friday – Jan 9

Bergen came in like a lamb & went out like a lion yesterday morning. During the forepart of the hour he was as soft spoken and encouraging as could be desired, but the last fifteen minutes he filled with more profanity than I have heard in a long time. He wants me to glide in for landings much faster than Thatcher did. Believe I shall be able to meet his requirements better next time.

Scrubbed woodwork, swabbed floors, and polished lockers for two hours this afternoon. Must confess that such drudgery dims for the moment a man's enthusiasm for the service.

Kauffman of the Star (K.C. Mo) interviewed me for five minutes over their radio station at 10:30 P.M. Col. Peters gave me special liberty until 11:30 P.M. It was good to get out for an up-town meal with all the trimmings.

An enlisted man by the name of Brostrom gave us an hour talk on Navy personnel which developed into a pep talk of the highest calibre. It was enthusiastically and well presented. What a joy it is to hear a man who truly loves his service exhort others to imbibe of the same spirit. He pointed out that we students are to become officers and urged us to realize right now what obligations and responsibilities such a position entails. He emphasized how important it is to gain the respect and affection of the men under you – then with conviction he stated that with the good Lord and the men on your side you can't lose. He expressed my sentiments exactly – but I would add this rule for becoming a good officer. You shouldn't ask your men to do what you won't do yourself. Where there is a dirty or dangerous job to be done a good leader is the first to volunteer.

Saturday – Jan 10

My ninth and last hour of dual instruction has now been finished. It was a good hour – even Bergen said very little. On Monday I shall check – and then solo. I am not perturbed – tests of all kinds should be viewed as opportunities to prove your merit, not as bugaboos to be avoided.

Several of the boys in my section have already soloed; several more will get their check on Mon. & Tues. Our small group remains intact except for one man, Stafford, who washed a couple of days ago. It is a sad day for those who can't make the grade, who are told they don't have an aptitude for flying.

Took 6.8 on a 7 w.p.m. radio test. Not bad – but am a little disappointed. Was rather sure I could take them solid at that rate.

Sgt. Caldwell gave us a little O'Grady drill at 1 oclock. It was some satisfaction to me to be the last man standing. Thats where a leader should come out – on top.

Bob, Ken, & I had a huge dinner in town and then went to see the movie, H. M. Pulham, Esq – not too sharp. We all look forward to getting to town for a sumptuous meal now & then, however.

Sunday – Jan. 11

Church in the morning, lunch with Bob at the Hereford Grill, and then back to the barracks to leisurely read the D.M. Sunday Register.

Man, did I have a good deal this evening! By far the best since I have been in Kansas City. I am referring to my date with Merle McKay. She turned out to be just as comely, just as shapely, and just as nice as I had remembered her at Iowa. Her family lives on the Kansas side of K. City out quite a ways in a fine residential district. Her father travels for a wholesale coffee company and wasn't home, but her mother and two younger brothers were on hand. I was well impressed with the whole family and happy to learn that [they] were Christian Scientists as I had heard. I knocked at their door about 6:15 PM and was graciously asked to come in by Mrs. McKay. We all visited for an half hour or so then

Mrs. Mc. took the boys out to supper somewhere and left Merle and me to have sandwiches, milk, etc. in front of the fireplace by ourselves. Not bad, not bad – a fine home, good radio music, a pretty girl, and a fireplace fire, what could be better. Unhappily, since I had to be at the base by ten I was compelled to leave about 9:15. Would like to pursue this possibility a little further, but there are several things which militate against it. First, she has play practice every night in the week, second, I won't have any more free Sat. nights if I solo today because I'll be flying Sundays, thirdly, I have a haunting hunch she may be tied up with a certain Sigma Nu in D. Moines. The first two reasons will bother me considerably more than the third, however. Happy day – I sure could take a few more nights like that.

Can't help making the observation that the college athletes that I know of at this base are the ones who do the least bitching at work detail to be done and who most energetically attempt what is required of them. It is quite a relief to a section leader who is responsible for the completion of certain routine work to have a few such boys around.

Monday – Jan 12.

Today, finally and at last, I soloed. My check flights with Mr. Bergen and Mr. Jenkins were nothing to crow about, but happily they gave me upchecks. Almost before I could collect my thoughts the red sock was on the plane, and I was clambering in to start my solo. Takeoff, once around the field, and land, that is all there was to it. I was considerably less on edge for my solo than I was on my check flights. Following all this the flight office permitted me to go up for a full hour of solo. What a joy it was to cruise up and down the valley free from the intoning criticism of an instructor. Now I shall be able to experiment a little and really get the feel of flying. Am forced to confess that it is something of a relief to be successfully by this first barrier in my flying career.

Tuesday – Jan 13.

Was sorry to find that I wasn't scheduled to fly today. The quicker I can get in my solo hours the better chance I'll have to get home for a day or two before going south.

Bob and I went over to the radio room tonight. I got some excellent practice sending to him for about an hour and a half.

Wednesday – Jan 14.

Took 8 words a minute in radio this morning. After yesterday's performance it was quite a happy surprise. Hope I can keep it up.

Was permitted my second hour of solo this afternoon. Rather a sad exhibition, I'm afraid. There was a rather treacherous cross wind which made landings somewhat difficult. Certainly, I didn't have too much confidence on the few that I made. Judging from the number of ground loops today I wasn't the only one having trouble. As a matter of fact, it was a sad day all the way around for section 50. Haugebak was temporarily grounded for flying over the municipal airport, and part of Kansas City, Quillen & Hotchkiss ground looped, and Perkins got two downchecks – the latter will probably get extra hours, however.

Bob got his 1st hour of dual instruction today. Was quite enthusiastic over the prospect.

Thursday – Jan. 15.

President Roosevelt has a big, big job ahead of him. I have been pretty much in accord with his foreign policy, and I suppose a fellow shouldn't be too critical if he is remiss here & there in handling a situation of such magnitude. However, if he doesn't coordinate this defense effort and properly head the production supply angle pretty soon things aren't going to go so well. He has an excellent opportunity to further unify the nation and bolster the defense program efficiency by appointing a couple of Republicans to important posts. The men I have in mind are Willkie and Hoover. The former is of proven merit and has been big enough to support Roosevelt's foreign policies despite the censure of the old heads of the G.O.P. Hoover had incomparable experience in the last war and is of undoubted ability. We need a coalition gov't of some kind as well as the services of the best men in the country regardless of party affiliation. Whether Roosevelt is a big enough man to do this, I don't know. He seems to have unconquerable aversion toward those who have opposed him. I'm afraid he carrys many petty prejudices, and I know he protects those of his political family at the expense of the most efficient results. He sure has sloughed off Willkie unpardonably.

Wonder if Singapore can hold out? Each day finds this vital base in greater danger. How much, much tougher it will be to win this war if the Japs manage to take it. I rather think that somehow or another it will hold out. Australia must be praying and hoping that the little yellow men will be halted short of Singapore. For years the people of that vast, empty continent have feared an invasion by the teeming millions grubbing out a living just above them.

Two men of section 50 have now been washed – Stafford & Perkins. Westbrook and Ledbetter are hanging in the balance. They will find out today whether they make it.

And now my *third* hour of solo has passed. Again my performance was none too good – especially landings. But despite this I feel that I got the hang of it a little better. May have an hour & a half check coming up tomorrow so I had better have improved.

It is some satisfaction to see that my Penn. R.R. stock has recovered just about what it lost when the war started.

Friday Jan 16.

This was a thoroughly good day all the way around. From the standpoint of my own performance and from that of what I learned, my hour and a half check with Bergen was the best yet. This check is given each student at the end of his first three hours of solo. Because my last two solo hours were none too sharp, I thought it wise to be very much on the ball for this check. Happily, I climbed out of the plane at the end of the period well satisfied. My emergencies, air work, landings and takeoffs were ever so much better. Bergen, also, showed me flipper turns, rolls, flying upside down, "washing" a field and carrier landings. I enjoyed it all to the fullest extent – especially flying upside down at 1000'. Am beginning to get the "feel" of the plane more and more each time. Of course, with this brief instruction flipper turns are the only maneuvers which I will be permitted to practice on solo hops.

The McKay's asked me out for dinner – and how enjoyable it was. We had fried chicken, peas, excellent mashed potatoes, and upside down cake. It seemed almost like home. The children kidded their mother, and the youngest talked all the time much to the embarrassment of Merle, and Billy. And speaking of Merle, what a fine looking girl. I wish to goodness I had called on her sooner. I was just as well impressed this second time as I was the first which is of some significance. Too bad she is so busy with her dramatic work and I with my flying.

After dinner Mrs. McKay and I attended a Christian Science lecture by Florence Middaugh while Merle went off to play practice. Miss Middaugh is an extremely tall woman, over six feet, I am sure, but nonetheless, graceful, poised, and of fine bearing. Her message was simple, straightforward and good. I am so glad I went.

Saturday – Jan. 17.

This was another very satisfactory day. I managed to take 8 words per minute again on the test that was given. In fact I got 76 characters in a row without an error. Although 8 wpm is the radio requirement for graduation from this base, I'll be disappointed if I don't take 10 wpm before I leave.

My solo hour was more enjoyable than any other up to this time. I had more confidence and a better feel of my ship. My landings still weren't real good, but they are coming along.

At 9 P.M. I met Bob Hogan at the R.R. station. He came down to see Commander Wright about some special commission in the Navy. We drove out to the plaza for some ice cream, and then back down to the Hotel Dixon where we met K. Pettit. Inconveniently, Bob had a watch to stand at the base and couldn't be with us. We dropped into the Town Royale for about 45 minutes. At midnight when they closed up every one was singing the good old songs and in general having a very glowing good time.

I think it would be well to mention the men who are in command of this base, the U.S.S. Fairfax. The captain is Lt. Comm. Tomlinson – a man who, according to the men around here, has more hours in the air over 30,000 feet than anyone in the world. The executive officer next under him is Lt. Comm. Helm. Lt. Peterson is in charge of flight operations, and Col. Peters of the Marines is officer in charge of ground school. All very likeable men, and quite competent as far as I can tell. Ensign Adams and Ensign Solfisburg are a couple of ninety day wonders who are helping Col. Peters with his administrative work and also teaching math. They both had excellent college educations in the east, majoring in engineering, I believe, and, now, are doing their part in this war but not in a field which they would prefer.

Sunday, Jan. 18.

Attended services at 3rd church located at 40th [and] Grand this Sunday rather than at 1st church as I have done heretofore. Mrs. McKay spied me before church started and asked me to sit with her which I gladly did. Must have been some experience for her to hear me sing. Luckily, however, there was a woman right across the aisle who lustily and vigorously drowned out what little volume I had. After services I met Mrs. McKay's oldest girl Mary Alice who is now married. She, too, was exceptionally nice looking. They are [a] nice family in every respect. My acquaintance and association with them has been much to my liking. Took Merle home only to find that she had play practice that night outlawing our tentative date. She is quite serious about her dramatic work, I guess. A career girl, perhaps. Am getting something of my own medicine. I used to be so wrapped up in football that I quite willingly forewent most social activities.

I must admit that there is nothing I enjoy more than the companionship of a beautiful woman who also possesses breeding, grace, charm and wit. There have been a few such women in my life but not enough. There may have been a time when I was in love with love – but no more. However, I shall not consider my mortal existence complete until I have loved and won a woman who commands my admiration and respect in every way. It looks as if it will be some time before that comes about.

Had lunch with Bob Hogan, drove him through the fine residential district along Ward Pkway, then picked up Bob H. & Pettit at the base following which we saw the movie "Hellzapoppin," had supper, shot the bull for awhile, and finally to bed.

Monday – Jan. 19.

This morning was absolutely perfect for flying. The air was smooth as silk, the sun shone brightly, everything was just right. No one who has not flown on such a day can appreciate the feeling of exultant joy it gives.

Officially assumed my duties as Right Wing Commander today. Things went along quite well. Don't believe it will involve as much work as I first thought.

After supper I sent some radio code to Pettit, Rissmiller, and Hobbs.

Receiving is sometimes hard but sending correctly is even more difficult. It is good practice for me, however, as well as helpful to the
other boys.

Tuesday – Jan 20.

Another fine day for flying. Spent fifteen or twenty minutes landing
up at Sherman Field – not too hot – adequate, but not good.

Rec'd a fine long letter from Uncle Chas. in which he quoted a fine
poem by Emerson very pertinent to these times. It started out – "In an
age of fops & toys,

> Wanting wisdom, void of right" And ended –
> "When duty whispers low,
>   Thou must,
> The youth replies, I can"

Took the charming Miss McKay out to dinner at Blue Hills, a nice
little place on the south side. Had a very fine time, and I think she did
also. Anyway we are going to do a repeat performance on Thursday.

Wednesday – Jan 21.

Nothing apart from the usual routine happened today. Flew in the
morning and went to class in the afternoon. Did manage to get 10
wpm. in radio. Hope I can master *12* before leaving. The fine weather
continues and everything is going well. Like this life very much.

The flight office told Henry Bucello, the Left Wing Commander and
my present roommate, that they were "washing" him. He couldn't
land the plane, I guess. It is tough business, this getting washed-out.
The boys really hate to leave. At the end of 6 weeks a man just gets
well acquainted with everyone and the flying bug is in his blood – it is
with a sad face that a student leaves.

Must get a new license for my car one of these days. Somehow that
little requirement always takes second place behind my dates with
Merle.

Thursday – Jan 22

Had my second hour and a half check with Bergen today. Things went quite well. He even went so far as to mutter a word or two of commendation. Some concession for him, although I'll have to admit he has been very decent with me all the way through. If I can improve my cross wind landings a little I shall feel that I have mastered pretty well that which I have thus far been taught.

Effective this date the student personnel is not secure until 5 pm an hour later than heretofore. The whole right wing was on cleanup detail between 1600 & 1700 this afternoon. The Colonel talks as if this may be a daily procedure – perish the thought!

Because of all this I was a little late getting over to McKay's for my date. Mrs. McKay was gone so Merle put on the dinner – pork chops, french fried potatoes, peas, hot rolls & strawberry jam – *mighty* good. I ate with gusto and was as appreciative in my remarks as I knew how. Have I said that she, Merle, is very charming and that I enjoy her company much? Almost was late getting back to the base. I lingered a little longer than I should have and in my haste on the way back took a wrong road. Finally, careened up to the gate with only a minute or two to spare.

Bob will be up for a check tomorrow, and only after 5 hours of instruction. He evidently has done quite well.

Things continue to look worse around Singapore. Surely the Allies will begin to stem the Japanese advance soon. I wonder what really is going on inside Germany. Rumors are rife and the Russians continue to kick them around on the Eastern front. Spring will bring strenuous and bitter action on all fronts.

Friday – Jan 23.

A haze hung over the field most of the morning canceling all solos and checks, including Bob's. He will undoubtedly get his chance again tomorrow, however.

The phys. ed. instructors have been giving strength tests to all students the past few days. I made my effort today with pretty satisfactory results, to wit, 8'2" in the standing broad jump, 31 back levers, 16 chinups, and 40 pushups for a total of 354 points, 80 points higher than anyone else yet tested. How long my record will stand, I don't know, but the instructors seem to think it is a pretty good mark to shoot at.

Section fifty was assigned two hours of field day this afternoon. I found that my position of Wing Commander relieved me of most of the routine work of this sort, for which I am most appreciative.

We had company drill at 4 oclock. Can't say that I handled my duties as platoon commander with as much confidence and precision as I should have. However, next time I think I could do quite well.

Spent the whole evening after supper writing letters, and even then didn't catch up on all my correspondence.

Saturday – Jan. 24.

My plane wouldn't start this morning so had to wait until the 3rd hour to fly, the mechanics working on it in the meanwhile.

Took a disappointing drop in my radio code this afternoon. On Wed. of this week I took 10 wpm and today I only got 9.2. That can be chalked up to indifference of thought when I walked into the code room. I was inalert, and not keyed up at all, not on my toes. Will see what can be done next week.

We had personnel inspection followed by company drill around 3 oclock. Did fairly well, and certainly as well as most of the Marine sgts did their jobs. They aren't too sharp on their company drill commands by a long shot. The right wing finished up the day cleaning up lockers. Kind of a useless and meaningless job – don't blame the boys for not turning to with more enthusiasm.

Can't refrain from observing once again the lack of leadership and organization around here. Just where the fault originates is hard to say. I guess we are all a little unfitted for our job, right down the line. Nobody seems to know for sure just what should be done under a given set of circumstances. Too often in a military organization leadership is gained through seniority or political appointment and not merit itself. Superimposed leadership is seldom successful.

The headlines in tonight's papers put the blame for the Pearl Harbor catastrophe on Admiral Kimmel & Lt. Gen. Short. The committee headed by Ass. Justice Roberts indicted both men for failure to work together and for complacently refusing to recognize the danger of such an attack despite the fact they were warned time and again by

responsible men in the gov't & in the service. This failure to work together, to compromise, to recognise merit in others, this small mind
pettiness seems to be a historical characteristic of government and
military men. Inexcusable!

Bob & Ken went to a movie after supper and I spent a couple of
hours at the Reading Room.

I wonder if the North American bomber plant just across the road
thinks it is fooling anyone. Every other day or so they roll out that same
bomber they finished 3 weeks ago, warm it up, taxi it around and then
it disappears for a day or two. Everybody around here knows it is the
same plane and that they haven't produced any since. Also, I am wondering if they are operating on Sundays. I didn't see much activity
around there yesterday. It is a crime if they aren't.

Sunday – Jan 25.

Flew the 1st hour this morning and the 1st this afternoon. In the
A.M. the air was smooth as silk, the sun shone warmly, and the visibility was almost unlimited. It was a beautiful and glorious day. By
afternoon a brisk cross wind had arisen and it was a little tricky landing. In fact there were about five ground loops – happily, I was not
among them.

Shared the company of Miss McKay again this evening. Picked her
up about 6:30 PM, drove out for a bite to eat, and then over to Blue Hills
for a few dances. Had a fine time and regret that in a very short while it
will all be over. She is *quite charming* and *quite a cagy little rascal.*
Yes, delightfully clever in fact!

Monday – Jan 26

A heavy blanket of fog hung over the field all morning grounding the
A.M. flight wing, however, our wing was able to fly during the afternoon. I didn't get up until the fourth hour, but it turned out to be one of
the best hops yet. My landings were all quite good. I think I have the
hang of it for sure now.

Bob, Ken, & I went to town for our supper tonight, then returned
early so Ken could study his math. He hasn't been doing too well in
this subject. In fact he has to take a special test today.

The papers indicate that the allies are beginning to get in some good licks in the S. Pacific even though the Japs continue to move ahead. The quicker we can halt the advance of these little yellow men the easier the job will be.

Tuesday – Jan 27

My radio still was not very sharp today, and our final test is tomorrow. Hope I have it when the chips are down.

Passed my final check with Lt. Kraft in a pretty satisfactory manner. This terminates my flight training here at Fairfax. In the eight weeks that I have been here I had seven hours of instruction under Lt. (j.g.) Thatcher, two hours of instruction and a tenth hour check under Lt. Bergen, a second check by Lt. (j.g.) Jenkins, three hours of solo followed by an hour and a half check by Bergen, 4 more hours of solo, another $1\frac{1}{2}$ hr check by Bergen, then 5 hours of solo, and a final check by Lt. Kraft. It has been fun and as a whole things went quite smoothly although not without a tense moment or two. The completion of this first step in my endeavour to become a Navy pilot gives me much satisfaction and happiness.

Tomorrow we have our final in math, as well as radio. I expect to get things lined up so that I can go home from Friday until Monday. It will be great to see the family again. I really hadn't expected to get home again for quite awhile when I bid them goodbye at Xmas time.

It was reassuring to hear over the radio tonight that the Germans counter attack against the British in Libya was mostly a gigantic bluff. I hope that analysis is correct. It would be too bad if Britain lost once again her fine advancements there.

Most of the boys, including Pettit, have now passed their final check. The remaining few will finish up tomorrow. Sure hope we don't lose anyone at this late stage.

Wednesday, Jan 28

We had our final in radio and math today. I took 9.8 on a 10 word test in the former and received a 4.0 in the latter. Quite satisfactory, I guess, but am a little disappointed that I didn't get 10 wpm solid in radio.

Sections 49 & 50 were conducted through the North American bomber plant across the road late this afternoon. We found it to be a building covering 27 acres with almost no partitions. They evidently haven't gotten under weigh in earnest yet, probably due to lack of raw materials. In any event there didn't seem to be much activity. It was in complete contrast, for instance, to the picture of interminable industry presented by the Ford plant in Detroit when I visited it a few years ago. There were only about 5 bombers that looked anywheres near completion. Gearing American industry to war production is a slow and enormous task.

Most of section 50 took off for home tonight. Westbrook is still around because he has a final flight check tomorrow. I am staying until Friday to help get the new Wing Commander started, and, also, to enable Bob to ride home with me if there should be no flight operations over the weekend. Ken headed for Iowa City all aglow over the prospect of seeing his heart interest.

Bob & I went over to K.C. Mo. for dinner and then to a punk movie. Home early and shortly to bed.

Thursday – Jan 29

Having finished up both my flying and ground school, I did little but loaf around today. Did drive over to town and buy a couple of foot lockers for Ken and me.

Took Merle to see Ted Weems' stage show at the Tower then up to the Drum Room for awhile. Must say I'm not much of a nightclubber. Everyone was doing the conga and rhumba – I felt like a fish out of water. Had a wonderful time, though – sorry in this respect that I am leaving K.C.

Well, section 50 lost no one on final checks or final exams. Our little group is intact at ten. It is amazing how attached you can become to the men in your section. I think we have a particularly good bunch – they are a swell outfit of happy-go-lucky fellows.

Here is a list of them:

> Pettit, Ken
> Tamisiea, Jack
> Westbrook, Wellington
> Hotchkiss, B. D.
> Quillen, Vincent
> Haugebak, Marvin
> Agan, Al

Ledbetter, Lou
Barker, Bill
Kinnick, Nile

By golly, I have had a good time at this base. Have met a lot of mighty good acquaintances, learned to fly to a degree, and still have had time to get out a little now and then.

Once again I say that my football and college experience in general has been excellent training for this period of my life. Being constantly on the go, getting cussed out frequently, keeping going when you're tired, none of these are novel experiences for a college football player. And am I glad I got my studies quite well as I went along! It is making things infinitely more easy for me now.

I believe I have made some good friends among the enlisted men on the base, both in the ground school and flight office and on the line. Why, those fellows on the line really took care of me – offered me their gloves and overshoes on cold mornings when all the regular gear was checked out, helped me get the rudder pedals and safety belt adjusted on those 1st few hops, etc. The boys in the ground school were just as good to me in other ways. For some reason I value these acquaintances and friendships very highly. I take more pleasure in being recognized and helped by the enlisted men than by the officers.

Just for fun I am going to record the names of some of these enlisted men. A good many of them are going to sea, perhaps, I'll run into them again before the war is over.

Among the line crew:
Bill Willetts – to Norfolk, Va.
Glen Rausch – to San Diego.
Curry –   "
Tony
"Fordham," (Schultz)
"Red"
Marvin
– and many others.

Among the ground school force:
Frank Carpowitz
Ed Klein
Holmes
George Chandler

Finch

Joe Palermo

Schaeffer – in the flight office, from Dows, Ia.

Friday – Jan 30

Loafed around the barracks all day waiting until Bob was secure. Finally, at 1600 the base was secured, and we took off for Omaha. It was a very enjoyable ride despite the fact I only got 3 hrs sleep last night. I'll never cease to be thankful for my car. There we were speeding along at a good clip, warm and comfortable, listening to the best music the radio had to offer. Real luxury.

We got into Omaha about 8:40 PM, and stopped to get some flowers before going on home. I purchased a dozen jonquils for my mother, and Bob got his a potted plant, a cyclamen, or something like that. It was sure good to get home again. Mother fixed me some sausage and scrambled eggs and a fine salad. We visited till late and then finally to bed.

Saturday – Jan. 31

Slept late for the first time since I was last at home. Strange, yet a good thing, the way man can become accustomed to changed circumstances. I seldom feel the need of extra sleep while at the base even though we arise at 5:45 A.M. regardless of what time we get to bed. And yet, the moment I get home a ten hour snooze seems most welcome.

Spent a very leisurely day around home. Did have my car washed – it has needed a lathering for a good long time. Bought a book on how to speak Spanish – hope I have the time and ambition to make use of it in the next few months. Read a few more of Churchill's speeches in the volume "Blood, Sweat, and Tears." None of them ever fail to leave me thrilled and inspired.

Bibba sent me a copy of the dedication she wrote for her Hawkeye. I thought it exceptionally fine and said so to the best of my ability in the return mail.

Father helped me make out my income tax for the past year. I didn't make as much as last year but paid more, nonetheless. I am not filing a state income tax this year since Nebraska has none and since I am no longer located in Iowa City. Trust that I am within the law in doing this. By the time I have paid my income tax, re-imbursed father for my car license plates, and taken care of my gas & oil expense from K.C. and back I shall have made a pretty good hole in my exchequer. Hope that my service check is in when I get back to the base.

Hard for me to realize with what unconcern I tell the folks of my social activities. It was not always thus by a long shot. Must admit my present attitude is much more normal – and makes mother much happier. Why I never truly enjoyed the company of women until the past two or three years I'll never know. Given half a chance, I'll willingly endeavour to make up for lost time.

Sunday – Feb. 1

How typical this Sunday morning was. While I still languished in bed mother was up and around getting ready to leave for the church, all the while urging George to hurry up so he wouldn't be late for Sunday school. With the noon meal finally in the steam cooker mother and George were off. Shortly thereafter I arose and leisurely perused the morning paper, whose headlines proclaimed Singapore was preparing for a last ditch stand. At 10:45 father and I headed for church. It was the last time I'll hear mother read, for her term is up in April. She has done an excellent job and enjoyed it very much, but, nonetheless, I'm glad it is coming to an end. It will give her more time – she has been pretty busy these past three years.

George and I went to the movie "They Died with Their Boots On" late this afternoon. It was the story of Gen. Custer and his heroic last stand against the Sioux Indians. It was quite good, and I enjoyed it very much. I always wonder, though, just how historically accurate such shows really are. How times and personal convictions change! I can remember writing in a college theme that I was tired of hearing of a nation's manifest destiny and of the often inevitability of war, and that, I would fight when I saw the tanks coming up #6 highway and not before. What an immature view! But more than that I now find myself moved strongly by feats of courage and battle heroism as depicted in such movies as "They Died with Their Boots On." I find myself anxious to do the same, to engage the enemy, and to comport myself with outstanding skill and daring. Truly nothing stirs the imagination of a redblooded youth like the prospect of battle.

Monday – Feb. 2.

Bid mother goodbye at 9:45 AM, stopped at the F.L.B. to have my income tax report notarized and to have a last brief moment with father, then took off for Kansas City. It snowed last night and I found the first 80 miles or so pretty slippery. Down around Auburn I started to speed up a little and almost got hauled in front of a judge. As I passed through the middle of town I noticed a patrolman following me, and slowed down to a snails pace, but the damage had evidently already been done for he promptly signaled me to a stop. The list of offenses he recited was quite awesome. It seems I passed him on a hill, was driving too fast for the condition of the roads, passed the next car in an intersection, and was doing 40 through a 25 mph. zone. Following my usual procedure when so accosted I was meek as a lamb, repentant, and talked tenor throughout. Happily, once again I got off with nothing but a lecture.

Got into Kansas City about 2:30 PM, devoured a hamburger, and then since my suit wasn't yet finished at the cleaners, I dropped over to the Public Library and read the play, "Stage Door" in which Merle has a lead. It was very enjoyable and had a great many fine lines. Speaking of plays I wish that I might have seen "Arsenic & Old Lace" which played in K.C. over the weekend. It was a riot, I guess.

Dropped out to McKays about 7:30 PM. For the first time since I have been going out there *Mr.* McKay was at home. He is a fine man – I liked him just as well as the rest of the family. After some chit-chat with the folks Merle & I went out for awhile. Dropped into a place on the south side where a couple of drunks recognized me & quite noisily said so. Seems if we hadn't beaten Notre Dame I would have been a better guy. It had been quite some time since I had been recognized & accosted in this manner. Seemed like old times for a moment. Finally, and regretfully, I was bidding Merle an affectionate, and somewhat difficult, farewell. It was with a mutual feeling of reluctance that we parted. Our little affair has come along rather rapidly this past week. Just where it stands now, or where either of us wants it to stand, I don't know. It has been grand. I only hope nobody's feelings get hurt.

And so ends my stay in Kansas City – pleasantly and happily. To-morrow I head for New Orleans – and with very little sleep this night.

Tuesday – Feb. 3rd

Up at 5:45 AM as per usual hoping that we might get an early start for the south – but no such luck. They kept us hanging around wait-ing for our orders until after two oclock in the afternoon. It was en-couraging to have those men who had been quite aloof during the training period come around and wish you the best of luck. Both Mr. Thatcher and Mr. Bergen bid me Godspeed and expressed an interest to hear from me. Mr. Adams, also, was most cordial in our last conver-sation. But once again I want to say that it was the large number of enlisted men who gathered around to say goodbye which gave me the real thrill. Just before we left Commder Tomlinson gave us a little talk which I thought quite good. He advised us to always pick out a particu-lar spot on which to land regardless of how large the field might be. Then he told us that he thought we would be ahead of a lot of the new men reporting at the same time we do, because he had never secured flying at Fairfax because of a cross wind as they do at a lot of bases. He said he didn't believe in starting a man out the easy way. His parting shot was, "now lets lick hell out of those damn Japs."

Finally, about three oclock, Pettit, Agan, Haugebak, & I drove out the gate and turned toward the southland. We took highway #71, to #35 to #13 and thence into Springfield, Mo. where we had supper at Davidsons Cafe. We took #60 out of there, hitting #63 at Willow Springs. About 9:30 or 10 oclock we ran into 50 or 60 miles of gravel road in the state of Arkansas. Now, on the map, it looked to be a pretty decent road, it was a state highway, etc, but, evidently, a gravel road in Arkansas isn't the same thing as in Iowa. Why this road was nothing but a wagon trail, full of sharp curves, narrow bridges, chuck holes, boulders, steep hills, etc. It was a horrible road – and lonely. We hardly saw a house or a light all the time we were on it. I thought my poor car was going to fall apart. Certainly, it took a beating. The next morning I discovered the cause of the hissing sound made every time I stepped on the accelerator – the air filter had been jarred loose from the top of the carburetor – truly a rough road. At last we hit pavement again and could pour in the coal. Around twelve oclock we hit Jonesboro, Ark. where we decided to stay all night. Man was I sleepy, having had only three hours sleep the night before. We got a tourist cabin with two big double beds in it for $2.50, and although Pettit weighted down one side of the bed so badly that I was lying on a side hill, I slept like a log.

Wednesday – Feb. 4

It was not very easy to get up this morning. It was raining outside, and the bed was, oh, so comfortable. We finally made it about 8:30, however. None of us bothered to shave, nor did we stop for breakfast. We just hightailed it for Memphis, Tenn. right off the bat. Can't say that I think much of the state of Arkansas, at least what I saw of it this morning – poorly surfaced and poorly marked roads, swamps and clay gullies galore, sterile looking land, small one or two room unpainted clapboard houses, lots of mules, rickety fences, and most of the people look like hungry coon hounds.

Crossed the Miss. R. into Memphis before noon. Didn't linger long, but took out immediately on #61 for Vicksburg. It didn't take us long to get out of Tenn. into Mississippi. The latter state in short order left these impressions on me – flat, unfenced, land worn out and crop weary, livestock along the road all the time and almost as many colored folk. Have never seen so many Negroes before in my life. We passed through town after town in which the number of colored people we saw far exceeded the whites. Here again we saw a countryside covered with small unpainted shacks in which the colored folks live. Not infrequently we would see a duplex affair in which the colored family lived on one side & the domesticated animals on the other. On first blush, seems rather humorous, but in reality what a serious social problem it is – and probably getting worse. I have never seen such poverty in the country before – in the city, yes – but not out on the land. The colored folks literally banked the highway in a constant moving throng to and from the small towns and their shacks. The distances were not short, but apart from a bicycle now and then, or a mule or a horse they were always walking.

We stopped in Clarksdale, Miss. for lunch. Our whole surroundings seemed so much less prosperous than in the north – but a pretty passable meal, nonetheless. Next on to Vicksburg where Grants "victory in the west" turned the tide for the North back in the early '60s. The view of the Miss. R. from the high bluffs around this city was majestic to say the least. Such a vista made you realize why this river is called the Father of Waters. Soon we wheeled into Natchez, that historic old river town of beautiful homes. We didn't have time to look around much, but we saw a few of the homes which give it its reputation.

By constant driving we got into Baton Rouge, Louisiana around seven oclock. The highway took us by the capitol bldg, so we stopped and got out for a little bit. It sure is a grand structure, but what held our interest was a bronze statue of Huey Long bathed in the spotlight shining down from the very top of the capitol. What a colorful and contradictory figure he was – bitterly hated and dearly loved, ruthless yet kind – nonetheless, a typical dictator. He did everything on a fear and favor basis. After a dinner of steak and french fries we began the last leg of our trip – 83 miles to New Orleans. The outskirts of this fabulous city reminded me a great deal of Los Angeles – wide, 4 lane highway, many neon signs, tourist cabins and drive-in spots galore, warm climate, and everybody driving like mad. All of us were quite well impressed with what we saw as we drove down Canal street. The newer part of town, at least, looks clean, modern, interesting. We all remarked how much larger it seemed than K.C. (pop. N. Orleans = 499,000, & K.C. about 400,000.)

We took a room in the La Salle Hotel which isn't the classiest hostelry down here by quite a bit – but quite adequate. After shaving and cleaning up a bit, we sauntered out to look the town over and see if we could find any of the boys who came down on the train. Although we looked in every bar on Canal st., we couldn't find any of them.

Finally, about 12:30 or so we turned in, tired and ready for a good sleep. I did all the driving on this trip – 8 hours straight yesterday, and 11 hours today – have had enough driving to last me for quite awhile.

Thursday – Feb 5.

Arose quite late and not with much alacrity even then. Wrote rapidly and not too coherently in my diary, trying to get it up to date before everything slipped my mind.

We had lunch at Morrisons cafeteria – quite a nice eating place – then dropped over to the De Soto Hotel to see the boys who came in on the train. They had a pretty "rough" time on the way down and were still at it today.

Around 1:15 PM. we drove out toward Tulane U., then back through the French quarter. The latter area was particularly interesting and picturesque. The streets were extremely narrow, being one way affairs for the most part. The buildings were unpainted and of a period long since past. Nearly all of them had small iron railed balconies just like the movies of the old South portray. We spotted Arnauds & Antoines – those two famous restaurants claiming to have been in business for 100 years or so. Hope to have an opportunity to eat at both places before being assigned to another base.

Around 3:30 PM. we reported aboard our new base located on Lake Pontchartrain. Lot of building going on around here. They evidently are intending to enlarge this base considerably. From all I can gather the liberty around here is going to be practically nil. Boy, am I going to miss K.C. & Merle the Pearl.

Friday – Feb. 6

The first thing this morning we had a routine physical check, and then around noon a radio test just to see how much we had forgotten since leaving E. base. I didn't do too well – can attribute it to carelessness. Must begin to snap out of it in radio unless I am to be satisfied with doing just fairly well. In the afternoon we had a lengthy lecture on the 11 general orders for guard duty. On coming out I noted on the bulletin board that I am listed for the "dog watch" (12–4 AM.) on Sunday. That being a holiday I'll have to stand from 12–4 PM also. Nice life – and in a hurry!

This base augurs to be a not too pleasant place – not much liberty and lots of watches and ground school. I am going to miss K.C. – and how. From here on out the play is out, I guess.

Can't think of anyone whose looks I liked better on 1st appearance than the present Wing Commander (S.B.O.) Radabaugh. He is a giant of a man, pleasant, affable, unaffected – and doesn't know me from Adam – doesn't even speak to me – but, nonetheless, his action & speech impress me. Can't say the same for many boys I have met in this service.

The sgt. who gave the lecture on guard duty answered his own question of what happened to a man who shot an intruder in line of duty – eg, shooting a fellow who refuses to halt. First, he is summoned before a summary court martial, fined $1.06, sent to another base, and probably promoted. The $1.00 fine is to prevent him being tried by any other court in the country, and the 6¢ is for the shell used. How accurate all this is I don't know?

Saturday – Feb 7.

Not much doing today – just more routine. In the morning we drew the ground school textbooks we shall need, and then listened to a lecture on the use of a riot gun (sawed-off shotgun) while on guard duty. The sgt. in charge had us all load the gun & then remove the shells without firing. I'm no Dan Boone with a gun, but some of those guys scared me stiff by the way they handled it – many of them must never before have touched firearms. We also had a little field day workout – not as bad as in K.C. but, nonetheless, irksome. In the afternoon we just hung around waiting for word on whether we were to get liberty. About five oclock the final decision was that no one was allowed off the base regardless of what uniform a man might have. This is the second weekend in a row this entire base has been restricted. Looks like a lot of foolishness to me.

A few of us did get off from 6 to 10:15 PM to play a basketball game. As a matter of fact about 25 went off the base, but, of course, very few showed up at the Y.M.H.A. where we played. What a night – a good deal of festivity preceded and followed the game – even during the game itself. We weren't very well organized and were beaten 21–17. Its the 1st game I can recall in which I only played two quarters, & the second in which I didn't get a field goal. It was a lot of fun, though, and it was good to get some exercise again.

Sunday – Feb. 8.

We were permitted to sleep until 9:30 A.M. – very welcome to all of us. Couldn't get off the base for church so wrote a few letters and looked up a bunch of definitions for navigation terms. About 10:30 A.M. some guy phoned saying he was Cap't Johnson from Iowa and that he would look me up, etc. Have only a vague idea who it is but if he knows his way around New Orleans I'll be glad to see him – when & if we ever get off this base. A bunch (50 or so) sailors came aboard last night. Most of them are young fellows fresh out of boot camp at Great Lakes, Ill. It turned out that most of them are from around

Iowa – many of them recognizing me and enthusiastically stepping up to say. Was glad to see all of them.

Signed up for my cadet uniform tonight. Am having it tailormade to insure a decent fit even though it will cost a little more.

Haven't seen a paper for several days – am losing out on the news – hope the Allies are still holding fast in the S. Pac.

Mon. Feb. 9.

Stood a watch last night bet. 12 & 4 AM. I was captain of that particular watch detail and had to get up at 11 PM and start waking the rest of the boys – sure didn't get much sleep for I was up at 5:30 with the rest of the boys. In the morning we had Physics, radio, & drill; in the afternoon, Fundamentals of Naval Service, and Navigation. Physics & Navigation look like they might be pretty rough. We go to class from 7 to 11, & from 12 to 4 – this schedule plus frequent watches is a pretty rigorous life.

Mel Ott was aboard this afternoon as a sort of publicity stunt. Lt. (j.g.) Gilbert introduced me and had us stand for a picture. Ott is about my height and build – appeared to be a very nice chap. Lt. Gilbert asked me to play a little bb. with him at 1700. Couldn't very [well] refuse but sure didn't feel much like it. After supper tried to do some Physics problems but found I wasn't very sharp. Decided to hit the hay about 9:30 PM. and study some other time. Feel rather low tonight – so much to do & so little time. Seems as if I have been hurrying all my life. Gets kind of old sometimes.

We were told today that our class leaves for Pensacola on Mon, 2/16 – just a week away. That means we are going to be shot through with all possible haste. It looks as if I won't even have time for my personal correspondence – and look how poorly I am writing up my diary these days. The battlefront is coming closer for us prospective aviators. Almost before we know it we will be in the thick of it. Sometimes I wonder what it all means. But I know of no honorable course except ahead and through. May God be with me.

Tuesday – Feb. 10.

Go, go, go, all the time – from dawn till dark. No time for anything except study & classes. Radio not going too well. Did pass the checkout test in Physics with a 3.4 which relieves me of going to class for two weeks – will help some. Navigation thus far is not difficult to understand, but very painstaking and takes lots of time. Haven't seen a paper for days – don't have any idea how things are going. Am behind on my correspondence – don't know whether I'll ever catch up. Such is life in the Navy.

Now for some names around this base.

Lt. Comm. Gillespie is the captain of the base.

Lt. (jg) Pike is in charge of ground school, I believe.

In other capacities are, Lt (j.g.) Gilbert, psychologist; Ensign Chase, Kellog, Knox, Lt (jg) Castleman.

Wednesday – Feb. 11.

During the two hours in which I didn't have to go to Physics I wrote a few letters, wrapped a pr. of Hobbs' pants for mailing which I inadvertently carried off, took care of my laundry, etc. Radio still not going too well. Finally managed to get the summer pants which they failed to give me in Kans. City. Now if Bob sends me my pants which I left at Fairfax I'll be all set to leave for Pensacola on Mon. Incidentally, there is a Marine Sgt. here who came from Pensacola. He tells me they will probably keep me down there all through the fall for the football team – even though I may get my commission in June or July. I definitely would not like that!

The Cap't Johnson who called up by phone last Sun. came aboard at noon to see me. Upon seeing him I did recognize him as an interne at the S.U.I. hospital who used to hang around the practice field. He was most cordial and wanted Ken & me to go back to the officers club at La Guarde Hospital with him. Too bad we can't get off. It is worse, though, not to be able to get off the base to see Harry Bremer. He is staying at the Roosevelt Hotel in New Orleans for a few days before going to Florida. He offered, even insisted, that he take us out to Antoines in the French quarter with all the trimmings. He says he will stay over till Sat. night if we can get out then – here's hoping.

Never have seen a place where the student officers so flagrantly take advantage of their positions – favoritism, partiality, drinking in their rooms – all wrong – but I'm afraid a bit typical of men hastily thrown into positions of some responsibility.

Each day I more fully realize what a terrific job it is to get this country on a full time war basis. The Navy is expanding so rapidly that each man – officers & men alike – have so much to do in such a short while that nobody does a really good job & everyone is trying to pass the buck in order to relieve his own load a little. It is a difficult situation – takes an even temperament & then some to remain civil to everyone.

Played basketball in the evening – or rather practised – at Loyola gym. This guy Radabaugh put on a drinking feat I have rarely seen equalled.

Thursday – Feb. 12.

Regular routine again today. Radio went a little better – I passed the Navigation check out quiz satisfactorily.

Those who have cadet uniforms (blues) are going to be given liberty this Sat. night. I don't have mine, but I think I have a deal fixed up so I can get out. If H. Bremer will just stay over in New Orleans another day it will be a fine evening. Haven't had any letters from anyone since I came down here – maybe tomorrow will bring some.

Friday – Feb. 13.

Checked out of radio at 10 wpm without too much trouble. Believe I am beginning to get the hang of it now. Should make rapid progress soon after getting started at Pensacola.

Phoned Harry Bremer about tomorrow night, but, unhappily, he had decided to go on to Florida Sat. morning. Am planning to go into town with Haugebak and eat at Antoines. Radabaugh, Student Batt. Comm., found a suit of blues that some kid who washed out left behind for him to turn in. He is going to let me use them over the weekend – they happen to fit pretty well.

After secure at 5 oclock today we all (7) turned to for field day. Darndest thing I ever heard of – work all day & clean up barracks before & after supper.

Had a watch last night between 4 & 8 AM. It got cold as the dickens – or so it seemed. A biting wind off the lake chilled me to the bone. Made me wish for a warm fireplace, or a bed with lots of covers.

Saturday – Feb 14.

St. Valentines day – patron saint of lovers – which still leaves me outside the fold – how sad. Feel a bit rankled today. The first thing I saw as I came down the ladder was my name on the watch list for Sat. night – also Haugebaks and Ledbetters. Rather unfair, inasmuch as we all had guard duty Thursday night. Evidently, the student officer who makes up the list decided the older students, those of his class, should get the weekend off. The new class on any base always gets the shaft – weekend watches and worst cleanup details.

We all had to turn to again for an hour this morning, putting the finishing touches on the barracks & grounds for the Captain's inspection. At 9:45 A.M. we mustered for inspection. Then the blasted skipper let us stand on that concrete for one hour and forty-five minutes before he showed up. Inspection wasn't over until noon – what a dismal morning.

The main things I'll remember about this base are the all too frequent watches, and the dirtiest silverware I have seen anywhere. I am plenty glad we are pulling out for Pensacola Monday.

Have been so busy that I haven't heard whether Singapore has fallen or not. Do know, however, that it is generally believed to be only a matter of a little while. This war is apt to be long, costly, bloody beyond any anticipations – all because of lack of foresight the world over. When will we learn!

Sunday – Feb. 15

It started raining about 2 AM this morning & has kept it up most of the day. The boys on watch early this morning got drenched.

Did nothing but lie around and write a few letters today. Hope that we get a chance to look N. Orleans over Mon. night before leaving for Pensacola.

Churchill spoke this afternoon, but I didn't know it until after he had finished. Once again he had to explain defeats & reverses, bolster & encourage. How he must wish for the day when the tide will turn, & he can tell of Allied victories.

Had a letter from father today saying that Ben had passed the physical at K.C. & had enlisted in the Naval Air Corps, but wouldn't be called until after his graduation in June. So glad he made it ok & that he will be able to get his degree.

Still raining like mad outside. Hope I'll be able to get my car out of the parking lot tomorrow alright.

This talk about southerners resenting the presence of northern boys is quite exaggerated, I believe. A few feel that way no doubt but most of them are quite friendly once you get to know them.

Monday – Feb. 16.

Spent most of the day getting checked out – bedding turned in, jackets returned, also books, etc. Around three oclock everything was taken care of and Haugebak, Agan, Pettit & I headed up town for a look around. First, we all got a haircut, next to a movie, & finally down into the French quarter for dinner at Antoines. I tried their famous oysters on the half shell ala Rockefeller – they were excellent and should have been for the price. About 8:45 we took out for Mobile, Ala. with the intention of staying all night there. It rained to beat the band most of the way and lightning intermittently lit up the whole countryside. Despite the rain we were dry and comfortable inside my good old '41 Ford, listening to fine music from the radio all the while. We passed thru Biloxi & Gulfport, famous resort towns on the Gulf, and even at night you could tell it was beautiful country. There were no rooms to be had at the hotels in Mobile so we kept going until we hit a nice-looking cabin camp 7 or 8 miles east of there. We got a fine cabin with two double beds for four bucks. It then being 1 AM and raining pretty hard we hit the hay at once. Quite a life – now here, now there, seeing new places & new people – I like it.

Tues. Feb. 17.

Arose rather late, dashed off a letter to Merle, grabbed a bite to eat and away we went again. Pulled up at the Pensacola Base gate at 11:55 – just five minutes to spare. We were due in at noon exactly.

The buildings, hangars, etc are quite a long ways back from the main gate. The ensuing drive to the base proper reminded me of a national park – pretty country, fine trees, asphalt roads. The central area of the base including barracks, classrooms, officers quarters, hangars,

& all the other buildings are arranged in such a way as to remind one very much of a college campus. More bldgs and closer together, to be sure, but similar to college grounds, nonetheless. We had chow right away, and very good it was, then started the familiar routine of checking in which will take two or three days at this base, I understand. My assigned roommate is Jack Wright, one of the left wingers from K.C. His home is in St. Joseph, Mo. and his actions & temperament on the effeminate side. Quite harmless withal, and I'm sure we'll get along alright.

Went to a movie on the base after supper. It was no good, but the theatre is a fine bldg which is a statement of not much sense – right? They have a gym, bowling alleys, and many other recreational facilities right here on the base – not much need to go ashore for a good time.

Ran into several of the fellows who were at K.C. when I first went aboard up there – also, Tony Bremer, & a kid by the name of Ingrahm from Iowa, and Red Monaghan who attended Benson High way back when.

Things are well organized around here. I'm going to like it I'm sure.

Wed. – Feb. 18.

Continued checking in today and also got measured for the G.I. blue uniform. Was notified that my physical exam would come on next Friday morning.

Met a few more boys from up in Iowa and a good many other fellows who have mutual friends with me. No trouble getting acquainted and making new friends. Wyman Hayward came up to the room around noon today. Hardly recognized him he has matured so much since last I saw him. We had a fine visit for 20 minutes or so.

Have been amused by two common expressions on this base – "has he got the word," meaning does he know whats going on, is he "hep" to everything, and the other – "he is a little too *eager*," meaning too great an effort at being military, too much use of authority, etc.

Thursday – Feb 19.

Lounged around in the morning except for getting my camera tagged. Spent most of the afternoon filling out mimeographed sheets

of personal information – most of them concerned insurance, benefi-
ciary, whom you wanted notified and where you wished the body sent.

Wandered over to the gym about 1700 to watch basketball practice.
The Pensacola team is entered in the A.A.U. tournament in New Orleans starting next week, I believe. Some pretty fair players on the
squad – not like a good college team, however. Ran into York who
used to play football at Wisconsin. He has been here about 5 months –
only a few weeks to go. He is flying OS2Us – they are pretty slow – an
observation ship operating off battleships – derisively called "clay
pigeons" by some, meaning they are easy picking for enemy fighter
planes.

More and more impressed with the physical plant they have here.
Ken & I took a long walk this evening trying to get everything located
in our minds.

Was pretty cold today – not different from Northern weather in the
early spring. Rumored that it will get down to 18° tonight. Can hardly
believe it!

Received a copy of the "Life of Will Rogers" by O'Brien from
grandma today. There was no accompanying letter. I don't know what
prompted her to send it. Doubt if I'll be able to find time to read it. Very
thoughtful of her, however, as always.

Friday – Feb 20

Most of the morning was taken up by the physical exam. It was
pretty exacting as are all Navy tests, and it was a relief to get the ok
sign. They certainly go over a fellow with a fine tooth comb. A lot of it
seems pretty unnecessary, and there is no doubt that some of the best
flyers couldn't measure up in some respects, just as many of the best
athletes don't seem to possess the necessary physical requisites; however, where the selection has to be made in such a short time from
such a large group, any other method would hardly do. It has been my
observation that if a Navy really wants a man of evident ability, they
readily waive minor physical deficiencies.

This afternoon those cadets who had received their blue uniforms
formed into battalions, marched out to the parade ground, & while we
in khaki looked on, the names of those to graduate this week were read
off. It was a rather impressive sight to watch these young men swing

by in perfect cadence & step, chins up, chests out, arms moving in perfect unison.

Went to the basketball game after supper between the N.A.S. & Millsaps College of Jackson, Miss. The Goslings had no trouble with them, whatsoever, having them far outclassed. Its a little late in the season, but I think I shall report for basketball tomorrow, if for nothing more than the exercise & to avoid standing watch duty.

As has been true for the past two weeks I haven't been following the war news very closely, but it seems to me that it is about time the United Nations assume the offensive a little bit. If we continue to fight delaying actions until there is no doubt of our personnel & materiel superiority, the Japs will be at our very shores before we get going. It will then be at a terrific price which we recover all that we are losing.

A man is frequently lonely who has not become strongly attached to a fine woman by the time he is 23. I am not going into this war with the idea of losing my life, but, nonetheless, I could more easily face the obvious risk if I were deeply in love with a clean, wholesome girl in the bloom of young womanhood. This sounds like reverse reasoning, that I should, rather, hesitate to leave someone so dear. However, I should expect the woman of my choosing to send me off to battle with her chin up and reassuring words, fully expecting me one day again to embrace her when it was all over. Were I in this position I would feel that I had tasted pretty deeply of this mortal life in just my 23 years.

Each passing week, now, as I move from one base to another, meet old friends & make new acquaintances, I begin to realize what a great game football really is – and I get the urge to get in the harness again. I must elaborate this and comment more fully in the near future.

Saturday – Feb. 21

At the request of C.P.O. Huff I reported to the athletic office at 0800 for a picture shaking hands with Mr. Stack the football coach here at the base. Stack formerly played at Yale and is now an AVS with an ensign's commission. In our ensuing conversation he suggested that I come out for baseball on Monday, and after he told me of their schedule I made haste in assuring him that I would. They play La., Mich. State, Alabama, several other colleges & the Jacksonville base team – ten games in the first two weeks. They really go for athletics down here – hope I can make the club – it has been 5 or 6 yrs since I played any baseball.

Checked out my ground school book which leaves me all set to get started on Mon. A little better than half of our class has been designated to skip the customary two weeks indoctrinational period and start immediately on ground school. I'm not too sure if it is a good idea, but in any event I had no choice, and I will get out of the two hr. drill period each day.

Ken & I played some basketball in the afternoon with several other students. Just a makeshift game on an outside court but a lot of fun & good exercise.

After supper we attended the movie. It was a wild west affair called "Texas." Might have been good in Adel 15 years ago but not much to my liking now.

Sunday – Feb 22

Washington's birthday and the Sabbath didn't keep the planes on the ground today – they were hard at it all day. I remember reading a letter that Washington wrote his mother right after his first Revolutionary War battle in which he said, "I have heard the whistle of bullets past my ears & I have found it not unpleasant." Wonder what my first reaction will be!

Provided my own church services this morning by reading my lesson. First time I have read it clear through for over two weeks. Am better situated to get some studying done now.

Ken & I dropped down to the Cadet club for awhile this afternoon. Very pleasant little place with a fine bar, leather chairs & lounges, and two pool tables. Saw a movie about 3:30 PM – not very good.

As a follow up on the comment I made a couple of days ago that athletics were of much value, I want to say this. It provides a wonderful opportunity for initiating acquaintance. Regardless of the degree of our civilization people still thrill to physical combat & admire the man who excels. He who is of proven merit in the field of major sports has shown to all that he is possessed of strength, vigor, stamina, and courage. The great majority of people want to know such a man. What that man does with such an opportunity to make friends depends on his common sense, his character, his temperament, and his sense of proportion. How well I have taken advantage of the football reputation it was my good fortune to gain is for others to judge, but I personally am very thankful for the whole experience and the fun & friends it has brought me.

How peoples personalities do differ. What is pleasant & quite natural to one man would be offensive & out of place in another – and it shows rare good judgment to recognize this fact. For instance, constant profanity is not exactly an admirable trait, and yet the conversational profanity of some men seems quite natural, not in the least offensive, and frequently very amusing. Nonetheless, were I to adopt this as part of my personality makeup it would end in dismal failure, I am sure.

Monday – Feb. 23

It was raining when we got up this morning and has been hard at it ever since. As a matter of fact it has rained a good deal all the time that we have been in the south. There has been more than a little chilly weather, also – temperature of 35° during the night has not been uncommon either here or at New Orleans. Nonetheless, the grass is green and the countryside verdant, quite in contrast with the north at this time.

We started ground school this morning, and it bids to be intensely interesting. For the most part our study will be concerned with engines, a field which was not in my college curriculum at all. How glad I am of this opportunity to fill that void in my education – at least to a degree. I believe I am more interested in learning than at any other time of my life. I would so much like to speak a couple of foreign languages, take more math & physics, be more conversant with good literature & history. What a pity it is that a man doesn't make better use of his time when such subjects are presented in the course of his formal education. College exposes a man to courses in a great many fields, it opens up new vistas & possibilities but it is the continuous reading & study a man does after he graduates that determine whether he will ever be educated or not. There [are] a good many things I don't like about military life – and there undoubtedly will be more. But, nonetheless, the education and experience gained in military service is invaluable, I am sure. I believe I would like to have my boys attend West Point or Annapolis after a couple of years of L.A. school, if they so desired.

This afternoon we listened to a three hour lecture on high altitude flying and the effect lack of oxygen has on pilots. It was rather interesting, but also left one feeling enslaved to the physical forces – hardly, God's man with "dominion over the fish of the sea, the fowl of the air, the cattle, and everything that creepeth on the earth." Tomorrow morning I take my hop in the low pressure chamber to see if I would be fit for high altitude flying. I don't anticipate any difficulty, but just the same I wish I didn't have a fire watch tonight from 1:15 AM to 5:30 A.M.

Tuesday – Feb. 24

What a long day – from 1:15 AM to 10 PM – this is no place for a guy who needs 8 hours of regular sleep. Happily, the adjustment isn't too difficult for me – or at least so it seems thus far.

More engine theory and engine construction this morning. How I am enjoying it! Ben & father would take all this in stride, but for me it is a new field. Four hours at a stretch in one class room with only ten minute breathers each hour is a long sit. Sometimes it is pretty hard to stay awake.

Had my hop in the low pressure chamber after lunch. We took a small psychological test at sea level, went up to 18,000 without additional oxygen and took another, then on up to 28,000 with oxygen masks and still another test. All of this was directed at showing us the effect of lack of oxygen on our comfort and muscular & thought efficiency. My reaction was about normal, I guess. Am all in favor of oxygen masks, however, it helps a lot.

Went out for baseball around four oclock for the first time. Hadn't had a baseball suit on in five years, but wasn't long in getting the feel. It was good to toss the old apple around again – now if I can only hit.

Received 8 letters today, the ones sent to New Orleans having finally caught up. It was fine to hear from the folks back in Iowa – McGrane, Ashby, etc.

Wednesday – Feb 25

Followed regular class routine in the morning.

In the afternoon we spent 3 hours at the gunnery range. First, we listened to a j.g. by the name of Atkins on the imp. of gunnery and how we were here to learn to kill and not just pleasure. He tried to make it sound pretty grim but somehow he wasn't very impressive. Perhaps, it was because he didn't look inherently tough himself. Having been in the oxygen chamber yesterday I was sent to the pistol range where the majority of the class had already had their turn. Because of a shortage of .45 calibre pistols we shot .22 Colt Aces – a nice little gun. Our target was a cardboard silhouette of a mans upper torso and head. We were firing from 25 yards – 1st deliberate and then rapid fire. I did no better than average, I'm sure. Was better at rapid fire than when I took my time in aiming.

Baseball from 3:30 to 5 PM and a show after supper. The movie was quite good, starring Edward Arnold as Dan Webster & Walter Huston as Mr. Scratch, in "All that Money Can Buy." It was based on the old New England conception of the evils of avarice, a man's battle with his conscience, and the legend that Black Daniel could outtalk the devil himself. It was well put together and cleverly allegorical to the end.

Vol II

Herein is contained a record of my service in the
U.S. Naval Reserve Air corps beginning on Dec 4, 1941 –

>Nile Kinnick jr.
>
>5024 Hamilton St.
>
>Omaha
>
>Nebraska

Thursday – Feb. 26

Four hours in the same classroom listening to lectures on the same sort of material is a long sit, but we do it every morning – broken only by ten minute breathers at the end of each hour. How I wish that I had studied engines more in civilian life! Nothing but careless indifference brought me this state of ignorance. I was exposed enough to get at least a general knowledge but, oh no, I paid no attention.

This afternoon we shot clay pigeons (trap shooting) with a twelve gauge shot gun, using #$7\frac{1}{2}$ shot. My exhibition was ludicrous, I couldn't hit a thing. They didn't even record my effort, advising me to try again at a later date. It is humiliating to do no better than I did. Why I haven't learned to shoot at least fairly well in the past 10 or 12 years I'll never know. Of all things a man needs to be good at in a war, it is shooting. I must remedy this deficiency – and soon. There is no reason in the world why I can't be proficient in shooting as well as in other things. It is nonsense. I hope I get a chance tomorrow. Tests tomorrow in engine theory and engine construction. Studied all evening.

No baseball this afternoon because of rain. – No mail either – I wonder what the folks are waiting on – and Ben, I had expected to hear from him by this time.

Friday – Feb 27.

Didn't shine in the tests I took this morning, but got by alright, I suppose. Found out that I only made one mistake in the radio test given yesterday, hence, have one leg toward checking out. The requirements for complete checkout in radio receiving are – 8 words plain, 6 mix, and 10 wpm press, ie, a message taken without a mistake.

We took up the Browning .30 calibre machine gun in gunnery this afternoon. We must learn to take it apart, reassemble it, and know all the parts by name. I didn't suppose such a small mechanism could have so many parts – !

Went out for baseball again today – just a light workout – a little throwing, a little running, and then to the showers. What a contrast to college football practice! I'm all for it.

Lolled around in my room after supper fanning the breeze with Pettit & Noonan. About 8 oclock we went down to the cadet club and played some bridge. I really should have been studying gunnery or answering some of my correspondence.

Saturday – Feb. 28.

Viewed some pictures of airplane engines in operation this morning. It is marvelous how they can slow down such rapid movement – they even had slow motion shots of the gas combustion causing the power stroke.

This afternoon we fired the Browning .30 calibre machine gun, first at a stationary target, then as it moved back and forth in an 180° arc. My accuracy when firing a single shot at a time wasn't so bad, but when firing in bursts of five I had no little difficulty, as did everyone else.

Rapid firing really makes it jump all over the place. I can now understand how it is possible to miss with such a gun. Heretofore, it has always looked like duck soup to score with a machine gun.

Baseball again, and then a little bridge after supper.

Sunday – March 1

Up at the regular time by necessity, a quick breakfast, then back to bed for awhile. Don't have my blues yet, therefore, can't get off the base, so didn't get to church again this Sunday. Spent an hour or so reading & studying my lesson then wrote a few letters. Played some bridge after lunch and studied awhile.

Studied again after supper. It started to rain about six oclock & was still at it when I went to bed.

Monday – March 2

Shot the machine gun again today. This time we fired out of the slip stream of an airplane prop. Just to give us an idea of what it would be like in actual combat. Believe me accurate aerial machine gunning must take a lot of practice. Henceforward, I shall have more respect for those pilots recorded in the paper as having downed a certain number of enemy planes.

No baseball today – too windy and cold. Didn't quit raining until noon. Can't say much for the Florida weather thus far.

Went to a movie after supper when I should have been studying. It wasn't a bad picture, however – the "Night of Jan. 16."

It is rumored some more of the K.C. boys are due in here today. Sure hope Hobbs is among them.

Tuesday – March 3

Fired the machine gun again this morning – this time through the prop. itself. No record was kept of our hits which saved me further embarrassment. Aerial gunnery is a fine art. I have much work ahead of me if I ever am to be any good.

Major Passmore, the baseball coach, put me behind the plate for the first night of batting practice. It was the first time in five years I had caught with a mask & protector. Got along pretty well but I hope my blinking & lunging on strikes wasn't as evident to him as to me. Also got to hit a few – could hardly say my eye was sharp.

Some more boys from New Orleans came in today, but none of the K.C. men were among them. According to reports Hobbs is still stationed at N. Orleans. It would be a crime if he were sent to Corpus instead of over here.

Time passes quickly – the days tumble over each other in their eagerness to end the week. "E" base training at K.C. seems like ancient history.

Wednesday – March 4

Active gunnery is finished for awhile, I guess. Today we listened to lectures on gunnery theory in addition to the other ground school classes. Pretty tedious sitting in class rooms all day long. They are beginning to really throw it at us – must begin to get on the ball a little more.

Just missed by *one* lousy character checking out of radio today. Get another chance tomorrow. Sure hope I make it – would give me just enough extra time to do the necessary little things, such as getting an haircut, etc.

Rain interrupted our ball practice this afternoon. Our prospects to date are about as dismal as the weather has been. Perhaps, we will be better than I think – lets hope so.

Thursday – Mar. 5

Rain, and lots of it, again this morning. If this is the sunny south, I pass.

Carburetors & magnetos occupied part of our time in ground school today – two little mechanisms which are supposedly simple in theory but rather intricate when completely analyzed. What a course this meteorology is – looks like a study in hieroglyphics there are so many symbols for different states of weather & visibility.

Had my picture taken for the Flight Jacket today, all decked out in white. Hope it turns out well, and I shall have some prints made up for the folks.

Cadet Nile Kinnick in Pensacola, 5 March 1942. Negative, Kinnick Collection.

The war picture grows more grim. Valiant is the stand being made in Java, but courage is not going to be enough it appears. Where is the Japanese advance going to be checked – Australia, India? Certainly these two places are next in order for attack. All this talk in recent years of Hitler's plan to march around the oceans & join hands with Japan was not just idle speculation. Undoubtedly, there will be an all out bid in the spring by the Axis powers to join forces through India and that general area. The year 1942 will be critical – we must not falter or fail. How I would like to be in on the action by next fall!

Friday – March 6

Tests today – in gunnery, and carburetor & ignition – didn't do too well. First pay check as an aviation cadet received this noon. Won't be much left by the time I have paid my mess account here & New Orleans. The K.C. boys have a lot of back pay coming one of these days. Sure would like to get my hands on some of it.

No baseball for me this afternoon because of personnel inspection. Am anxious to get a chance to bat again – believe I have something figured out.

How wonderful it would be if I could set down in a clear and interesting manner the funny things that happen and the rough humor of the conversations in the hallways and barracks. For example, the peripheral vision of some fellows during an exam & their comments afterwards is wonderfully funny. And the tale some of the men are telling of the way the tetanus shot is administered and the reactions of the more timid is great listening. Memories of these days will make interesting retelling some time.

Am getting a yen to join the Marine Corps & fly fighters. I wonder if that is where I will end up.

Saturday – Mar. 7

Routine class work plus some more shotgun shooting out at the range. Still couldn't hit those clay pigeons at all – very sad!

My blue uniform was delivered by White & White today. It fits pretty well, I believe. Plan to get into town one of these nights and give the city of Pensacola a "gander."

Played bridge after supper. Am getting a little better and enjoy playing very much.

Sunday – Mar. 8.

Up late, read my lesson, studied a little, looked through the Readers Digest, napped and played bridge. Wish Sunday came around oftener.

Monday – March 9

This week we are studying airplane performance, radio, materials, accessories, aerology, and test stand observation. Will have to study a little more this week.

All of [a] sudden the baseball team begins to look pretty good. Several boys who played last year, mostly enlisted men, are now out. Shouldn't be surprised if we had a pretty good outfit. Last year's catcher, out for the first time, impressed me as being plenty good. Expect I'll have to make the grade at some other position. Don't seem to mind the prospect particularly – does that mean I've lost my competitive urge? Well, not necessarily, I guess. Its just a matter of how much effort baseball is worth at this stage of the game. Its somewhat of a relief to feel that it isn't imperative to do my utmost every minute I'm out on the field. I never want to work as hard at athletics again as I did in the fall of 1939. It paid dividends & was a great experience – but never again.

Tuesday – Mar 10

General routine with an intra-squad game in baseball at 4:30. I didn't get to play because of my finger. It is no fun sitting on the sidelines – thank goodness I haven't had to do much of it during the past few years.

Saw Deanna Durbin in "It Started with Eve" after supper. What a vibrant, stimulating smile she has – and when she sings, oh my! It is a real joy to watch and hear her sing.

I am experiencing a greater degree of anonymity here than at any time for the past three years, perhaps, longer. It is not unpleasant. In fact, in many ways it is downright enjoyable – less pressure, less responsibility, less expected of me. Having enjoyed an unusual degree of publicity and popularity at one time I can see how an athlete has some difficulty in making the adjustment when his career is over. People even speak to you in a different tone. That deference once accorded is no longer observed. All that is as it should be, but, nonetheless, it is a change, nay, even a letdown. Happily, I didn't have to make a real abrupt adjustment. The curtain has come down rather slowly – the eclipse wasn't immediate or total.

Wednesday, March 11

A young 2d lieutenant in the Marine corps stopped me today and introduced himself as John Howard, saying he used to room right across the hall from me at the Quad. Didn't recall him but was glad to meet anyone from Iowa. His mother is living with him at Warrington, a little jerkwater station between the base and town. He asked if I would like to come out for dinner some weekend to which I replied in the affirmative. Sure would be nice if he knew some nice girls around here. Am getting a bit lonely for that sort of thing.

The football coach here at the station was sounding me out for next fall this afternoon. Said they had a fine schedule lined up, might even play Purdue. He wanted to know how I would like to stay around here as an instructor and play football. As politely, and yet as firmly, as I knew how I told him I never again wanted to play any football, and that I would really rather go to the fleet than remain as an instructor. All of which is a true representation right now. Mayhap, I'll change my mind before I'm designated.

Another bad crackup out in squadron one today. This training is no picnic – plenty of the boys are shipped home feet first.

Thursday – March 12

This day's routine was just like the one before it and the one that will follow. I shall be glad when we start flying.

More than once in the past few months, speeches that I have made have come to mind. It is strange that what I considered then as a pretty good talk now seems naive, unimpressive, possessing little merit. Sometimes I momentarily feel embarrassed – I wonder what others thought – would it all have been better unsaid? No, I think not, though undoubtedly there was plenty of chaff and hot air in most of the talks. It was fine experience and some good will come of it, in fact, already has.

The inequities in human relationships are many, but the lot of the Negro is one of the worst. Here in the south this fact is tragically evident. The poor colored people are kicked from pillar to post, condemned, cussed, ridiculed, accorded no respect, permitted no sense of human dignity. What can be done I don't know. Nearly everyone, particularly the southerners, seem to think the only problem involved is seeing to it that they keep their place, whatever that may be. We supposedly are fighting this war to obliterate the malignant idea of racial supremacy and master-slave relationships. When this war is over the colored problem is apt to be more difficult than ever. May wisdom, justice, brotherly love guide our steps to the right solution.

Some personal dislikes follow: – affectation, undue display of emotion of any kind, haughtiness, common argument full of statements of absolute certainty excluding all other opinion or possibility.

Friday – March 13

Tests today – and did I ever make a mess of the test stand exam. Shouldn't be surprised if I busted it and have to take it over.

Not infrequently I get to thinking about what I am going to do when this war is over. There are many possibilities – I wonder which I'll make a stab at. Today it occurred to me that some kind of a good salesman job in Iowa would be interesting. Don't know just what I would sell but I do know a lot of people out over the state & I do like to travel around to the different small towns.

Saturday – March 14

A dismal, foggy day – routine class schedule and a brief baseball practice.

Went into town for the first time right after supper. Not much of a place – don't anticipate that I'll be going in often. Did find a nice place to eat and dance (if you had a date) about halfway between the station and Pensacola. It is called Morton's – wouldn't mind dropping in there now & then. Didn't get in until awfully late – kind of a poor time, too. Will be glad when Bob gets in on Wed. – very glad.

Sunday – Mar 15.

Supposed to have a mate of the cock watch today, but got out of it because I'm on the baseball squad. Don't have to fall in for parades and inspections on Fridays either.

Feel kind of low today. Used to worry about getting into a field of life endeavour that would be sure & press my capabilities. Now I am wondering whether I didn't have a rather exalted idea of the extent of those capabilities. Probably won't take much to exhaust them. Service life and the prospect of the future kind of stifles the ambition – at least the tendency exists. One thing is certain – when this is all over I'll have a much greater appreciation for those things in civilian life which I used to take for granted.

Monday – March 16

A new week has begun and a couple of new subjects are on the schedule – communications (procedure) and ship & aircraft recognition. The latter is apt to be rather difficult but all important. More than once during this war aviators have bombed their own ships mistakenly. Why, the Italians even escorted some English ships through the Mediterranean thinking they were their own.

The fog still hangs on – there really hasn't been much good weather since we arrived here.

What a showdown there is going to be this summer! If the Japs aren't stopped short of India & Australia the length of this war will be longer than any sane man cares to contemplate. I wonder what Turkey will do? Sure as shooting Germany will try to march through the near east to India. I hope that the United Nations have been fortifying & supplying their positions in India & Australia. I just have a hunch that they have. Just as Germany failed to take England in the fall of 1940 so I believe Japan will fail to take Australia or India. And when she has been definitely halted – then will the tide turn, and the Allies will get under way.

Tuesday – March 17

Another foggy, rainy day – we wear raincoats, or, at least, carry them, half the time. No ball practice again today.

Am finding blinker a bit difficult, also, ship & aircraft recognition. The latter is hard because I am starting from scratch. Have never paid much attention to the different types of ships & aircraft prior to coming into the Navy. In fact my ability to tell the different cars was limited to distinguishing between a Ford & a Chevrolet.

Just about got a rib punched in at the supper table tonight. I ate beside a maniac. His elbows stuck out at right angles all the time he was in action – which was every minute. After awhile, with all the sarcasm I could command I said, "pardon me, bud, but don't let me crowd you." He didn't even slow down or look. He ate as if it was the last meal he expected to get on earth. I reiterate that the fare is good but you don't want to enter the mess hall without warming up. You don't have a chance if you do. Its every man for himself & devil take the hindmost which is an empty platter.

Have I yet said that my roommate is an inveterate gargler. Every night he takes a pull at the Listerine bottle, throws back his head and gurgles with gusto – and not for just a little while either. No sir, he keeps at it until a thorough job is done. Makes me feel as if my own personal toilet is quite incomplete.

Wednesday – Mar. 18.

Regular routine. Weather sunny & pleasant.

Bob Hobbs got in about noon, looking very snappy in his blue uniform. His tales of life at the New Orleans base jibe well with the impression Pettit & I got.

What the devil are the labor leaders & Roosevelt thinking about in refusing to repeal the 40 hr week law. Doesn't seem quite right to me. Looks just like the sort of thing that wrecked France.

Received another clipping on what life at Iowa City will be like for the new pilots who go into preliminary training there about April 1st. For three months they are to indulge in nothing but strenuous exercise & a little ground school. Cross country, wood chopping, etc. are supposedly in the program – and no liberty! Sounds nuts to me. You'd think our aviators were going to fight this war in hand to hand conflict. Knox & Tunney have gone berserk on this physical training business. Thank goodness they have been able to keep such nonsense off this base. Here we have no regimented calisthenics stultified by such exercises as the explosive punch, etc., but rather get to choose our type of athletics and participate at least three times a week.

Thursday – Mar. 19

Another fine sunny day – bright, warm, pleasant. This is more like it.

Blinker & semaphore are coming along better now, but it will be a close race to see if I can check out on Sat. when we are supposed to.

Took my turn at batting practice tonight & swung without discomfort for the first time since I hurt my finger.

Received a delightful letter from Merle today. She thoughtfully inquires if I would care for some cookies or fudge ala Merle!

Friday – March 20

We had tests today in Materials & Construction, and in Airplane Performance. I had to do a lot of guessing in the former but feel that I probably passed it alright. After getting a 2.9 in the Test Stand exam given last week it is hard for me to worry over any of these courses. If ever I wrote a poor exam that was it.

Anticipating rain & fog for tonight & tomorrow the commanding officer decreed that Saturday should be our liberty day this week and that we would go to school all day Sunday. Ken & I drove in to Morton's for supper, Bob not yet having received his gate pass couldn't go along. It was the best steak & french fries I have had in a good long while. Shall plan to go back again when the next liberty rolls around. We then went on into Pensacola for a little while returning to the station about 10:30 P.M. By that time the fog was thick & low obscuring all but the closest objects.

Saturday – March 21

It rained from dawn to dusk today without letup, despite the fact it is the date of the vernal equinox and, also, of Hobbs' birthday.

Spent most of my time writing letters and taking it easy. Jack & I *did* wax the floor this morning, however.

There seem to be several popular songs right now that I like a lot –

Elmer's Tune, Chattanooga Choo Choo, Blues in the Night, Moonlight Cocktail, White Cliffs of Dover, This Love of Mine. Can even recognize them without much trouble which is pretty good for me. Still like to listen to cowboy & hill-billy songs, though.

Sunday – March 22

Today didn't seem like Sunday at all. We dragged through a regular schedule of ground school then had baseball practice – no church, no afternoon nap – no, it wasn't Sunday as far as I am concerned.

Hadn't seen a show for quite some time so walked over to the theatre with more than ordinary anticipation right after supper. The name of the movie was intriguing – The Maltese Falcon – but it was misleading. It was no good at all.

Monday – March 23

Two new courses this week – Maintenance, and Parachutes. This Friday will be a tough test day, but it will mark the end of all day ground school, and I shall be glad. Will start flying next Monday.

We beat Mich. state in the opener 5–2 – without the services of one, N. Kinnick. First time I ever sat on the bench throughout an entire game in any sport any time. Didn't mind it particularly; but I can tell it would have been very irksome in college when I really wanted to play. We have two more games with Mich. state tomorrow & Wed. May get to play in one of them. If I could just hit a couple on the nose I'd be all set – neither one of the other catchers is too good a hitter.

Pettit & I played bridge with C.L. Wilson & "Jellybelly" Shelton after supper. Enjoyed it a lot, but I'm a bit obtuse when it comes to cards.

Rec'd a large box of toll house cookies from home, and a fine letter from Tait Cummins of the C.R. Gazette. He is a good gent, and it pleased me much to hear from him.

Tuesday – March 24

Another fine, warm day, this is more like the Florida weather you hear about.

We lost to Mich. state this afternoon, 4 to 1. And still I did not get to play. The fellow who caught today is the regular catcher from last year.

He is plenty good though not an exceptional hitter by a long shot. Perhaps, I'll get to catch the final game of the series tomorrow – hope so.

Wed. – March 25

We lost to Mich. state 6–3 this afternoon. Really a crime to be beaten by that outfit, particularly, by the pitcher who hurled the whole nine innings. He tossed them up there big as balloons. Major Passmore sent me in to pinch hit in the ninth with a man on second, one down, and us trailing by 3 runs. I busted the first pitch down the 3rd base line for a single. The 3rd sacker managed to knock it down, but he didn't even attempt to throw to first. The steal sign was given on the second pitch to the next batter, and I "streaked" for the keystone sack – no luck, they threw me out without much trouble. It had been so long since I had tried to run the bases I wasn't sure how big a lead to take off first. Anyhow it wasn't big enough, or I was too slow or something. The Major was far from pleased which doesn't augur well for my chances to play in the near future.

Once again in an effort to beat the weather they moved "Sunday" up a few days. Tonight and tomorrow were designated as liberty hours and Sunday is to be a regular working day. Bob, Ken, & I went in to Morton's for steak & french fries, then on into Pensacola. Wandered around a little while and drove back to the base about 10:30. There is absolutely nothing to do around this town. I don't like the prospect for what future liberty is granted.

Thursday – March 26

Rained all day – did nothing but play a little bridge, write a few letters, & read a couple of magazine articles. In Look magazine there was an interesting article on Stalin & Russia by Joseph Davies former U.S. ambassador to the Soviet. I cannot help feeling that despite the ruthless domestic policy of the Russian gov't & its world revolutionary tendencies that something good may ultimately develop out of this great experiment. At least, in my mind, Russia is a better country in which to live than Germany. The former deplores the methods it feels it must use to gain its end, while the latter holds that bestiality, race prejudice, war, and all the indignities which it has bred in the minds of its people is aim & end of the Germanic way of life. When such well educated & reasonable men as Joe Davies & Sir Stafford Cripps, former British Ambassador to the Soviet, both wealthy capitalists, have many fine things to say of the Russian experiment then I think there must be some merit & some hope in what we have called Communism. If it is gradually changing to an evolutionary movement where individual enterprise & initiative is recognized, as these men suggest, then surely they are getting on the right track. And while I am on the subject I can't help noting the difference in the pictures I see of Stalin & Hitler. The former has a kindly, cheerful looking face, he cannot be all bad, I'm sure. But Hitler is always the epitome of fanatical hatred, & prejudice. He looks like a maniac. I end this by stating my admiration for the courage & staying power of the Russian armies. I hope they have what it takes come spring.

Friday – March 27

Rain spoiled our game with Alabama, but, weather permitting, we'll play tomorrow.

Studied awhile for my final tests in ground school before starting to fly.

Joe Louis knocked out Abe Simon in the sixth tonight. The proceeds were to go for a service benefit fund. Joe was "fighting for nothing but my country" as he put it. He is one of my favorite athletes, and a truly great champion in my mind. He takes them all on anywhere, any time. They can talk all they want about the old timers, about the lack of good opposition, but I still think he is one of the best fighters who ever drew on a glove. But even more to his credit is the way he has conducted himself as champion. He has remained quiet and courteous throughout it all – no braggadocio, no alibis. Truly he has been a credit to the fighting game and to a downtrodden race. Good for him!

Saturday – March 28

Six tests today and all of them considerably harder than heretofore. Apart from radio communication procedure, and possibly meteorology, I think I got along quite well. In any event it is a relief to finish this all day ground school routine. Will start flying again Monday.

We beat Alabama 3–0 this afternoon. Sexton pitched the shutout, doing a good job all the way. Had not tests prevented my getting out until after [the] game I think I would have gotten to catch today. Doesn't seem to matter much to me whether I get to play or not – particularly catch. What I really want to do is bat. I wish he'd let me play in the outfield.

Quillen, Barker, Westbrook & I played bridge for a couple of hours after supper. Quillen & I held good cards and beat them soundly. Its a lot of fun when you are holding the good ones.

Sunday – March 29

We dragged through our regular schedule of ground school classes today. It was the seventh day of the week, but surely it wasn't Sunday. There was baseball practice, too. We chose up and had a little game, with me catching for one side. Did just fairly well – no hits, nobody thrown out, and worst of all no urge or ambition. Didn't realize how much I had concentrated on football to the exclusion of proficiency in baseball – and basketball – these past few years. Am more convinced than ever that DESIRE is 80% of success in athletics, probably in anything. Believe that I would be better off to quit baseball. There are at least two better catchers than I right now, and it wouldn't be worth the effort to try [to] outbest them. Furthermore, they are lengthening the day again. We are getting up at 5 AM now. There is no use adding the fatigue of baseball, & the time it would take, to a schedule that already keeps me awfully busy & draws off my energy.

Played bridge after supper. Held excellent cards again.

Monday – Mar. 30

Clambered into busses at 5:50 AM which took us out to Saufley field where squadron 10 training is given. It is a fine big field with "millions" of yellow N3Ns taking off & landing all the time.

We received a lecture on the course rules and the general program of training to be followed, then hung around doing nothing until noon. Spent the afternoon in navigation class. This is going to prove a more interesting & enjoyable schedule than the previous five weeks, I'm sure.

Tuesday – Mar. 31

Most of the boys got up for their first hop today, but mine was scratched. Did meet my instructor, however. His name is McCroskey, and he seems like a right good fellow. He is short, average build, pleasant faced, quiet spoken. His rank is full lieutenant in the regular navy. Started work on dead reckoning in navigation class – tedious work, but fun. Hit a few golf balls around 5 oclock – much better than playing baseball.

Wed. – April 1

Had my first hop today. Everything went well. We shot a few landings at one of the auxiliary fields, did a little air work, coped with a couple of cut guns & then called it quits for the morning. McCroskey said it was a good ride & talked of soloing me tomorrow. Was very generous in his compliment of the way I taxied – said it was the best job any of his students had done regardless of stage of training – then admonished me not to forget how I did it! Sure is good to get to fly again. Happy to find that most of what I learned at K.C. has stayed by me. Practiced a little radio sending after coming down. Dealt with running fixes & corrections of radio bearings in navigation this afternoon.

Have quit baseball definitely – am positive it is a wise move.

Shot the "bull" with Hobbs for about hour & half this evening. Very enjoyable for us both – wish we were rooming together.

Thursday – April 2

Quite well pleased with my flying again today. Landings are causing me no trouble whatsoever. McCroskey speaks well of them nearly every time. He is a good little gent, liberal with the encouragement, and makes every effort to see that you improve. He is sending me up for a solo check tomorrow.

Started some celestial navigation today. Very interesting and wonderful to realize what can be done with it. Father would enjoy so much this sort of thing. Sure would like to have him for my navigator. He'd be a honey!

Not much sleep or leisure these days. Have to work on my navigation every night. Feel fine, however, and thankful that things are going so well.

Friday – April 3rd.

Passed my solo check successfully today. There wasn't much to it – one cut-gun, two landings, nothing more.

Navigation is getting a little tougher. I must stay on the ball.

Saturday – April 4

Three hours of solo this morning – most enjoyable and yet fatiguing, too, it is so necessary to be on the alert for other planes all the time. I was first man up on the 6:30 hop and winged my way northward for Kingsfield, up near the paper mill, arriving in time to shoot a few landings before it became too crowded. It was a wonderful morning, and I reveled in the joy of flying and in the wonderful view in all directions. Military flying has its unpleasant aspects, but flying just for pleasure would be hard to beat.

Tomorrow being Easter we were granted weekend liberty for the first time in several weeks. A bunch of us went to town, stopping at Mortons on the way in for steak & french fries. Bob & I returned early, there being nothing to do as always. I'm getting pretty tired of having nothing of interest to do over liberty – perhaps, its my own fault?

Stayed up late last night & read through Steinbeck's short novel "The Moon is Down." Enjoyed it very much – it is pleasantly written and presents a theme that stirs the soul of any man, to wit, a free people cannot be permanently conquered. Apropos of Germanys situation in the countries she has conquered he says – "the flies have conquered the fly paper" – pretty good.

Sunday – April 5.

Easter Sunday – significant day, beautiful, warm weather. Rose late and went to church for the first time in all too long.

After dinner I wandered over to the library and checked out a volume of Kiplings poems. I really like his stuff, particularly right now. He understood the thoughts & experiences of servicemen perfectly.

Always enjoy reading "Tomlinson" again, and that scornful line – "there's sore decline in Adam's line if this be spawn of earth."

Also, "the race is run by one & one, never by two and two" – "the sin you do by two and two must by paid for one by one." How well I remember Prof. Sayre quoting those lines in class one day.

Monday – April 6

Our class is flying in the afternoon this week. I didn't get up today, my instructor didn't show up at all.

Hit some golf balls over at the driving range during athletic period this afternoon. It is a wonderful game and one which I shall play much whenever time once again permits.

I don't believe that I have yet mentioned that Jack & I have a new roommate, making three in our little nest. His name is James Walker and [he] hails from Longview, Wash. Seems to be a pretty nice chap. There are apt to be three, perhaps, four, in every room before the summer ends.

Tuesday – April 7

And still I didn't get to fly – I was scheduled again today, but my instructor didn't show up. I am getting tired of that old noise. Perhaps a full lieutenant flies just when he wants to.

The weather man predicted rain for tomorrow, so we were secured at 5 oclock. Bob, Ken, & I went to town, but came back pretty early. Bob & I stopped at Simpson's and were measured for white uniforms. Don't think I'll trade with White & White any more. They screwed me on my blues, I'm afraid. I ordered a tailor made uniform, and got nothing but a full drape model, size 42 right off the rack.

Wednesday – Apr 8.

This being "Sunday" for this week I slept late and spent the remainder of the morning writing letters. Bob & I drove to town, he, to get his radio fixed and make some purchase, I, to do some studying & reading at the C.S. welfare room located on the second floor of the San Carlos. He & I hit some golf balls in the afternoon – both thoroughly disgusted with our inability to hit them straight & true. Read several articles in the Sat. Eve Post after supper. The weather men missed on their prediction for it didn't rain at any time all day long.

Thursday – April 9.

Flying secured at noon today – the rain predicted yesterday arrived today. Slept a little this afternoon, and wrote several letters.

Borrowed the "Last Puritan" by Santayana from the library this evening. Have read about fifty pages and find it exceptionally good. Believe that I shall [be] reading more now than at any time for the past 7 or 8 years.

Am getting fed up with keeping this irony. It involves tedious monotony and is evidence of personal vanity, I'm afraid. It would be much better to record what I do and think in my correspondence to others, then only that would be saved which merited it. However, since the folks seemed so interested in what I had set down while at K.C. I shall continue to keep it up.

Friday – April 10.

Man, I'm really a whipped puppy tonight. My instructor did about 20 successive lazy 8s with me this afternoon, then gave me an inverted spin, and followed that with instruction on slips to circles. All this made me a bit woozy, and I didn't feel a whole lot better when I went up for an $1\frac{1}{2}$ hour solo shortly afterwards. Found that I could neither slip nor do wingovers as he had taught me. Felt thoroughly disgusted and submissive when I came down. For the moment I feel quite low, almost uninterested in flying. You could buy me for a nickel tonight and no haggling. Don't even believe I could fly a kite. Trust I shall feel & do better tomorrow.

Sat – April 11

Flew three hours of solo today. Did pretty well on wingovers, but not so good on slips to circles. Was pretty well bushed again when I came down. Not as bad as yesterday, however. I can see how it takes lots & lots of flying hours before you have any business calling yourself a pilot.

Bataan peninsula has fallen to the Japs. Heroic men, those Americans and Philippinos, how long will they be able to hold Corregidor commanding the mouth of Manila Bay? When will the Allies take the offensive? Sometimes this war looks to be an interminable mess.

In what little leisure time I can find I am reading the "Last Puritan" by Santayana. Wonderfully well written. It holds my interest keenly.

Sun – April 12.

Received another hour and a half instruction today, followed by a solo period of equal length. My instructor seemed to think I was coming along pretty well, and in addition to wingovers, & slips to circles, he gave me some work on small field procedure. My solo period proved to be the most productive of any I have yet flown. Really seemed to be getting the word on wingovers & slips.

Having finished most of my navigation I read for a couple of hours after supper. Am enjoying the "Last Puritan" a great deal. What a masterpiece of ability a good book represents!

Mon. – April 13

My three hours of solo today were most enjoyable – my wingovers were good & I successfully slipped to the circle time and again. Also did my first solo spin today, just to enhance my confidence. In fact I experimented in several ways today just for the fun & practice. Got a faint idea of what a dive bomber's perspective is by nosing my plane *straight down* and holding it there for awhile before pulling out. It is great fun, the trees come hurtling up at you, the wind screeches by; all this at 120 knots, I wonder what it feels like at 250 kts. Flew around over the countryside at about 3 to 400 ft for a little while. Not a very good idea, but I couldn't restrain the impulse.

Tuesday – April 14.

My instructor was gone on a ferry hop, so I didn't fly at all today, because my 3rd period of instruction on my twenty hour check was scheduled (Horrible sentence structure!?) Five hours at the squadron with nothing to do is an awful bore.

Navigation is getting tougher, & the instructor, a 1st class heel, is pouring it on. Notebooks are due on Friday, and a test is also to be given. Should have everything whipped into pretty good shape by then – I hope.

Wed. – April 15.

Had my 3d period of instruction on my twenty hour check today. Only had time for slips to circles and wingovers before the clouds closed in, but during that short while I gave him a good ride – he said so when we landed. We climbed through [a] layer of broken clouds to get up above for our wingovers. In the short while we were up above, the weather closed in almost completely making it a little difficult to get down stairs again without the use of instruments. It was a good practical experience for me showing how quickly the weather can close in, and what danger lies in flying in or around clouds. Up above everything was sunshiny and nice, but below the situation was quite the reverse – low ceiling, gloomy, foreboding.

This period was called incomplete, and I shall get the rest of my instruction tomorrow.

Thursday – April 16

Didn't do so very well today – my small field procedure was anything but good. McCroskey didn't complain much, but, nonetheless, it didn't satisfy me by a long shot. He took time out to show me some things I had asked about not included in the general instruction routine – carrier landings, night landings, landing on one wheel, taking off in a minimum distance, side slips, etc. He is an excellent flier – it is a treat to ride with him and watch him operate.

Final test in celestial "nav" tomorrow. Must get to bed and so I'll be a little bit sharp tomorrow.

And still no letter from Merle. Its been a long time now, and I can't imagine why!

Friday – Apr 17

Had a pretty good day flying – 3 hours of solo – practiced slips, wingovers, flipper turns, carrier landings, – lot of fun but rather tiring.

Received a 3.4 in my celestial "nav" final. Sounds like a pretty good grade, but in navigation 4.0 is the only really satisfactory mark.

Had the inevitable parade at 5:30, it being Friday. Must say I detest them.

Retired early, but slept poorly. Will make up for it Sat. night, if we don't fly Sunday.

Saturday – April 18

Soloed 1½ hours, then had a period of instruction. Things went well, and I should get by my 20 hr. check on Monday ok.

We had our first liberty in 12 days tonight. Had a late dinner in town with Bob, Ken being in the hospital with an arm infection, then drove back to the base and a short lookin at Mustin Beach. Rather good to mingle in a party atmosphere again – dancing, pretty women, drink, and all that sort of thing. Wish that I had a date.

Sunday – April 19.

Rose late, attended church, took some magazines down to Ken, and then strolled down to the beach with Bob. Lolled in the sand soaking up the sun's rays. Very comfortable, wish I had time to do more of it. Wrote a very long letter home, went to a movie, and retired not very anxious to meet the coming week.

Monday – April 20

Passed my twenty hour check today. Wasn't a very masterful job by a long shot – neither good nor bad, just an average ride, I should say.

Started work on plotting board in navigation. These same instruments are being used in the fleet right now. I hope I have enough sense to work for proficiency in its use.

Tuesday – April 21

Received my first instruction in acrobatics today. McCroskey showed me how to do a snap roll, a loop, an immelmann, split "s", a falling leaf. It was a lot of fun, but a very confusing experience until I began to get the word on what was happening and how it was being done. After spending about 45 min. on acrobatics he showed me how to do pylon 8s, and "s" turns to circles. By that time the hour was up and we landed. He then told me to go up for an hour and practice the stunts he had just showed me. This is a perfect example of how fast everything is being shoved at us down here. Inasmuch as I didn't know a snap from a cinnamon roll before entering the navy it was hard for me to see myself trying to do acrobatics with only that much instruction. However, I plunged into them during my solo hop and managed to do every one of them in a crude sort of way. Sure would like to ride Gus thru a few of them.

Wednesday – April 22

Couldn't find one maneuver that I could do well today, neither stunts, pylons, nor acrobatics. When I go up for another instruction hop tomorrow McCroskey will ask what in the devil I have been doing the last two or three periods.

Don't seem to get much mail anymore – rather disappointing, too, there are several people who owe me letters.

Thursday – April 23

Gave McCroskey a fair ride today. My stunts went better than yesterday by quite a bit. Pylons and small field work need improvement; wingovers are much better.

Friday – April 24.

Had three hours of solo today. Everything was much improved except immelmanns, haven't quite gotten the word on them yet. Feel that I can give McCroskey a good ride tomorrow. I had better, it is the last instruction before my 33 hr. check.

We are still dealing with plotting board in navigation. It certainly is an ingenious way to find your way around the ocean & back to a carrier.

Pettit is on the road to recovery from his arm infection now. They will keep him at the hospital for another week though. Too bad he had to be slowed up this way.

Saturday – April 25.

Did pretty well on my last instruction hop today. Always easier to do a good job for your own instructor, however. Bob and I went into town for a while tonight. Walked out in the middle [of] Betty Grable's show "Song of the Islands" – should have known better. Stopped in at Mustin Beach for a short while then turned in for a good long sleep.

Sunday – April 26

Up late and to church. Afterwards Stuart Hemingway and I went over to Pensacola beach for the afternoon. There was a good surf running and we had a good time riding the breakers in. Played a little touch ball, some one-o-cat, lolled in the sun, and in general took it easy. Wish Sunday came oftener. Trust my very pink back will soon turn to tan.

Monday – April 27

Was supposed to check on my 33 today, but a low ceiling kept down all but one flight. Will get my chance tomorrow, I suppose. If I am on the ball I shouldn't have much trouble.

Pettit is up and around now, and should be released from the hospital in a day or two.

Tuesday – April 28.

Successfully passed my 33 hr check this morning. Not a good ride, not a bad one – didn't [do] too well on my first cut gun and wasn't too sharp on my wingovers, otherwise, pretty fair. My final check will be up before the week is out. Boy, they sure stick it to you fast around here.

Bibba sent me a Hawkeye which arrived today. On the front leaf the editor had written – "to the greatest Iron Man of them all." Quite generous of her, as always, and made a tremendous hit with my vanity. Really an excellent yearbook – one of the best I have ever seen.

Wednesday – Apr. 29.

McCroskey was gone on a cross country hop so didn't get my final instruction. Didn't put my extra time to very good use – conked off on the leather davenport most of the morning.

Received a long air-mail letter from Ben saying that he and Ellie were very much that way and that he was thinking of proposing, etc, what did I think, and please let him know by Friday. Flattered that he should ask me, and did hastily pen my views on the situation, sending it special delivery air mail.

Found a letter from the commandant's quarters in my box late this afternoon. Couldn't imagine what it could be about, opened it with avid curiosity. It turned out to be an invitation from Mrs. Read, wife of the skipper, asking Ken and me to drop in on them Friday at 5:30. You could have knocked me over with a feather, and Pettit just about expired. It seems Dr. & Mrs. O'Brien of the University Hospital in Iowa City had written that we were down here. The only Dr. O'Brien I can recall was killed about 2 years ago or so. I *must* know this fellow, however.

Thursday – April 30

Didn't get any instruction today either, McCroskey not having returned from cross country.

Test in voice procedure tomorrow – don't know straight up about it. Sure am fed up with ground school.

Don't know what I am going to do for a white uniform tomorrow. Impossible to go to the Commandant's without whites. Mine were ordered some time ago, but haven't yet arrived. Will try to borrow a set from someone.

Friday – May 1

Got my final instruction today. Gave him a pretty fair ride, but am going to have [to] work on those S turns to circles. Told McCroskey I'd have a brother down in the fall & sure would like to have him get Ben for a student. Said he would keep his eyes open for him.

The Commandant's shindig turned out to be a cocktail party with lieutenants & commanders thicker than the sands of the seas. Ken & I had a good time. Would like to go again some time. I borrowed Quillen's whites for the occasion.

Test in plotting board tomorrow, but I'm going to bed early, nonetheless.

Saturday – May 2.

Only flew one hour this morning because of fog. My s turns to circles were better but not too sharp. Couldn't do a decent snap roll in 5 tries. Am going to have to snap out of it for that final check on Mon.

Didn't do very well in plotting board – got rather careless. Sure hope I don't have to take it over.

Having no whites, neither Bob nor I, we took a stroll, conversed awhile, & retired early. Loaned Pettit my car, and he & Quillen went into town.

Finally, got a nice long letter from Merle, with explanations & sentiments satisfactory. Sure glad to hear from her again – a fine gal.

Sunday – May 3

Had no whites so didn't get to church. Bob & I went down to the beach for a couple of hours this morning. Mighty pleasant lying around [in] the sun – wish I could do more of it. Slept most of the afternoon, and read in Carl Sandburg's "The Prairie Years" of Lincoln after supper.

Monday – May 4

Successfully passed my final check in primary squadron this afternoon. Felt that I gave my check pilot a pretty darn good ride. Nice to get that one out of the way.

Had night flying after supper for a couple of hours. It is a lot of fun to land in the dark along a lighted runway. Have to keep on the ball though.

Tuesday – May 5

Kind of dull day. Had a sandbag hop the last period today – that is a solo flight from the front cock pit with a sandbag in the rear to keep the plane balanced. Should start formation any day now.

Bob & I hit some golf shots during athletic period. Can't understand why the folks don't send me my sticks as I have asked.

Wednesday – May 6

Had my first formation hop today. Am flying with a boy by the name of Scott from Arkansas, and one, Hollows, from New Jersey. They are both quite good. I stunk during the instruction period, but got along pretty well on our solo effort.

Received a notice from the R.R. Express Agency that my golf clubs had arrived. Hope I have time to use them now & again.

Corregidor has fallen, India is being menaced worse each day. It looks like a long summer. Trust the British won't have too much trouble with the French in Madagascar.

Thursday – May 7.

Clouds closed in about the middle of the afternoon and caused the cancellation of our formation flying. Practised a little radio sending, read a couple of articles in the Sat. Eve. Post, napped briefly.

Received a most flattering letter from Bibba in reply to the commendation I gave her on the Hawkeye. She has been awfully frank in the nice things she says about me ever since I met her – almost embarrasses me sometimes.

Also had a letter from Kilmer Bortz who is now getting fighter training at Miami. He is very enthusiastic, and makes me much the same way. Carrier duty would be exciting, adventurous, full of action, requiring the utmost in skill and daring. All of which suddenly recalls to me a statement of Richard Hillarys in his fine book Falling through Space – "in war one can swiftly develop all one's faculties to a degree it would take half a lifetime to achieve."

Friday – May 8

No flying at squadron today because of rain and clouds. Studied a little for the test tomorrow in strategy & tactics.

Received a fine letter from Celia this afternoon, and one from another comely lass of my acquaintance. The female front seems once more to be all in order. Oh, for a nice long leave!

A terrific naval battle is raging between the U.S. & Japan northeast of Australia. The length of this war may in a great measure be determined by its outcome. Conflicting reports are being [sent] out, but the first round seems to have gone to the U.S.

Sat. – May 9.

Flew three hours of formation today. Things went pretty well, but don't believe I did quite as well as the other two boys. We will get some instruction in echelons on Monday.

And still I have no whites. Loaned Pettit my car for a trip to town. Bob & I stayed for about ten minutes of the movie showing at the station theatre and then wandered back to his room for a bull session. It broke up early, and I was in bed by 9:15 – can you imagine that on a Sat. night.

Had a letter from Barbara in the afternoon – short, and not too well pleased with the tardiness of my last letter.

Sun – May 10

(I have fallen behind in this record rather badly. I am writing this on Friday, May 15.)

Bob & I hit some golf balls in the morning and went down to the beach in the afternoon. A lazy day of which I could take more.

Monday – May 11.

We got instruction in echelons today and in touch & go landings in formation, followed by two hours of solo. Things went pretty well, which is gratifying, since we check tomorrow.

Tuesday – May 12

Successfully passed our formation check the last period this morning. Apart from the first takeoff it was a pretty good ride.

Wednesday – May 13

Drove out to squadron with Scottie & Hollows and finished checking out. We are supposed to take another pressure chamber test, have some X rays of the chest taken, and report to squadron three quite soon. We have decided to "conk off" for a few days, however.

Butch O'Hare was on the station this afternoon and gave a little talk to the assembled cadets at 5:30 PM. Quite a modest chap, hardly mentioning his exploits. This one statement of his struck me as being particularly American – "once I was up there with no one to help, there wasn't anything else I could do but get after them." What a contrast to what an Axis flying ace would probably have said. He made fighters sound like pretty good duty. Rather think I shall put in for them.

Thursday – May 14

Loafed around most of the morning. Wrote a letter or two, read a little, and slept a little. Had a test in general information about the Navy this afternoon. Did better than I thought I would.

Saw the movie "Captain of the Clouds" in the evening. First show I've seen in a long time – pretty good. There were some beautiful technicolor shots of the Canadian wilds.

Friday – May 15

Put in for my preferred duty today – fighters first, "P" boats second, and VO-Vs third. Also took my pressure chamber test – went up to

18,000 ft without oxygen, then donning our oxygen masks, on up to 35,000 ft for 40 minutes, and finally up to 40,000 ft for ten minutes. I got by ok. It must be some experience to actually fly around 35 or 40,000 ft above the earth.

Wrote a few letters, read and snoozed.

Sat – May 16.

Had a test in scouting & search today. Might have done pretty well, but you can't tell for sure till you see it in black and white.

Still no whites, so Bob [and I] spent a very quiet evening together on the base, and to bed early.

Sun – May 17

Up at 7:30, read my lesson, then over to the golf course for 9 holes. Did fairly well for the first time out. The fairways were awfully narrow though.

Down to the beach in the afternoon for a couple of hours, and then 9 more holes of golf about dusk.

Russia still continues to sound good on the eastern front, but the real storm hasn't broken yet. What will Turkey do? We *must* hold fast this summer!

Mon – May 18

Just this one week more, then the end of ground school. Boy, that will really be great.

Checked in at squadron three today. Will probably start my "Link" hops tomorrow.

How rapidly the weeks have gone. Soon I shall have been in the service 6 months. It hardly seems possible. Should get my commission in Aug. some time. Man, how I would like to get back up into Iowa for a few days at that time – via K.C.

Tomorrow, or the next day, I should be able to find out what duty I got. Hope it is fighters.

Tuesday – May 19

Well, I got fighters alright, that is, I shall get VC training at Miami. I may end up in dive or torpedo bombers, however.

Had my first hop in the Link trainer at squadron three today. Didn't do very well. The technique is entirely diff. than in operating an airplane. Can't seem to get excited enough to do my very best.

Wednesday – May 20

More Link hops today – still not very sharp. This instrument flying could drive a guy nuts.

Can hardly imagine that I once thought the mess was excellent here. Hardly anything really appealing appears before me any more. Just eat out of necessity any more.

Man, will I be glad when ground school is over the end of this week.

Thursday – May 21

Still flying the Link – a little better today.

Suddenly found myself with an overwhelming urge to join the Marines today. It may now be too late, but I am going to try to get my application in tomorrow.

Finished Sandburg's Prairie Years on Lincoln (vol II). Found it extremely interesting, actually an history of the period as well as a biography of Lincoln. Want to get started on the War Years soon.

Friday, May 22

Managed to get by the U track exam in the Link and thus qualify to start work with the radio beam. Still don't like to fly in the Link – it reacts like a mechanical toy rather than an airplane.

Had an enthusiastic letter from Ben telling me of his being tapped for Cardinal Key. How wonderful this spring has been for him. I am so glad – he has worked awfully hard.

Saturday – May 23

Had my first hop in an SNJ-3 today. It felt good to get into the air again – and what a fine ship it was. Got along pretty well, but really didn't do much. Once again I have been fortunate in getting an instructor who has been to the fleet and has had lots of experience. His name is Coffman (Lt. j.g.) and a mighty fine gent. Soft spoken, patient, 100% for the student.

Bob and I went out for dinner having finally received our whites. We ate at a little place called Martines out on the Mobile highway. Had the biggest steak they offered, and man was it good! After three weeks of nothing but station food such a meal seemed fit for the gods.

Sunday – May 24

First to church, then down on the beach, and in the late afternoon 9 holes of golf – so went the Sunday. Bob & I went back out to Martines for supper.

Monday – May 25

From now on I shall be out at squadron all day for ground school is no more – happy day.

Am working on radio range orientation in the Link and primary instruments in my actual flight work. This is exacting work but invaluable experience. If I should come back to Pensacola as an instructor I would like to get in this squadron.

Tuesday – May 26

More time in the Link but no air hop for some reason or another. Am not too sharp in my Link operation, but am learning the proper radio range procedure which is the main thing.

Wednesday – May 27

Had another air hop today. Didn't [do] too well. The daggone air speed seems to be my biggest bugaboo.

Bob & I went out to Martines for supper. He is now working on formation flying & will be out of squadron one this week. Has sailed through without any trouble. Pettit seems to be having some difficulty. He had to ask for squadron time on his 33 & now is in the same position on his final.

Thursday – May 28

Finally finished all my Link hops – what a relief. Had more time in the air again today – this I really enjoy.

Quite by chance I ran onto Eddie Lynch the other day. He was end coach at Iowa under Solem when I was [a] freshman. Right now he is a full lieutenant in the reserve in charge of the enlisted flight student battalion.

Friday – May 29

Finished up my primary instrument work in the air today. Will start radio tomorrow.

Bob had his formation check in squadron one this morning & got by ok. He will be over at squadron three on Mon.

Pettit got an up on his 1st check on squadron time. Has only to pass the 2d check tomorrow & he will at last be past his final.

Saturday – May 30.

My 1st radio hop in the air went pretty well today. Of course we didn't do much but bracket a beam & one letdown.

Had a watch at the ACRAC from 5 to 7 & 10:30 to 12 so couldn't do much this evening.

Bob & I had reserved a boat for tomorrow afternoon & Stuart Hemingway had two girls lined up so we have decided to all get together for a sail tomorrow afternoon. Hope it turns out to be a good deal.

Sun – May 31

It did *not* turn out to be a good deal. First of all there was some mixup on the reservation, & we couldn't get the boat. Secondly, the would be glamour gals were too young, too broad, too simple – I pass.

Bob & I went out to Martines for supper then dropped over to Mr.

McCroskey's house for a little while. Had a nice visit & an invitation to come back again.

Mon. – June 1

My air hop really went quite well today – hope I can keep it up.

Secured at one oclock, went back to the barracks & dashed off two or three long letters.

Tues – June 2d.

Flying just went fair today – kind of doped off down near the cone.

Secured at one again & went out & played 18 holes of golf with Bill Barker – pretty soft. Bill Johnson former end at Minn. dropped up to the room after supper for a chat. Seemed like a fine fellow.

Wed – June 3

Some guy by the name of Hopkins substituted for my regular instructor this morning. Man, was he a wrong guy! – whacked off all the time & wouldn't keep his feet off the rudder pedals nor his hands off the stick. I flew the worst flight of any time since I came down here.

Bob, Ken & I went out to Martines for supper. The longer I eat at the cadet mess the greater desire for good food I get – and Martines meets that desire perfectly.

I check tomorrow – and will be glad to get out of there.

Thurs – June 4

Checked successfully this morning – not too good a flight but passable considering the weather. There was a strong wind, rain, & clouds.

Appeared before the Marine Selection Board after supper. Really thought that I would get in ok, but unhappily the selection was determined entirely by lottery and I wasn't among those pulled out of the hat. Felt quite disappointed at the time, but now don't regret it at all. If the Marines are getting their men by lottery rather than merit that branch of the service loses most of its appeal for me.

Drove out to Ellyson field after the meeting & checked in to squadron two.

Friday – June 5

Listened to several short lectures, had a cockpit checkout in an SNV & OS2U in the morning & then went out to the skeet range in the afternoon. At the beginning my shooting was no better than ever, but toward the end it improved. Believe that I am beginning to get the word.

Saturday. – June 6.

Stood for personnel inspection in whites at 7:30 AM. Nothing is more obnoxious & tiresome to me – I loathe them.

Finally got my first instruction in an SNV at 3:15 in the afternoon. My instructor is Ensign Stewart, a young fellow from Kansas. Seems like a pretty good gent. He showed me the stall characteristics of the plane & then let me shoot a few landings. Got along pretty well.

Drove back to the base about 6 oclock & picked up Bob, then went out to Martines for supper.

Sunday – June 7

Stayed all night at the main station. Went to church in the morning, wrote some letters right after dinner, then played golf with Barker & Westbrook later in the afternoon. Hobbs, Hotchkiss, Barker & I drove out to Martines for a buffet supper. It was excellent!! Drove back to Ellyson field after taking Bob home in time for the 10 oclock bunk check.

Mon – June 8

Had two more periods of instruction in an SNV then a check which I passed ok. Wrote several letters after supper.

Received a note from Earl Hall of the M. City Globe-Gazette saying he had met the folks at the Iowa State graduation ceremonies. He spoke very highly of them which made me quite proud. Also he mentioned sitting across from Ben at a Cardinal Key banquet. He is a good gent – I think the family must have enjoyed meeting him.

Tues – June 9

Soloed for three hours in an SNV this morning. The ceiling was never higher than 1000'. It was a new experience soloing under such conditions. Got along ok, however. In the afternoon I got a cockpit check in an OS2U. Will have an hop in one of them tomorrow.

Wednesday – June 10

Had an hour of dual, then a period of solo in an OS2U today. Can't say that I am particularly enthused about the plane. Prefer the SNV many times over. Understand they are still using some of these old OS2Us in the fleet. What a crime – I'm glad I got fighters.

Took a bunch of the boys to town with me after secure. I then drove out to the base, picked up Bob & Ken, and we went to Martines for supper. Ken had tough luck in the low pressure chamber, getting "bends" at 37,000'. He will probably get VO-Vs now that he has been eliminated from the possibility of fighter training.

Thursday – June 11

This morning's paper quotes MacArthur as saying that the United Nation fighting forces would soon be moving north, and there is continued talk of an invasion of the European continent. I wonder if this is all talk, or whether we are actually ready to move. The worst of the war will be fought this summer in all probability. A precipitous end to it all is not an impossibility, but I should certainly be personally opposed to anything smacking of a peace short of complete victory. Really think, still, that next year is when we really will get in gear, finishing up the job in 1943.

Read a couple of articles in the Sat. Eve Post by a wealthy U.S. merchant who escaped from the Japs after capture at Hong Kong where he was at the time. He paints them a bloodthirsty, heartless lot. Some of his stories sound almost incredible, but they are true, I fear. The lot of a prisoner of war is not very good at best, but treatment at the hands of the Japanese is bestial!

Flew an hour of solo then a period of formation (3 plane) with an instructor in the lead. Can't say that I did too well.

Friday – June 12

Shot 50 more rounds of skeet this morning. Only broke 26 of them but that is better than heretofore, and augurs for improvement.

Had three hours of formation today – 3 plane. Things went better, I believe.

Sat – June 13

This was a bad day for me from start to finish. On my 1st formation hop up above the clouds I got lost, more or less, as were the other two boys, but I happened to be leading. The chase pilot, a little snipe of unreasoning tongue, about had a fit when we got down & threatened to order a special check for me. He didn't think I did anything right. On the next hop a diff. chase pilot gave me hell when we got down. Its true I hadn't done very well, but not that poorly – most of the trouble lay in the fact that my radio wasn't working well, & I couldn't under-stand what he said while we were in the air. About that time the officer in the tower wanted to see me, saying that I had taken too long to get off the ground when leading off the formation, which was very true. He was quite reasonable about it, however, even though it was a rather dangerous miscue. Then I proceeded to run off to shoot some trap & forget all about a board watch I was supposed to stand. In the evening on the way out to Martines a cop stopped me for driving in the middle of the road. Happily, I got off without a ticket. What a long, long day.

Sun – June 14

This is flag day, I believe, and Old Glory really means more to us & to all the world than at any other time in U.S. history. May we carry that grand banner to complete victory and soon.

Stayed at the main station last night. Went to church in the morn-ing, down to the beach in the afternoon, and out to Martines for supper.

Mon – June 15.

This was a long flying day – didn't quit until 7:30 PM. Now have only one 9 plane formation hop left. Things went a little better today, but, nonetheless, I shall be glad to get out of this squadron. Should be leaving for Miami about Fri.

Tues – June 16.

Rained most of the morning, and the first hop didn't go up until around noon. Had my last formation flight (9 plane) during the middle of the afternoon. It was quite smooth, & things went pretty well. Checked out and got back to the main station shortly after seven oclock.

Wednesday – June 17

Spent a good part of the morning catching up on my correspondence. Wrote 4 or 5 rather short letters that should have been tended to quite some time ago. In the afternoon I started checking out of ground school as required before leaving for Miami. Happily, my navigation was all up, and I managed to check out of radio on the first test given. Really should be leaving tomorrow, but am going to try to delay things until the forepart of next week so that a couple of the K.C. boys who aren't quite through yet can ride down with me. Bob & I ate supper at Martines, & then on the way back I left my car at the Ford garage to have a little work done on it – motor tuneup, wash & simonize, grease job.

Thursday – June 18

Didn't get up until around 7 oclock. Spent most of the morning reading magazine articles. In the afternoon I hit a couple of buckets of balls, then went down to the beach. Bob & I lazily conversed after supper until time to retire.

Friday – June 19

Did a little more checking out today. Found out I couldn't leave for Miami until Tuesday even if I wanted to – my orders haven't come in from Washington yet.

Down to the beach in the afternoon – this is the life. At 5:40 PM we had a dress parade in whites for the benefit of [a] cameraman. I detest marching & all that sort of thing. Glad I'm not in the infantry. Bob & I caught a bus immediately afterwards, getting off at the Ford station halfway into town to pick up my car. The new wax job makes it look pretty snappy, & the motor tuneup & grease job puts it in tip-top shape. Got off pretty reasonably, too.

Bob should finish up at squadron three today & will report at two on Sun. night. He will be down to Miami before long.

After flunking the low pressure chamber test Pettit expected to get VO-Vs, but happily enough got VP, which will be more to his liking.

Saturday – June 20

Ordered my officer uniforms through Simpson & Co. today. Am getting them about as reasonably as possibly can be done, but it still is robbery. Its a crime that the gov't doesn't handle the uniforms.

Bob, Ken & I went to a show after supper – not much good.

Sent a telegram to Gus for father's day.

Sun – June 21

Up late – didn't go to church for it was raining to beat the band, & I had already checked in my raincoat.

Bob & I went to the movie on the station about 3 oclock – no good. We went out to Martines for their Sun. night buffet supper. Did there meet Stuart Hemingway's girl whom he gave an engagement ring just a few days ago. Nice, refined looking sort of girl. Nearly all the boys with commission only a few weeks away are thinking of marriage. Sounds good.

Drove Bob out to Ellyson where he starts in tomorrow. Bid him farewell about 8 oclock.

Mon – June 22

And still no orders – am enjoying the rest & yet anxious to get on to Miami. Rained most of the day. All of the squadron except four were secured. Bob came back to the main station from Ellyson, and I drove Haugebak & him back out after supper.

Tues – June 23

My orders didn't come in today either so Garton, Bird, & Wright, who were going to ride down with me, went on ahead on the train. Wrote a letter or two, lolled on the beach, took my blues into Simpson & Co to be converted. Also ordered the rest of my uniforms from this same outfit, in anticipation of the day of my commission. Now feel completely mortgaged. Selling gov't uniforms is not a business but a racket.

Wed – June 24

At last my orders arrived, but I still won't get out till Friday – the station says Tues. & Fridays are the only two departure dates. Haugebak finished up yesterday and is going to ride down with me, also, a kid by the name of Carlson from Philadelphia.

Pettit & I went to see a show, the Invaders, in town this afternoon. Not too sharp.

Picked up a biography of Mr. Churchill just recently written by Philip Guedalla. Read it right straight through and found it extremely interesting, as I always do anything that concerns Britain's sturdy Prime Minister. He is the man in history who has completely caught my fancy and imagination. I read his every speech and writing with absorbing interest. He is a man of thought, of action, of resolution, and the man of the hour in the world's greatest crisis.

Thursday – June 25

Finished checking out except for that which can't be done until the day I leave, tomorrow.

Played nine holes of golf by myself. Not nearly so enjoyable as when you have companionship.

Went out to Martines for supper with Hotchkiss, Barker, & Glen Carlson from Chariton. Will be the last meal I'll take out there for a long time.

Kay Kyser and troupe were on the station for their weekly evening show. I had no ticket so couldn't go. Guess they were very good.

Said goodbye to Len Swett & Welsh two good boys now in P. boats.

Friday – June 26

Got off for Miami just about noon. Stopped over night in Tallahassee in a very comfortable little cabin camp. It was a hot, uninteresting drive – no pretty scenery, no traffic, no nothing. After supper we took a turn about the Florida State Teachers College ogling the girls with more than passing interest. Remained quite passive, however. Saw the show "Moontide" later in the evening – *fair*. Coming out on to the street again I ran into Bob Vernon who used to teach my geology lab at Iowa when I was a freshman. He now has a wife, 25 lbs more flesh, & a job as ass't state geologist.

Though the trip over was quite dull, my thoughts turned to farming & how I would like that kind of a life up in Iowa. Where to get the money to buy a decent farm – that is the problem. Man, I get eager of the prospect sometimes.

Sat – June 27

Got started out of Tallahassee about 9 AM and with constant driving drew into Ft. Myers about 5:15 PM. Nothing of unusual interest happened along the way – quite hot though.

Had to stay all night in a hotel, because we could find no decent looking cabin camp. Didn't rest very well because of the heat.

Sun. – June 28

Didn't get under way until about 10 oclock. While crossing the Everglades an unhappy incident occurred – the right hind tire blew out – or rather a large portion of the rubber was torn away although the tube didn't blow out. Didn't take long to get the spare on, however, and we were soon under way again. Pulled into Miami about 12:30. Drove around a little then registered at the Caribbean Hotel in Miami Beach. Went swimming in the ocean for a couple of hours, then went out for a bite to eat & a show.

Mon – June 29

Up late for a fine breakfast in the hotel dining room right next to the ocean. Spent the next hour & half writing a long letter home. We all went to a show in the late afternoon & another that night. The first, "This Gun for Hire" was only fair; the second, "Tortilla Flat" was pretty darn good.

Much sobered to hear the news that Matruk had probably fallen to the Axis. Things are really going badly for the Allies in Lybia. To lose all there, would be a terrible blow.

Checked in at the air station about 9:30. Haugebak & I are rooming together which is fine.

Tuesday – June 30

Began the usual routine necessary to check in at all Naval stations. Ran into a couple of sailors from Iowa who recognized me, called me by name, saying they were glad to see me aboard, etc. Such incidents serve as morale boosters. Wrote a couple of letters in the evening.

Wed. – July 1

Finished checking in. At one of the offices a woman stopped me saying that she stayed with Mr. & Mrs. Eastman who used to farm just outside Adel, & that they wanted very much to see me some time. If they knew how many times I used to steal watermelons from their patch they might not be so anxious.

Heard a brief talk from Lt. Comm. Thomas who welcomed us to the station and made the point that at this base the sole purpose of the training was to teach us to fight & that we shouldn't be anticipating instructors jobs nor ferry command, etc. He put it well, free from dramatics, but, nonetheless, forcibly. Sounded like good sense to me. Am all for it.

Reported in to squadron late in the afternoon. There will be lectures tomorrow.

Thursday – July 2

Our runway observation tour was canceled this morning. Had our first taste of the athletic program on this station which includes everything from swimming to hand to hand combat. All ok if not overdone. Looks like a good program even though it lasts for over an hour each day. We had swim test at 11 AM. Had to stay afloat (could move arms & legs) for five minutes without a rest. Sounds simple, but I found that 5 minutes can be an awfully long time.

In the afternoon I managed to check out of blinker leaving radio sending & receiving, semaphore ditto, & radio procedure. We had a tower observation tour about three oclock.

Friday – July 3

Listened to some more lectures on course rules, characteristics of the SNJ airplanes, passed a semaphore receiving check-out quiz – and did a lot of sitting around. Should start flying on Sunday. Liberty for different groups of men comes every eighth day. Haugebak & I are in liberty section six & have from secure today until 9:30 tomorrow night.

We left the station about six oclock. Were delayed on the way in by a practice air raid drill. Registered at the Patrician Hotel in Miami beach, got a bite to eat (poor) & went to a show (poor). Haven't been able to find a good place to eat around here yet.

Saturday – July 4

Independence Day! – current events bring its glory into sharp relief. Allied victory in this war will mark an important milestone in world independence from tyranny.

Slept late, went down to the beach behind the hotel for an hour or so. Sat in the sun in lazy reverie (wishing Bob were also here) & then had a little breakfast served to us. After showering I bought three magazines – old standbys – Time, Life & Sat. Eve Post. We sat around reading until 1:30 then went to see "Sergeant York," a truly good movie. It is the first really good cinema entertainment I have seen in a coon's age. I laughed & wept & thoroughly enjoyed it.

Drove back to the base, stopping along the way for a malted milk & a sandwich. They don't seem to know how to make a thick malt down this way.

Read awhile before going to bed. Finished St. Exupery's book "Wind, Sand, & Stars." Found it full of adventure & philosophy &

quite enjoyable. Couldn't follow him always in his philosophical wanderings but some of it was appealing & thought provoking.

Sunday – July 5

Flew 4 hours today – 2 hrs of dual instruction in which I was shown the stall characteristics of an SNJ, then an hour of cut-gun landings (check) & an hour of power landings (practice). Did not do very well at all. In fact haven't done any very good flying for quite a spell. I had better snap out of it.

Had a letter from Jimmy George in which he said he had been assigned to the Mechanized Transport Division of the Marine Corps – and he learned to drive a car only a couple of years ago!

Mon – July 6

Had my check out in inverted spins in an N3N this morning. Lt. Knudson was my instructor. His affable & encouraging manner gave me a much needed lift. He showed me also an inverted falling leaf & a slow roll, the latter of which I tried several times myself without much success.

Got my power landing check in the afternoon. Did much better than yesterday.

Wrote a letter to Clarke & one to Bob Stacy after supper. Spent the rest of the time before lights out reading several D.M. Registers which had been forwarded to me from Pensacola. That is certainly a fine paper, excellent in fact.

Tues – July 7

Had a couple of hours formation work today (3 plane). In addition to refreshing ourselves in routine formation flying we learned how to execute cross over turns in open echelon & ABC formation. I got along moderately well. Don't seem to pick up this formation stuff very quickly.

Received a card from Bob this morning. He expects to arrive here on this Friday. He mentioned that Hemingway is getting married on the 18th & that his orders are for San Diego. Will be flying Coronados between there & Australia.

Wed – July 8

My birthday – 24 years on this mortal coil – happy, strenuous, endeavoring years – and what of the future? Can't view it with pessimism despite the circumstances.

Started division cruising today, 9 planes kind of complicates things.

Discovered that Jim Carroll, a boy with whom I went to S School years ago in D. Moines, is an instructor here. He is a fine, big, pleasant looking chap. Also, ran into Don Frame who played football at Tee Jay in Council Bluffs while I was at Benson. He is taking a refresher course & then going back to Jacksonville to help get a fighter training squadron started there.

Thurs – July 9

It seems I got mixed up on my dates somewhere. Today is the 9th & my birthday, not yesterday as I first recorded it. Received a telegram & fine letter from father today. Letters from home have become almost precious. How I enjoy hearing about what is going on back there. He mentioned that Ben has been assigned to R111 out at St. Mary's – the same number as mine. What a strange coincidence.

Only had one hop today & that division cruising. Still am not too sharp – must do better tomorrow. Did check out of radio sending & radio procedure, however. Getting those requirements out of the way is quite a relief. Had another chat with Jim Carroll. He gave me a little dope on this formation – and also asked me out to dinner Sat night. It will be wonderful to get some home cooking again.

Bob arrived today and how glad I was to see him! We talked all evening forcing postponement of the letter I was going to write home.

Friday – July 10

Had an hour of acrobatic instruction followed by an instructors check. Can hardly imagine how I passed it – really a punk exhibition. Went out for some more practice in the afternoon. Everything went better except the slow rolls.

Wrote a long letter home after supper & talked with Bob.

Saturday – July 11

Had another hours practice on stunts. Still haven't mastered the slow roll very well – one more hour in which to get the word. Our flight had a final check in ABC formation the last hour today. We didn't even get joined up – about everything went wrong – have to take it over I guess.

Went to supper at Jim Carroll's. Enjoyed thoroughly a home cooked meal. Checked in at the Patrician Hotel about midnite.

Sunday – July 12

Slept late & then did some Science reading for an hour & a half. Read more in Pringles biography of Theo. Roosevelt until Marvin came in about 1 oclock. He stayed at the base last night & took a bus downtown around noon.

We went down to the beach for awhile & then to a movie. Had a fine supper at the Seven Seas & then back to the base.

Monday – July 13

Final check in ABC formation work and also in acrobatics. Got by both ok though not in a very imposing manner. My flirtation with mediocrity in flying the past month or so has settled into something more permanent. Am not discouraged with my progress, but it isn't quite as sharp as it might be. However, it may be just as well to proceed at this gait. Certainly, it is easier on the nerves and energy.

Tuesday – July 14

Bastille day in France – note by the evening news reports that they kicked up a little excitement for the Nazis just to prove the spirit of the French Revo. still flames.

No flying today – have to wait awhile before starting gunnery. Read at length & finally finished the biography of Theo. Roosevelt by Pringle. Don't believe U. Chas. in his devotion to T.R. would thin! much of the presentation. Not having read much about the "Trust Buster" I don't know just what to think. Pringle doesn't show him in an unfavorable light but neither does he pull his punches concerning Roosevelts weakness. Certainly he was a man of boundless energy and ambition, patriotic, possessed of much ability, a great American, and all that, but he was also vain, vindictive, contradictory. I don't care for his style of writing much.

The news tonight is that the training syllabus has been changed and that we shall be here twelve weeks with more ground school thrown in. The prospect doesn't appeal to me. Had hoped to be commissioned in late August.

Wednesday – July 15

No flying today either. Sat around & read most of the time. They started the ground school stuff today. Most of it seems to be repetition, drier than fallen leaves.

Thursday – July 16.

Still no flying – waiting for a gunnery hop. More sitting around, more ground school lectures, more reading.

Sec. Knox was on the station today looking around.

Friday, July 17

At last we flew again – a dummy gunnery run. However, I piloted the tow plane & didn't learn much. Will probably start flying tomorrow.

Finished Steinbeck's "Grapes of Wrath." It is coarse in language & episode, but realistic, and a tough protest against an unjust situation. The humor was rough but good – I laughed a lot.

Wrote a long letter home.

Sat – July 18

It is now July 21st – haven't penned a line in here for four days. Doubt if I can recall in proper order just what has happened. Do know that I have felt pretty low for the past few days. Rather hard to explain, too, – just have been in the dumps for no apparent reason.

Didn't fly at all today – ground school & time on our duff.

Spent an hour after supper observing night flying landings.

Sunday – July 19

We had another dummy run again – every one did poorly – not much fun when the chase pilot is climbing all over you most of the time.

Marvin & I had liberty beginning at 5:30 secure. Drove into town for a movie & then to the Patrician for a bed & bath.

Monday – July 20

Up late, read some, wrote a letter home, swam a little, a movie, something to eat, & then back to the station. Oh yes, I bought myself a small radio which should be much enjoyed by the both of us.

Tuesday – July 21

Had a strafing flight – quite a bit of fun. How anyone could strafe helpless refugee columns, though, I can't imagine.

Two hours of night flying after supper – good experience – wonderful view of the surrounding area at 3000′. Miami didn't look like it was having any blackout.

Wed – July 22

Fired at the sleeve today – great fun, but no hits for Haugebak or me – disappointing to both of us – but perhaps tomorrow.

Started reading Tolstoys "War & Peace," the greatest novel ever written. It is 1350 pages long, hope I have the desire & perseverance to finish it.

Thurs – July 23

Had a strafing run the last hour in the afternoon. Night flying called off because of bad weather. How fine to have a couple of hours relaxation after supper.

Friday – July 24

Fired on the sleeve again. I couldn't seem to get "on" it & only fired twice, & at that managed to get one hit. Marvin got 7 or 8 which is pretty good.

Spent two hours in section practice after dark. On my last landing I ground looped, the first time anything like that ever happened to me. No damage was found for which I am very thankful.

The war news is awfully dark these days. If Rostov hasn't already fallen, it looks like it would at any moment. What a grim prospect is ahead of us.

Sat – July 25

The officer who was to be our chase pilot was forced down out in the area just before our hop so it was canceled. Understand he made a nice landing on the highway.

Finished up night flying including a simple, 40 minute cross country flight.

Am 300 pages into "War & Peace" now. Find it very good, but oh so long.

Sun – July 26

Managed to get 4 hits on my gunnery run today which isn't too good but, nonetheless was high in our group. We have more time in which I am going to really do my best. If I get quite a few hits I think I'll ask for fighters.

Bob was in the room after supper. He and Marvin argued politics with some force. Bob can express himself with considerable logic in opposition to the present administration.

Monday – July 27

I was awfully disappointed today when my gun jammed after firing only 5 rounds. Really thought I was getting "down" on the sleeve too. Did manage to [get] 3 hits though. Will probably tow next time (the last), hence, my record is already in, and unimpressive it is. Think I shall put in for fighters anyhow & see what happens.

This being my night off & Marvin being restricted I drove up town by myself. Saw a movie & then sat out behind the Patrician for awhile enjoying the moonlight & sea breeze. It was a beautiful night such as only poets can tell about.

Tuesday – July 28

Up late, studied awhile, wrote a couple of letters, then a swim. Stopped at Eddie's tire shop for my tire that I had left to be fixed a week ago. Found he had ruined it completely in trying to put it in shape, but he says he'll have another just as good for me next week. Hope he won't gouge me too deeply. Was able to get an "A" gas rationing card with a minimum of trouble. It will give me 4 gal. a week which will meet my needs quite nicely. In the late afternoon saw a putrid show & returned to the base.

Wed – July 29

Last gunnery run today – I towed. Marvin got 11 hits which makes him a fighter pilot for certain. I also put in for fighters, but doubt if I get them.

Wrote a couple of letters after supper.

The Germans roll on – the prospect is sure grim – and all the while continues Allied speculation about a second front.

Thursday – July 30

By golly I got fighters and now find myself very glad that such is the case. Must really bear down from here on out & become just as skillful as possible.

Flight two had a little get together at the Officers club for supper. A rollicking good time was had by all.

Friday – July 31

No flying today – still waiting for flight #3 to finish up gunnery, then we shall join with them to makeup our fighter flight.

Picked up my uniforms at the supply dep't where they had been lying for several days. Total cost equals $217 & they don't fit too well either – this uniform racket is scandalous.

Wrote a long letter home after supper, also got one off to Tait Cummins.

The Russians are stiffening their resistance again, especially around Stalingrad, and the RAF is bombing German industrial centers about every night. Hope this combination will do the trick, for I fear we aren't really ready for an invasion of the continent.

Sat. – Aug 1

Still waiting to get our fighter flight started. This all too frequent waiting around is tiresome & annoying. Surely we shall fly tomorrow.

Had a very enjoyable chat with a boy from New Zealand who was quite interested in American football. I found that he was well acquainted with the names of our good teams & players. Shall look forward to becoming better acquainted with him. He is a nice looking chap, well built, & resembles Ted in the face a great deal. Don't know his name yet.

Sun – Aug 2
Mon – Aug 3

Still no flights for fighter class #2. Wait, wait, that is all I've done since coming into the Navy. At this rate I won't get home before Xmas. Had the duty as mate of the deck on Mon. Managed to read quite a bit in War & Peace.

Tues – Aug 4

We flew four hours this morning, one right after the other. This is more like it.

Went out to Jim Carroll's for supper, then down to the Patrician, it being my night off.

Wed – Aug 5

The tireman having ruined my tire, I stopped in to see if he hadn't gotten me another yet. He had, a pretty fair one, & charged me only $3. Left my uniforms at City Tailors to be altered. Hope they can shape them up a bit.

Got back to the base about 6:30. Groused with Bob for a couple of hours & then wrote a letter to Merle from whom I heard on Mon for the 1st time in quite awhile.

The world picture continues gloomy & foreboding. The Germans continue to advance in the Caucasus, the Japs are showing increased activity around Australia, India threatens to begin a civil disobedience campaign if Eng. doesn't grant them complete freedom immediately, U.S. production is in need of steel, the shipbuilding program is in a bad way, nothing looks very good except the Allies slowly seem to be gaining air superiority everywhere – and that should eventually win the war.

Thursday – Aug 6

Just one hop – but it went off pretty well. If we don't start getting more than one hour a day we won't *ever* get out of here.

Had a surprise telephone call from King Clarke about seven oclock this evening. He has been transferred to Camp Murphy about 100 miles north of here. Hope we can get together for a visit before long.

Friday – Aug 7

Rec'd a note from Mrs. Jack Riley (formerly Mary McHugh of Soo City) asking me to look them up. Jack is connected with the FBI & now stationed here in Miami. It will be good to see some Iowa people once again.

Spent two hours on six plane division work. We got along pretty well.

Wrote several letters after supper.

Have now finished Tolstoy's monumental work War & Peace. Found it enjoyable throughout its 1300 odd pages. His range of interest and knowledge seem illimitable, and he can so simply describe a scene or character. Can easily see why nearly all critics proclaim it the greatest novel ever written.

Sat. – Aug 8

Today is Ben's birthday – best wishes, old buddy.

Had a two hour hop this afternoon – a formation check – went off pretty well.

Letters arrived from Tait, Stace & mother. How fine it is to hear from all these folks. Stace is to be sent to Detroit for training as an electrician. That is about like King becoming a radio repair man.

Sun – Aug 9

Two hours of course flying – just enough to indicate how precise your navigation must be if you expect to get back to the carrier.

Rec'd an unexpected call from King about 7 oclock. He had caught a ride into Miami & was at Union Bus Depot. I drove down to see him but we could spend only about an hour together for I had to be back at 9:15. It sure was good to see him. He looked about the same as always and none the worse for wear.

Mon – Aug 10

Four hours today – a two hour relative search sector & a two hour cross country up to Bell Grade, then to Fellsmere & back. Start gunnery tomorrow.

Tues – Aug 11

3 hours again today, this is more like it. One & half hrs of dummy beam runs (I towed), then $1\frac{1}{2}$ hrs of firing. I got the pattern ok, but didn't hit the sleeve very well.

Wed. – Aug 12

Three hours of beam runs – now ready to start camera gunnery.

Went out to Rileys for supper. Jack was over at Tampa, so Mary had Jim Dower come in to make a third. It was quite a surprise for me, didn't know Jim was in the FBI too. Had a wonderful time – good meal, good people, enjoyable exchange of stories & experience.

Thurs – Aug 13

Stayed at Patrician – rose late, studied awhile, and then in for a swim. Saw the movie "Mrs. Minniver" in the afternoon. It was one of the finest cinemas I have ever seen. It brought forth in me more heartfelt emotion than I have felt for a long time. Greer Garson & Walter Pidgeon are both so good. Back to the base at 6:30 – wrote a letter home & listened to Marvin & Bob argue rather aimlessly about the war effort.

Friday – Aug 14

Two camera gunnery hops with no film. Both useless hops, nobody knew what was going on nor why.

The rumor is that we are to finish up in Brewsters. Glad of the chance to fly a faster ship, but there are so few of them in commission at a time we probably won't finish for three weeks – lamentable prospect.

Sat – Aug 15

Had the duty today as mate of the deck, a boring, useless, thankless job. Am getting so tired of this training life I can hardly stand it.

Just before bed time I dropped down to Bob's room & helped him work on a terrifically big box of cookies, candys & nuts he received from Elsie.

Sun – Aug 16

Last shot at camera gunnery – beam runs – kind of a poor exhibition all the way around – then in the afternoon 3 hrs of uninteresting, dull, senseless ground school – ugh!

Mon – Aug 17

Two hours of instruction in combat, ie, dogfighting – quite a bit of fun – did pretty well.

Allied cause is looking a little better now. The Russians are stiffening, particularly around Stalingrad, & the Solomon Islands engagement appears to be a victory for the United Nations thus far.

Tues – Aug 18

Haven't written a line in here for almost a week. Had almost forgotten it altogether.

Finished up combat work. A checkout in Brewsters next.

Wednesday – Aug 19

Lecture on the F2A airplane which under 10,000 feet will perform pretty well with the F4F.

An half day of this awful ground school as per usual.

Thursday – Aug 20

A cockpit checkout in the Brewster, then we shot landings for half an hour.

Drove up to W. P. Beach to meet King & Mary Jane, it being my night off. We had dinner together in the air conditioned dining room of the Geo. Washington hotel, then visited till 12:30 when King had to head back to camp.

Friday – Aug 21.

More landings in F2A & familiarization air work. Chandelles & loops easy but a slow roll awfully hard.

Sat. Aug 22

More familiarization work.

Sunday – Aug 23

Ditto

We have the duty tomorrow – what a shaft!

Bob's outfit hasn't had a watch yet! They are going through to dive bombing in SNJs and are up with us right [now]. May even finish ahead of us.

Mon – Aug 24

Another hour of familiarization & then a landing check. The days creep by – will we never finish?

Tues. – Aug. 25.

Two hours of section work – attack tactics tomorrow.
"Nothing worries and wearys a man so much as trying to achieve absolute certainty in human affairs."

Wed – Aug 26

Again I have failed to write here for several days. My neglect of this record bespeaks my interest in this last month of training. I am tired of it all & anxious to get home.

Thurs Aug 27
Friday   28
Sat   29
Sun   30

These days were spent on attack tactics, only two hours left now, then 5 hours of glide bombing.
Just after we came down today it rained torrentially, one of the hardest rains I have experienced in a long while.

Monday – Aug 31

Got off to a good start in dive bombing today – 4 out of five were hits. Should finish up tomorrow.

Tuesday – Sept 1

All through!! Can hardly believe it! Should be commissioned on Thursday & ready to start home on Friday. Happy day!

Vol. III

The Story of Philosophy – Will Durant

A Time for Greatness – Herbert Agar

Biographies of Great Men $\left\{\begin{array}{l}\text{Jefferson}\\\text{Wilson}\end{array}\right.$

Good Set of Encyclopedias

Good Atlas & Globe & Dictionary

World Crisis – Winston Churchill

Glimpses of World History – Nehru

Good Books on Civil & World War & the League of Nations

American Strategy in World Politics – Spykman

Reading I Have Liked – Clifton Fadiman

Historical Novels

Good texts on history, economics, money & finance, taxation,
corporation law, municipal law, constitutional law, inter-national
law

Good Volume of Prose & Poetry

Good history of Iowa

Foreign language study – Mathematics

Close study & analysis of the constitution

National Anthem, America, Battle Hymn of the Republic

Peace & War – gov't document on U. S.-Jap relations *1931–41*

Let the People Know – Sir Norman Angell

A Time for Greatness – Herbert Agar

Currier & Ives Lithographs.

Combination Radio & Victrola

Heathen Days – Mencken

Good books on Russia since Revolution.

This is My Best – edited by Burnett

Van Loon's Lives

Woodrow Wilson and the League of Nations.

Time

Life

Readers Digest

Sat. Eve Post

Fortune

Epic of America – James Truslow Adams.

Macaulay, Carlyle, Gibbon, Prescott, Parkman.

Oriental history & thinking – particularly Chinese.

Snow Goose – Paul Gallico

*War & Peace – Tolstoy

Aesop's Fables

Arabian Nights

Chinese proverbs & wit

Folklore of Capitalism – Thurman Arnold.

The American Language – H. L. Mencken.

Jean Christophe – Romain Rolland

A Shopshire Lad – A. E. Housman

Famous Supreme Court Decisions

Walter Duranty on Russia

"R. E. Lee"
⎱ Douglas Southall Freeman
Lee's Lieutenants ⎰

History of South.

Literature on the party system and practical politics.

Book on flora & fauna of the U. S. – partic. in mid-west.

Odyssey

Southern Regions of the U. S. – U. of North Carolina

1943

1/1 to **4/25** – In training at Q. Pt.

4/26 – Q to Nfk – 18 planes

4/27 – Landed aboard – back to Q.

4/28 – Q to Nfk – 36 planes

4/29 – Landed aboard – back to Q.

5/2 – Q to Nfk – 36 planes – pilots walked aboard at Portsmouth.

5/3 – Ports. to H. Roads – tugs – harbor buoy – leaden sky – rain – wind.

5/4 – Am. demo. was founded & can only succeed on a thoroughly moral basis – common respect for innate dignity of man nec. – a profound sense of justice for all – closely knit family life & sound, efficient local self-gov't required.

5/5 – Avoid the complex & fancy in thought, speech and action. Put your faith in simplicity & plain common sense. Our social & econ. prob. are fundamentally moral. Their ultimate solution depends on the home, school & church. However, we must eternally seek those laws & institutions which will most readily implement our ideals & reduce to a minimum the conditions tempting the frailties of human nature. – Sunset in the harbor – a suffusion of gold & scarlet lingering over the bank of purple clouds in the west – freighters at anchor – blinking semaphore signals, silent but articulate – ferry boat – strange, clamoring cry (squeak) of the sea gulls – quiet, peaceful.

5/6 – Order vs liberty – vigor, efficiency, incentive of private enterprise & ownership vs organizational power of gov't & its assurance of greater social & economic equality & justice – how to reconcile them? Imp. of the middle class in the progress of society? How to make nationalism serve the cause of internat'l cooperation?
Diff. bet. a colony & a mandated area?
Correlation bet. self-interest and the moral obligation to respect the dignity of your fellow man, to deal honestly & fairly? Even the broad minded members of the privileged class are prone to worship stability – need to be shaken from their apathy, shamed from their apprehension of change.
Has capitalism – as well as Christianity – been given a fair trial?
Can the prospect of power, prestige, recognition, take the place of profit incentive?
"How can you ever have political & econ. freedom where the state owns everything." (Willkie)
A man must *never* cease growing, developing, looking ahead. Be alert, be vigorous, cultivate the mind & memory continually – laugh a lot.

5/7 – Friday

If the general standard of living is increased thru gov't ownership & control why be alarmed at the bureaucracy & inefficiency, debt increase, etc? – or do they bring disaster in the long run? Are the old virtues of thrift, hard work, initiative no longer imp? A society must earn what it receives or it will disintegrate for lack of character. A gov't which ignores this demand is a deceiver and deception in gov't is the highest of crimes.

The sound, honest way to aid underprivileged individuals & nations is to help them help themselves, enable them to become strong and productive. Paternalism is but a stop-gap and a contemptible one at that.

What part should the state gov'ts play in producing a better society & way of life? How dangerous is the growth of tolls and excise taxes on traffic bet. states?

Profit is a legitimate incentive but it must go hand in hand with the grander aim maximum production at low costs. Monopolies formed for the purpose of restricting prod. & thus controlling the price structure is a crime against society and the free enterprise system.

How can any political candidate be really free & independent in thought & policy when he is dependent on wealthy backers for campaign funds? Is there any practical remedy for this seemingly inescapable situation?

Pro & con of patent rights?

How best to meet the Negro problem?

Is this war a people's revolution or a struggle for survival or both?

The Constitution is a magnificent instrument but it is not a dispensation from on high. We must not be afraid to let it grow & change, nor to fear a liberal interpretation in the interest of social gain & justice. However, let our aim & means be frank and honest. The danger lies in deception & crafty circumvention.

"Nothing of importance can be won in peace which has not already been won in the war itself" – W. Willkie.

Wonder why my folks voted for Hoover in 1932? Was he advancing any of the social & econ. remedies promulgated by Roosevelt? Was it a recalcitrant Congress which hamstrung him?

Why did Roosevelt torpedo the London Econ. Conf. in 1933? What were its prospects for inter-national co-operation & gain?

Heretofore, Am. political parties have automatically taken diametrically opposite views and the country has managed to progress regardless. This can no longer be true. In this respect W. Willkie has shown himself a man of much stature & character.

Great majority of our political & economic troubles arise from a lack of candor in our leaders. They try to be too smooth & adroit. They put partisan advantage above conviction.

Without self respect there can be no character

5/8 – Saturday

"brown bagger"
"yokel color"
"riders of purple haze"
"Bourby breath"

5/9 – Sunday – Mother's Day

Don't confuse resignation with patience.

Is class warfare nec. for social gain of common people? What is wrong with running a gov't on a fear & favor basis as the New Deal is prone to do – much needed social legislation has been passed hasn't it?

"From each according to his ability, to each acc. to his work" – this may point a workable mean between the extremes of capitalism & Communism. If we are to have an economy of abundance our productive forces must operate at capacity, but a man must always be made to earn what he receives, & those who produce more must receive more; also ingenuity & merit must be rewarded. A society which does not recognize this fundamental fact must surely disintegrate. Prices cannot be successfully controlled by legislative fiat, nor even by tyranny. It can only be done by competition of the buyer & seller in the free mkt. What gov't control may sometimes be nec. (in wartime, monopolistic inequities) can best be exercised by influence in the fundamental fields of demand & supply. For eg pchsing power can be curtailed through taxation & enforced savings. Supply can be regulated through rationing or subsidies. Monopolies can be broken by anti-trust suits or subjected to the competition of a gov't owned business in the same field.

The time to levy heavy taxes to meet a mounting war debt is during the war itself when the people are in the spirit to accept the sacrifice & when they are nec. anyhow as an anti-inflation measure. The New Deal is doing this country a disservice in this respect. If we expect to avoid disastrous repercussions in our economy after the war we must be as tough on the home front as we are on the fighting front. It is true that the common people will suffer more from such measures than the wealthy, but it will be a minor sacrifice compared to what they will have to endure if we are snowed under by a run-away-inflation.

The U.M.W. strike – euphemistically clothed in the phrase "we shall not trespass on comp. property without a contract" – is largely a pers. battle bet. Roosevelt & John L. Lewis. If a wage increase is granted Lewis once more will be top dog in the labor ranks. If the increase is refused, Roosevelt may lose the support of labor in the next election. He is in a tough spot, but mostly of his own making. Had the administration effectively applied their price controls long ago this situation could never have arisen. As it is the miners really need more money – which the operators can afford to pay because of an OPA permitted boost in coal prices – to meet the rising cost of living, yet of necessity the anti-inflation line MUST be held. The conditions under which these coal miners live – and the Negroes in the south – is a shameful blot on our democratic ideals and the potential standard of living in this country.

Bizerte & Tunis are now captured, the show in N.A. is about over. Presume the invasion of the continent will begin the latter part of June. Its success will depend on the overall strategy, air superiority, reduction of the sub menace in the N.A., and on the revolt of the people in the occupied countries.

Now there is the matter of the noisy, prolonged laughter at movies & stage plays which make it impossible to hear the succeeding remarks and repartee. Truly the loud laugh & the vacant mind travel hand in hand.

"Elmers Tune" – Katey Smith, Dec. '41 – K.C.

"Moonlight Cocktail" – Morrison's – Mar. '42 – Pensacola

"Blues in the Night" – Merle McKay – Jan '42 – K.C.

"White Xmas" – Anne Kanoy (rhumba) – Dec '42 – Greensboro

"As Time Goes By"

"Back to Where I Come From" – Ready Room – April '43 – Q. Pt. Flew up among the clouds today – tall, voluminous cumulus clouds – they were like snow covered mts, range after range of them. I felt like an Alpine adventurer climbing up their canyons, winding my way between their peaks – a billowy fastness, a celestial citadel.

"Chattanooga Choo-choo"

Wild dreams – lying in field with planes making forced landings & one turns out to be a horse; Neff & Roosevelt, Lindbeck & the snakes.

5/10 – Monday

"shall revive as the corn"

"blindness of their heart"

The Bible is a great and good book well deserving the reverence & respect it has commanded up through the ages. It is fine literature, interesting history, and full of the wisdom and experiences of a people who loved God. But best of all a spiritual understanding of its inspired word will bring the same comfort and healing that it did in the early days of Christianity. It is practical teaching & its application is sorely needed in the world today.

A gov't must do more than establish order, guarantee political liberty, and insure equal justice under law. It must stand ready to remedy abuses in the econ. system, to stimulate the econ. of abundance. However, in doing these things a *good* gov't will help the people to help themselves, never promoting the philosophy that the gov't owes its people a living.

"Comin' thru the Rye"

"restless as the sea"

I am learning once again to read leisurely, with patience and thoughtfulness.

Frank – small, snub-nosed – neat, correct, formal, adherent of discipline in small things, accustomed to a certain deference from his associates.

The recent meeting of the U.S. Chamber of Commerce (except for Pres. Eric Johnson) expressed satisfaction with the goal of "fairly constant employment" after the war, stating that full employment is possible only in a slave state. They had better devise some way to get full employment in their business system or it will never last. Max. production & full emp. can be had & some way must be found short of totalitarian measures.

It is not enough for the privileged to treat the less fortunate, or the whites to treat the colored people, with kindly tolerance and indulgent paternalism. All people of whatever creed, nationality, or color must be accorded equal dignity and human worth. Both Christianity & true democracy demand this fundamental acknowledgment. Social & economic & racial inequities cannot be solved in a moment, & in some respects it is best that we make haste slowly, but this truth is basic and is the starting point & foundation on which to build.

"grates on my classical ear"

A position of leadership & responsibility should mean more work, more sacrifice, not privilege & repose.

Parents should guide & discipline their children so that they will learn their lessons of life by minor experiences of grief & mistake. Too much warning, restrictions & prohibitions bring rebellion sooner or later with all its sad consequences.

No man, or group of men, is wise enough to rule a country in happiness & prosperity. It takes the wisdom & perspective born of the crucible of free debate & discussion of a demo. people.

"Mighty as a Rose"

"Take it off"

Movies & band on the hangar deck after supper –

The happy, peaceful, kindly mind is the one which loses all sense of self and takes no thought of the physical body.

Most unforgettable characters – grandpa Kinnick, grandpa & grandma Clarke, parents,

"close but no cigar"

5/11 – Tuesday

Under way at last after 8 days delay, around noon – beautiful day – sunny, good breeze, low scattered clouds. On the bosom of the deep – gentle pitch & roll of the ship. Scouts coming aboard at dusk, etc – exciting, adventurous is life aboard a carrier.

Give way easily in trivialities but stand without yielding in matters of principle.

A good sense of order is a fine thing, but in certain circumstances be willing to settle for something a little short of the ideal or you will be unceasingly annoyed. The imp. thing is to keep your thought well ordered – be able to see order in seeming chaos.

5/12 – Wed.

"Where wood is chopped the chips must fly" – War & Peace.
140 mi. west of C. H. at 0900
Water is deep, rich blue – good breeze always blows.
"plowing water"

Parallel bet. skippers threat to drop some of the pilots & a coach's threat to kick some of the boys off the fb. squad.

5/13 – Thurs.

Initiative – timely action based on sound thinking & willingness to assume the responsibility.

Wonderful similes of Tolstoy.

Passed through Sargasso sea this afternoon – had group tactics.

Lying on deck at dusk – wake of ship is a beautiful turquoise color – flying fishes.

5/14 – Friday

Now why all this excitement and criticism of the British Empire. It would be virtually as correct to refer to this country & its possessions, though not so widespread, as the American Empire. Our acquisitions, growth & development into a United States closely parallels that of the British Commonwealth. England fought for and won the territories of what we now know as Canada, Union of S. Africa, India, Australia, Egypt, etc, plus many islands. Many of these have grown to full dominion and independent status; some are still in the process, not having yet met the required standards. Where there has been no racial problem the transition has been steady & sure, eg. Canada & Australia. Our history has been quite similar though confined for the most part to the boundaries of one continent. From our original 13 colonies we advanced ever westward, acquiring the Northwest Terr., Florida, La Pchse, Texas, Calif, Oregon Territory, Alaska, Philippine Islands, Puerto Rico, etc. As each terr., or division thereof, measured up to certain stipulations they were admitted as states with full rights & protection under the constitution. Our growth to federalism has been steady and sure though not without its difficulties including a Civil War. As in the British Empire the real trouble has come where vested interests and racial differences are involved. Until we have put our own house in order (successfully & fairly met the Negro problem) we cannot well afford to criticize the British colonial policy – particularly in India where the situation is unusually complex.

"The fashions of this world are in continuous change & I would concern myself with things that are abiding." – Goethe.

Notes & References on the Epilogues to War & Peace by Leo Tolstoy – Inner Sanctum edition:

Foreword by Clifton Fadiman:

xxiv – quotation

xxv – 1st line

xxvi – 1st ¶

War & Peace full of recurrent human situations

xxxv – ¶3

xxxvi – ¶4

xxxvii – – ¶2

xxxviii – ¶1

xlviii – last 3 lines of ¶3

"No Nazi politically but one spiritually"

"sense of process" with respect civilized values.

"continuity of human events"

Plvi – last ¶

P670 – ¶3; P1256 – ¶4; P1257 – ¶9; P1258 – ¶3; P1264 – ¶1, 2, 3; P1356 – ¶2, 5; P1360 – ¶2, 4; P1361 – ¶1 (last sent), ¶3. P1314 – 2d¶; P1321 – ¶3; P1329 – ¶3; P1330 – ¶2, 3, 4;

"like a deaf man answer questions no one has asked."

The theme of War & peace is – what are the forces which move peoples & nations back & forth bet. war & peace?

Tolstoy claims there is no such thing as chance or genius.

P1330 – ¶1; P1332 – ¶4; P1333 – ¶2; P1334 – ¶3; P1335 – last ½ of page; P1336 – ¶3; P1337 – ¶2; P1338 – ¶2, 3; P1339 – ¶2, 4; P1340 – ¶7, 8; P1341 – ¶4, 5; P1342 – ¶5 (last line) P1344 – ¶2, 3; P1346 – ¶7, 8; P1347 – ¶4+; P1348 – ¶5; P1349 – ¶5, 7; P1351 – last 2¶s.

"sotto voce."

No flying today – low ceiling, frequent squalls. Water is dark, inky blue tonight.

Gunnery scores since commissioning of squadron were posted this afternoon. Mine was poor but not as bad as a lot of others. The skipper threatened to replace some of us if we don't improve, which is fair enough since a fighter pilot isn't of much value if he can't hit with his fixed guns.

What is so rare as a really good competitor who is unselfish

5/15 – Saturday.

At 2:30 PM we were 120 miles north by east of Barbados.

"enlightened selfishness"

"Let me designate the heroes of a nation and I care not who writes its constitution" – Thurman Arnold.

5/16 – Sunday.

Test run for ship up to 30 knots to note vibration. Murky day, low ceiling, frequent rain squalls. OS2Us came out to meet us. Entered Gulf of Paria, bet. Trinidad & Venezuela, through northern entrance (Dragons Mouth). Anchored around 2:30 PM.

5/17 – Mon.

Group tactics – S.B.D. cowling ripped off in dive. 5″ batteries on ship fired at sleeve towed by PBY in afternoon – very accurate.

Officers bunkroom – 2500 cu ft less space than minimum conditions permitted for prisoners in brig.

Beautiful night – full moon – distant lights on shore – light clouds – stars, etc.

5/18 – Tuesday

Talked to a jg (Young) who made the run to Archangel as Naval gunnery officer on an armed mchtman – tough go – naval gun crews got more liberty but less pay than the merchant marine sailors – union prevented the possibility of much military discipline. U. S. shipping can't compete with other countries bec. of higher wages (eg $80 to $40 min. for Eng) – need a gov't subsidy – Liberty ships too slow for peace time competition – Hurricane (!) only air protection they had the whole way.

Refueled destroyer this afternoon.

"Errol Flynn says its best with your shoes on."

Moonbeams were dancing on the water tonight in everchanging forms – a kaleidoscope of geometric pattern – without refocusing my eyes the shapes seem to grow to become permanent as if they were traced on the bottom of a pool of water about 6″ deep.

What is so rare as a really good competitor who is unselfish.

5/15 – Saturday.
At 2:30 PM we were 120 miles north by east of Barbados.
"enlightened selfishness"
"Let me designate the heroes of a nation and I care not who writes its Constitution" – Thurman Arnold

5/16 – Sunday.
Test run for ship up to 30 knots to note vibration. Murky day, low ceiling, frequent rain squalls. O92 U came out to meet us. Entered Gulf of Paria, bet. Trinidad & Venzuela, through northern entrance (Dragons Mouth). Anchored around 2:30 PM.

5/17 – Mon.
Group tactics – S.B.D cowling ripped off in dive. 5" batteries on ship fired at sleeve towed by PBY in afternoon – very accurate.
Officers bunkroom – 2500 cu/ft less space than minimum conditions permitted for prisoners in prison.
Beautiful night – full moon – distant lights on shore – light clouds – stars, etc.

From Nile Kinnick's diary, May 1943. Kinnick Collection.

5/19 – Wed.

"Always fake before you strike"

Desire for approval of associates deters the conservative, respectable people from advocating reform.

Both our Consti & our slogans have their worth and meaning, but we should not worship them superstitiously or permit them as moral argument for the suppression of the underprivileged.

As the gov't continues to play an even greater part in our econ. & social life it is imperative that we develop a good, sound, honest, efficient system of administrators.

The Consti. fathers were wise but also humble – I don't believe they thought they had formulated an infallible & unchanging law. It isn't a divine dispensation.

A demo gov't whose people will not permit it to arm & act against foreign & domestic enemy – both military & econ – is not fit to survive.

Such institutions as the church & family cannot very well sanction the easy compromise of principle and ideals because the frailties of human nature would soon run rampant and obscure the beacon which has pointed our progress. The reconciliation of practical needs and our aspiration must be made by the individual in good conscience and without fear.

"ex cathedra"

"sub rosa"

Everyone saluting the colors at sunset as they are hauled down.

5/20 – Thursday

Went to the beach today, operating out of Edinburgh field. Got 12 hits out of 79 – believe I've gotten the word on this gunnery.

"Navy phonetic alphabet."

"snafu" – "tarfu"

"gook money," etc

"sea stories"

"airdales"

"spooky nite"

Used to read at least 40 or 50 pages a day. Since some of us started playing bridge a few days ago I haven't read a word.

5/21 – Fri

Ken Kavanaugh & 3 other Army pilots were aboard observing today. They are flying B18s on patrol duty out of Trinidad. Tony Bremer, formerly a swimmer at Iowa, also was on board. He is flying PBYs out of here.

5/22 – Saturday

No flight operations today. All pilots went swimming – and drinking – at Maqueripe, an officers club and beach built by the British about 40 years ago and recently taken over by the Americans as a result of the destroyer (over-age) deal in the fall of 1940(?). Had an interesting talk with one of the native truck drivers. Seemed quite intelligent & fair minded. He philosophically opined that there were both good & bad Americans & British. The British educational system sounded pretty good. Compulsory up to 14 – elementary, secondary, & even colleges established. If a student is particularly apt he is sent to Britain for more education. All of it is free. I gathered that the econ. opportunity was not so generous. Where the white man's pocketbook & social & racial superiority is involved his humanitarian impulses are quick to recede.

The mind which demands "one or the other," "all or nothing" is the mind which can never successfully reconcile idealism with the practical need.

The desire for certainty – unachievable in human experience – frets so many people, wears them out, robs them of happiness & peace. Do the best that you can & the best that you know and fear not. That goes for prayer as well as other endeavour.

When writing or speaking don't attempt to be too precise and detailed. Leave something to the intelligence and imagination of your listeners.

If the gov't shouldn't enter into the production of goods, how about entering into the distribution

"slave to precedent"

"polar words"

Conforming or reconciling everyday action & thought to the demands of religious teaching is a potent stimulus to the active & conscientious mind.

Men are no stronger or braver than the women behind them.

"Take Me Back to West Virginia"

5/23 – Sunday

If you really want to win, never give a sucker a break. Press every advantage to the limit.

Safety in aviation demands a healthy respect for your aircraft, unceasing alertness.

5/24 – Monday

Were the labor strikes during the thirties actually more orderly than in previous depressions?

Gov't by force cannot last, it is too exhausting. An enduring gov't must be based on the faiths & loyalties of a people.

"emotional drive derived from ceremony"

Is profit an essential element of efficiency? Is he who works without a profit incentive inevitably bureaucratic? How about a professor, minister, scientist?

"Given a situation where the ideals are in contradiction to the needs, a sub rosa organization must develop." – Thurman Arnold in Folklore of Capitalism.

Christian Science, Yankee pragmatism, laughter are the tools with which I fashion my life.

"bete noire"

Realize that every close call with danger is proof of God's care and that the demands of a tough assignment are a challenge to your worth and courage. This kind of thinking knows no fear.

Learn to sleep soundly and efficiently regardless of circumstance if you would be a man of stamina.

5/25 – Tuesday

Night field carrier at Edinburgh – darker than pitch, but everything went along pretty well. Afterwards at Army Officers club I met two pilots from Iowa – Cap't. Teedie from Ottumwa & Lt. Gray from Sioux City.

Port of Spain – small, naked native boy eating watermelon & urinating at same time – "little squirt."

"industrial feudalism"

"tail gunners" – cartoon.

5/26 – Wed.

Tonite at supper met a young officer of the British Fleet Air Arm who was observing aboard. He was from N. Zealand & knew Neville Turnbull – a pleasant coincidence.

A letter from Pettit says Hobbs is on his way back to the States – sure would like to see him before heading for the Pacific. Enich is now a captain.

5/27 – Thursday

If you cannot meet the moral demands of abstinence and continence, then for goodness sake at least be temperate, discriminating, discreet – be civilized.

May there not come a time when economic security will become as an integral part of our Bill of Rights as pers. security. Of course it will mean that there must be max. production and that each man shall receive according to his work & merit. Such guarantees can never spring from the logic of biology and anthropology but only from a high sense of justice, common brotherhood, and human dignity

"tarfu"

Given a social need plus a respectable symbol, and the means, whatever they are, will be readily countenanced.

"waste" of gov't vs "efficiency" of private organizations

Patronage & political technique of private org. vs gov't?

Was the exploitation of labor by the big corp. & the robbery of stock & bondholders thru bankruptcy & reorganization proceedings the result of unscrupulous action by dishonest men, or of viewing these great org. as individuals competing in a free mkt without public responsibility.

Relationship bet. succ. issues of corp. sec. & fiat money printed by gov't? Investors holding defaulted sec. have sacrificed their money to the material gain of the corp, & public sanction is given to this. But what a howl greets the gov'ts effort to tax for similar purpose.

What would be wrong with a gov't lottery? gov't controlled brothels? or any gov't controlled activity now permitted sub rosa?

State & fed. highways really am't to a gov't subsidy for the auto industry

Selfish vested interests must clothe themselves with some respectable social myth, if they expect to form a powerful organization.

"tax evasion vs tax avoidance."

"spiritual conflict bet. actual needs & inherited folklore."

We are too often prone to judge corp. entirely by their successes & our gov't by its failures

Good & efficient gov't in an expanding sphere requires gradual development just like private organiz. It cannot be mature at the moment of birth.

Opinion of Justice Stone in AAA case.

Negative vs positive philosophy of fed. power.

Constitution should lead rather than instruct.

Social philosophies have significance only in relation to the conflicts out of which they arise & the institutions which they support.

P341 – 2d ¶ – Fklore of Cap.

"ad nauseam"

A good leader in gov't must be a good organizer, also tolerant & humanitarian

The poorer element of a city will support a corrupt political machine because it gets charity without humiliation.

By & large people prefer "financing" to taxation.

No one particular system of gov't can solve our econ. & social difficulties. Any attempt to base a philosophy of gov't on a universal truth or eternal verity (impossible in human affairs) will fail. An honest, just, humanitarian pragmatism is the answer – a realistic understanding of political dynamics.

Political gov't is a dramatic spectacle.

Supreme Court in their learned & august opinions are actually deciding political issues – that is, there is a limit to the judicial function.

What is the significance of Stalin's dissolution of the Comintern?!?

Dramatic contests give unity & stability to social organizations. War is a primitive type, & games (football) & judicial trial are civilized examples.

"as easily heard as your name."

P347 – ¶1 – Fklore of Cap.

"priesthood" in gov't, econ., industry?

Diff. bet. a science *about* law & econ. & a science *of* law & econ.

Generalizations in last chapter of Fklore of Cap.

"highly moral atmosphere of public investigation."

Abrupt change of institutional habits is no easier than pers. habits.

Is this an age where organiz. have largely replaced individ. as units?

Is it a mistake to personify a corp. as an individual? Its "prop." value is in its organization & not primarily in its tangible assets.

Are big businessmen who force their employees to work under poor conditions, pay low wages, sell their products at artificially high prices, & yet are great personal philanthropists – are they hypocrites or just observing a fundamental principle of human org.?

Under the influence of liquor men can justify action which they would deplore when sober. Similarly, under the banner of "laissez faire" & business competition men can justify methods which are entirely foreign to their personal nature.

An honest, conscientious reconciliation of conflicting ideals is absolutely nec. for practical efficient results.

Is it logic or organizations which rule an organized society?

"England seems to have a better understanding of the nec. inconsistencies of public ideals. It therefore on the whole is able to keep more humanitarian people in power because of its realization that gov't has two functions: (1) to put on a public show; (2) to be exceedingly practical behind the scenes. To this ability – to believe in principles & at the same time make them work for organizations, rather than compel organizations to work for principles – may be attributed a large part of the success of that small country in dominating a continent composed of nations far stronger in physical power." – P384 – Fklore of Cap.

"A governmental creed which enables men to face the facts about social organization without disillusionment & with positive enthusiasm for the opportunity presented is a prerequisite to the use of scientific method in gov't." – p389 – Flklore of Cap.

"editorial economics"

Those who rankle at the worship of Roosevelt's personality can destroy it only by advocating an attitude toward the function of gov't which makes that personality less imp.

How pitiful, that in our concern for the culture of the next generation we neglect the pressing problems of our own day.

P393 – last ¶ – Flklore of Cap.

"The greatest destroyer of ideals is he who believes in them so strongly that he cannot fit them to practical needs." P 393

5/28 – Friday

By mistake we simulated an attack on the Yorktown today.

"nom de guerre"

"wealth cannot be enjoyed without dishonor, or foregone without misery." G.B.S.

file

squad – corp.

platoon – lieutenant

company – cap't

battalion – lt. col.

regiment – colonel

brigade – brig. gen.

division – lt. gen.

army – gen.

corps area.

5/29 – Sat.

If a man would grow in character his battle with self must be unceasing

Is there a difference between modesty and humility? May not the former be an intellectual quality and the latter a spiritual?

Thought and action which centres around self can only bring unhappiness, vexation. Failure to honestly & courageously reconcile your ideals & present needs brings much distress, moral confusion. Expectation of absolute certainty in human affairs through prayer results in frustration, exhaustion. The spirit & the letter are complements one of the other, as are faith & understanding, but prefer the simple to the fancy or complex if you would triumph.

Be genuine, pleasant, tolerant – avoid pretense.

The enlisted men and mess attendants sure have it tough on board a ship. They are pretty much victims of the duty involved. It is hard to say how their lot could be bettered and still do the job that has to be done.

Big ball game on the beach this afternoon bet. VB 23 & VF 16 followed by a beer bust. We lost, but it was a lot of fun.

5/30 – Sunday

Letter from Celia – nice surprise

Diff. bet. power politics & collective security against an aggressor?

"Join the Army Air Corp & You will never Mind."

"celebrates Sun. by not shaving."

Sales in the South – must be a cheap luxury or a promise of cheap surcease from pain – eg-Coca-Cola & patent medicines.

"Expanding rings from a rock thrown into a pond."

"Here I go Again"

"technological efficiency plus cooperative organization"

"Men will choose wisely if they can choose freely."

5/31 – Monday

"anonymous naughtiness"

negative virtue

"Boy with the Silver Wings"

"punkin' in the oven"

"pay with the ring of my money for the smell of your roasting goose."

"Yesterday's Gardenias."

Privilege without responsibility soon becomes tyranny.

Poor whites in South feel vastly superior to the Negroes but have to compete on the same econ. level. This is the cause for *so* much bitterness & hatred.

"It is impossible to overestimate the stupidity of the American people." – A Hearst reporter.

"Good conversation is more rare than good food."

"loco parentis."

Is it generally true that the Southern Negro feels neither gratitude nor resentment? – impossible!

"freedom another name for hunger –

6/1 – Tuesday

"negat Butler" – nite flying at Jacksonville.

How I wish that I could sing and play the piano!

It is a sad mistake to try to be head man in everything you attempt.

The axiom "if its worth doing at all, its worth doing well" has its limitations. Stay on the ball most of the time, but learn to coast between moments of all-out effort.

"sans culotte"

People must come before profits!!

Notes to the Diary

4 December 1941

Pete Moeller: See letter 15.

5 December

Francis Heydt: Iowa '40; from Wichita, Kansas; letterman on the Iowa swimming team.

Paul Wolfe: Iowa '41; from Marshalltown; member of Phi Kappa Psi.

8 December

500 unidentified planes were over San Francisco: Kinnick himself believed this rumor by the following day, but no Japanese planes flew over San Francisco at any time during the war.

9 December

an editorial in the Mason City Globe Gazette: The editorial (scrapbook 2) quotes Kinnick's Armistice Day speech at the Old Capitol on the Iowa campus on 11 November 1941. The *Daily Iowan* reprinted it on 3 December (scrapbook 2).

Earl Hall: W. Earl Hall, managing editor of the *Mason City Globe-Gazette.*

John L. Lewis . . . captive-mine disputes: Lewis, the president of the United Mine Workers, foresaw war late in 1941 and sought a prior union-shop agreement for the "captive mines," that is, mines owned by the seven major steel companies (see Saul Alinsky, *John L. Lewis: An Unauthorized Biography* [New York, 1949], pp. 238–39).

12 December

Link trainer: Editorially capitalized here and hereafter in place of Kinnick's usual "link." This stationary trainer was manufactured by Link Aviation, Inc.

a clipping from Bob Hogan: An article recapitulating Kinnick's Iowa career, published in the *Cedar Rapids Gazette,* 7 December 1941 (scrapbook 2).

27 December

"Louisiana Purchase": See letter 19.

1 January 1942

"I would rather fail . . .: Attributed to Woodrow Wilson but not found in his works; see *Respectfully Quoted: A Dictionary of Quotations*

Requested from the Congressional Research Service, ed. Suzy Platt (Washington, D.C., 1989), p. 373.

"If you can talk . . .: Rudyard Kipling, "If – ."

"In war, Resolution . . .: Colin R. Coote says this motto is first found in *Amid These Storms*, published in 1932 (*A Churchill Reader* [Boston, 1954], p. 33), but I have not been able to locate it there. Churchill later used it as the "Moral" on flyleaves of *The Second World War* (6 vols., 1948–53). The word in square brackets is editorially supplied from the text of *A Churchill Reader*.

6 January

The female reporter: Macy Mong, in "Just Lookin' Around with Macy Mong," *Kansas City Kansan*, 7 January 1942 (clipping in scrapbook 2).

Merle McKay: See letter 21.

20 January

a fine poem by Emerson: Kinnick quotes the beginning and end of stanza three in Emerson's "Voluntaries," an 1863 poem honoring Col. Robert G. Shaw and members of the black Massachusetts 54th Regiment killed in an attack on Fort Wagner, South Carolina, 18 July 1863.

25 January

quite charming . . . quite a cagy little rascal: The italic underscoring is in red pencil, the text in blue ink, but the styling is regarded here as Kinnick's emphasis.

31 January

Bibba . . . her Hawkeye: Elizabeth Charlton was editor of the 1943 *Hawkeye*, published in the spring of 1942.

6 February

(S.B.O.): Inscribed above "Wing Commander," it meant "Student Battalion Officer."

Radabaugh: Kinnick spelled the name "Radebaugh" as well as "Radabaugh," but his more frequent "Radabaugh" is taken for the correct form.

11 February

Harry Bremer: See letter 28 and annotation.

17 February

Tony Bremer: Charles B. Bremer (Iowa '40), nicknamed Tony; was from St. Louis and was a letterman on the Iowa swimming team; no relation of Harry Bremer.

18 February

Wyman Hayward: See letter 22.

19 February

OS2U: An observation plane; see letter 32 and annotation.

21 February

an AVS with an ensign's commission: An AVS was an Aviation Specialist, a Navy Air Corps ground officer who might be in supply or intelligence, for example.

22 February

Washington wrote his mother: Washington actually wrote to his brother, John Augustine Washington, 31 May 1754, regarding his engagement with the French at Great Meadows, Pa. See *The Papers of George Washington*, Colonial Series (Charlottesville, Va., 1983), 1:118: "I heard the Bulletts whistle, and believe me there was something charming in the sound." Kinnick's error regarding the mother may have been in his source, for it was a common piece of misinformation.

23 February

dominion over the fish . . .: Genesis 1:26.

3 March

"E" base: Elimination base, the earliest phase of Navy Air Corps training.

9 March

test stand observation: A test stand was a stationary stand for testing aircraft engines. A detailed description of the procedure is in a letter from Kinnick to his parents of 12 March 1942.

18 March

Knox & Tunney have gone berserk: Compare letter 28, annotation 2.

21 March

Elmer's Tune . . .: All these popular songs came out in 1941. See also entry for 9 May 1943.

26 March

an interesting article: Joseph E. Davies, "Meet the Real Stalin," *Look*, 7 April 1942, pp. 13–15.

30 March

N3Ns: A primary trainer; see letter 32 and annotation.

5 April

Prof. Sayre: See letter 28 and annotation.

9 April

fed up with keeping this irony: Kinnick may have meant to say *diary* instead of *irony,* but *irony* is taken for an angry or contemptuous redefinition of what he has been writing.

18 April

Mustin Beach: The officers' club at Pensacola, named in honor of Captain H. C. Mustin, who was instrumental in the establishment of Pensacola as a Naval Air Station. In a letter of 19 April 1942 Kinnick explained to his parents that his advanced cadet status gave him access to the club.

20 April

plotting board: A navigational instrument; see Heflin, *Air Force Dictionary,* under "plotter."

29 April

The only Dr. O'Brien: See letter 23.

7 May

Kilmer Bortz: Unidentified; apparently not an Iowa student.

a statement of Richard Hillarys: From Richard Hillary, *Falling through Space* (New York, 1942), p. 123. Hillary was a fighter pilot in the Royal Air Force. After serious injury in the Battle of Britain in 1940, he returned to duty and was killed in action in January 1943.

8 May

a fine letter from Celia: Celia Peairs; see letter 15.

9 May

a letter from Barbara: Barbara Miller; see the introduction and letters 9 and 14.

13 May

Butch O'Hare: See letter 26.

15 May

"P" boats . . . VO-Vs: Patrol planes and observation planes.

19 May

VC training: Carrier training.

22 May

U track exam in the Link: A proficiency test in the instrument syllabus for the Link trainer.

23 May

SNJ-3: An advanced trainer with retractable landing gear; see letter 32.

30 May

the ACRAC: Identified in Kinnick's letter to his family of 2 June 1942 as the Aviation Cadets Recreation and Athletic Club.

5 June

SNV: The Vultee Vibrator; see letter 32.

11 June

articles in the Sat Eve Post: Jan Henrik Marsman, "I Escaped from Hong Kong," in the *Saturday Evening Post* for 6, 13, 20 June 1942.

19 June

VP: Patrol plane.

1 July

Mr. & Mrs. Eastman: The Eastmans farmed north of Adel. Stealing their watermelons was common among the local children.

7 July

Coronados: The PB2Y, a patrol bomber made by Consolidated.

1 August

a boy from New Zealand: Neville Turnbull, identified in Kinnick's letter to his parents of 13 January 1943; see also entry for 26 May 1943.

7 August

Mrs. Jack Riley: Mary McHugh Riley (Iowa '41) was a friend of Barbara Miller. Jack Riley, from Burlington, had been in law school with Kinnick (Kinnick to his parents, 8 August 1942).

8 August

Letters . . . from Tait, Stace: On Tait Cummins, see letter 28, and on Bob Stacy, see letter 32.

10 August

relative search sector . . . cross country: Search of a specific land area from the air. "Cross country," which was part of navigational training, meant flying between two specific points on land.

12 August

Jim Dower: Dower, from Marengo, had been in law school with Kinnick (Kinnick to his parents, 13 August 1942).

14 August

Brewsters: The F2A Brewster Buffalo was a navy fighter; see entry for 21 August.

25 August

"Nothing worries . . .: Source unidentified.

6 May 1943

In this entry, and through the entry for 10 May, Kinnick shows his involvement with Wendell Willkie's *One World* (New York, 1943), included in *Prefaces to Peace* (New York, 1943). All citations are to the pagination of the latter edition. Besides quotations, several topics and questions in the 6 May and later entries derive from Willkie.

"How can you ever have . . .: Compare Willkie, *Prefaces to Peace*, p. 56.

7 May

"Nothing of importance can be won . . .: Willkie, *Prefaces to Peace*, p. 121.

Why did Roosevelt torpedo the London Econ. Conf.: Kinnick accepts Willkie's account, p. 143.

9 May

"From each according to his ability . . .. Willkie, *Prefaces to Peace*, p. 54, reads: "'From each according to his capacities, to each according to his *work*,' was the slogan of Stalinist socialism."

the loud laugh & the vacant mind: Allusion to Goldsmith, "The Deserted Village," in Bartlett, *Familiar Quotations*, p. 250; see letter 16.

"Elmers Tune" . . . "Back to Where I Come From": For the first three songs, see entry for 21 March 1942 and annotation. "White Christmas" came out in 1942. "As Time Goes By" appeared in 1931 and was revived in the 1942 movie *Casablanca*. "Back to Where I Come From" is unidentified.

Anne Kanoy (rhumba): Kinnick wrote the parenthesis above the name, just below "Merle McKay" in the previous line. The parenthesis is taken to be in association with Anne Kanoy. See letter 29.

Neff . . . Lindbeck: Pilots in Fighter Squadron 16 (squadron photograph with Kinnick's identifications in box 3).

10 May

"shall revive as the corn": See Hosea 14:7.

"blindness of their heart": See Ephesians 4:18.

"Comin' thru the Rye": Sung by Marian Anderson when Kinnick heard her at the Met; see letter 35.

Frank: Frank Rogers, one of Kinnick's roommates on the *Lexington*.

"Mighty as a Rose": Evidently "Mighty Lak' a Rose," a song of 1901.

"Take it off": Refrain words from the song "Strip Polka" (1942).

Most unforgettable characters: At that time and for many years, a frequent feature in *Reader's Digest* was an article called "The Most Unforgettable Character I've Met," in which contributors discussed one such person in their experience. Kinnick wrote his parents on 8 August 1942 that he wanted to do an article on Arletta Clarke for *Reader's Digest* "entitled My Most Unforgettable Character."

12 May

"Where wood is chopped . . . . From Tolstoy, *War and Peace*, Inner Sanctum Edition, trans. by Louise and Aylmer Maude, Foreword by Clifton Fadiman (New York, 1942), p. 828. This is the edition Kinnick read; see entry for 14 May. All citations hereafter are to that edition.

14 May

"The fashions of this world . . .: Not located.

"No Nazi politically but one spiritually": See *War and Peace*, p. xlviii. Fadiman says this of a character in Rebecca West's *Black Lamb and Grey Falcon* whom he compares with Napoleon.

"sense of process": From the same Fadiman passage: "Gerda has no sense of process."

"continuity of human events": *War and Peace*, p. xlix.

"like a deaf man" . . .: In his Second Epilogue, Tolstoy says that "modern history, like a deaf man, answers questions no one has asked" (*War and Peace*, p. 1316).

The theme of War & Peace: *War and Peace*, pp. 1317, 1335.

no such thing as chance or genius: *War and Peace*, pp. 1257–58.

"sotto voce": *War and Peace*, p. lvi.

15 May

"enlightened selfishness": From Thurman Arnold, *The Folklore of Capitalism* (New Haven, 1937), p. 35.

"Let me designate . . .: Arnold, *Capitalism*, p. 34.

17 May

S.B.D.: The Douglas Dauntless, a scout bomber. On its shakedown cruise the *Lexington* carried F4Fs, SBDs, and TBFs.

PBY: Kinnick called this patrol bomber slower and more vulnerable than the PB2Y (letter to Ben Kinnick, 28 October 1942; see also entry for 7 July 1942 and annotation).

18 May

Hurricane: A British fighter.

"Errol Flynn says . . .: One of many Errol Flynn jokes that circulated in 1942 and 1943, during and after the actor's celebrated trial for statutory rape that began in 1942 and ended with his acquittal in

February 1943. The allegations concerned relations on his yacht with two underage girls.

19 May

our Consti & slogans: Compare Arnold, *Capitalism*, p. 79.

Such institutions: Compare this paragraph with Arnold, *Capitalism*, p. 114.

"ex cathedra": Arnold, *Capitalism*, p. 81.

"sub rosa": Arnold, *Capitalism*, p. 114; an expression used throughout *The Folklore of Capitalism* with regard to unofficial agencies that accomplish what public codes do not sanction.

20 May

"Navy phonetic alphabet": This may refer to the expressions that follow in the entry.

"snafu" – *"tarfu"*: Acronyms that originated in the service during the war and that were also in common civilian use. The first meant "situation normal: all fucked up"; the other, "things are *really* fucked up."

21 May

Ken Kavanaugh: An All-American end at Louisiana State in 1939, he was on the College All-Star Team with Kinnick in 1940.

B18s: A bomber, known as the Bolo, adapted from the DC3, the Douglas commercial plane.

22 May

The desire for certainty: Compare the quotation in the entry for 25 August 1942.

"polar words": See chapter 7, "The Traps Which Lie in Definitions and Polar Words," in Arnold, *Capitalism*.

"Take Me Back to West Virginia": Unidentified.

24 May

Gov't by force: See Arnold, *Capitalism*, pp. 193–94. The remaining topics discussed in the entry also derive from Arnold.

25 May

"industrial feudalism": Arnold, *Capitalism*, p. 347.

"tail gunners" . . . *cartoon*: Unidentified.

27 May

How pitiful: Compare Arnold, *Capitalism*, p. 393.

28 May

"wealth cannot be enjoyed . . .: From George Bernard Shaw, *Fabian*

Tract No. 2 (1884), in Edward R. Pease, *The History of the Fabian Society* (London, 1916), p. 41. Kinnick's immediate source is unknown.

29 May

VB 23: Bomber Squadron 23 on the *Lexington*.

30 May

Letter from Celia: Celia Peairs; see letter 39.

"Here I go Again": Kinnick possibly has in mind the opening of "Taking a Chance on Love," a 1940 song. The song titled "Here I Go Again" was not published until after his death.

31 May

"Boy with the Silver Wings": Kinnick possibly means "He Wears a Pair of Silver Wings," a song of 1941.

"Yesterday's Gardenias": A song of 1942.